The Methuen Drama Book
of Twenty-First Century British Plays

The Methuen Drama Book of Twenty-First Century British Plays

Blue/Orange
Joe Penhall

Elmina's Kitchen
Kwame Kwei-Armah

Realism
Anthony Neilson

Gone Too Far!
Bola Agbaje

Pornography
Simon Stephens

Edited and with an introduction by
Aleks Sierz

B L O O M S B U R Y
LONDON · NEW DELHI · NEW YORK · SYDNEY

Bloomsbury Methuen Drama

An imprint of Bloomsbury Publishing Plc

50 Bedford Square
London
WC1B 3DP
UK

1385 Broadway
New York
NY 10018
USA

www.bloomsbury.com

Bloomsbury is a registered trade mark of Bloomsbury Publishing Plc

This collection first published in Great Britain in 2010 by Bloomsbury Methuen Drama
Reprinted 2011, 2013

Blue/Orange first published in Great Britain in 2000 by Methuen Drama.
Revised edition published in 2001, © 2000 and 2001 by Joe Penhall
Elmina's Kitchen first published in 2003 by Methuen Drama
Reprinted in *Kwame Kwei-Armah Plays: 1* in 2009 by Methuen Drama,
© 2003, 2009 by Kwame Kwei-Armah
Realism first published in Great Britain in 2007 by Methuen Drama © 2007 by Anthony Neilson
Gone Too Far! first published in Great Britain in 2007 by Methuen Drama © 2007 by Bola Agbaje
Pornography first published in Great Britain in 2008 by Methuen Drama,
© 2008 by Simon Stephens
Introduction © Methuen Drama, 2010

British Library Cataloguing-in-Publication Data
A catalogue record for this book is available from the British Library.

ISBN: PB: 978-1-4081-2391-1

Library of Congress Cataloging-in-Publication Data
A catalog record for this book is available from the Library of Congress.

Typeset by Country Setting, Kingsdown, Kent
Printed and bound in Great Britain

Contents

Introduction   vii

BLUE / ORANGE
  Joe Penhall   1

ELMINA'S KITCHEN
  Kwame Kwei-Armah   119

REALISM
  Anthony Neilson   215

GONE TOO FAR!
  Bola Agbaje   285

PORNOGRAPHY
  Simon Stephens   373

Introduction

The Methuen Drama Book of Twenty-First Century British Plays is an anthology of five contemporary plays which together represent the latest trends in new writing for the theatre. The collection comprises outstanding work from the first decade of the new millennium, namely Joe Penhall's *Blue/Orange*, Kwame Kwei-Armah's *Elmina's Kitchen*, Anthony Neilson's *Realism*, Bola Agbaje's *Gone Too Far!* and Simon Stephens's *Pornography*.

Joe Penhall is one of Britain's leading playwrights and his debut, *Some Voices*, was the first to hit the stage in the now legendary 1994–5 season of new work that artistic director Stephen Daldry programmed at the Royal Court, and which culminated in Sarah Kane's notorious *Blasted*. Penhall's subsequent work includes *Pale Horse* (1995), *Love and Understanding* (1997), *The Bullet* (1998), *Dumb Show* (2004) and *Landscape with Weapon* (2007). He also wrote the screenplay for the film *Enduring Love* (2004). His typical motif of two men, often brothers, locked in struggle is usually expressed through muscular dialogue which, at its best, leaves naturalism behind and lingers for a while in the playground of wild imaginings.

His masterpiece, *Blue/Orange*, premiered at the National Theatre in April 2000, transferred to the West End, and won several awards, principally the Olivier Award for Best New Play 2001. It has since been revived several times. Like so many of the issue plays of the 2000s, its main theme is an engagement with the long legacy of Margaret Thatcher and the results of the disastrous social policies of the Conservative governments of the late 1980s and 1990s. As in *Some Voices*, the central concern is mental illness and the policy of Care in the Community, which led to the rationing of hospital beds for the seriously disturbed and the discharge of mental patients into the community. *Blue/Orange* dramatises this social problem as a power struggle between two male doctors, senior consultant Robert and his junior Bruce, over the treatment of Christopher, a troubled Afro-Caribbean youth. As Christopher reaches the end of his bureaucratically allocated twenty-eight days in care, Robert wants to discharge him and free up bed

space for other patients while Bruce argues that he is still
seriously ill. At first, Christopher's fantasies of being fathered
by Ugandan dictator Idi Amin sound almost plausible, but
when he describes an orange as bright blue his condition
suddenly seems much more serious. By this time, Robert has
lost patience with Bruce, his protégé, and persuades Christopher
to lodge a complaint against him for racism. One of the chief
delights of this tightly structured three-act play, in which the
action happens over twenty-four hours in an NHS psychiatric
hospital, is its exploration of character. The charismatic if
self-regarding Robert, who wants to publish his research on a
culturally specific 'black psychosis', talks like a well-educated
humanist, his range of reference including a poem by French
surrealist Paul Eluard and the Tintin adventure where a 'mad
professor' invents a bright blue orange that tastes salty. But he's
also capable of abusing his own power. By contrast, Bruce is
ethical and idealistic, if a bit gauche. The Darwinian struggle
between them is balanced by the thought-provoking ambiguity
of the character of Christopher, who may or may not be
seriously ill. In each case, Penhall's default position on character
is paradox, which raises the question: if a person can appear
to be so changeable, how can we ever really know them?

Originally directed by Roger Michell, *Blue/Orange* was
staged on a clinical white set that resembled an arena in
which Bill Nighy's Robert and Andrew Lincoln's Bruce
locked horns over the fate of Chiwetel Ejiofor's Christopher.
At the centre of the stage, a bowl of oranges on a low coffee
table seemed to glow with unearthly colour at every climactic
pause. Critics were enthusiastic about *Blue/Orange*, praising
the way that 'sympathy for the victim is perfectly matched
by Penhall's stinging satire on the arrogant assurance of
professionalism'[1] and his handling of the subject of 'race,
health, compassion and the sickness of the healers'.[2] But
perhaps the most incisive judgement on the play comes from
another playwright, Terry Johnson: 'This absorbing,
intellectual chamber piece is not so much about a probable
schizophrenic but about the issues that spring up around him:
issues of definition, diagnosis and control.'[3]

Kwame Kwei-Armah is not only a great writer but also a media star: an actor in the BBC drama series *Casualty* and *Holby City*, he was a Fame Academy graduate as a singer and is now also a cultural commentator. He sees himself as tri-cultural (African, Caribbean and British) and his trilogy of plays exploring the experience of black Britons began with *Elmina's Kitchen* (2003), continued with *Fix Up* (2004) and was completed with *Statement of Regret* (2007). All were staged at the National Theatre, and they explored the different worlds of a café on Hackney's Murder Mile, a radical bookshop run by a washed-up black activist and a contemporary think-tank riven with conflict. In 2005, Kwei-Armah was nominated for a BAFTA award for the television version of *Elmina's Kitchen*, which had already won the *Evening Standard*'s Charles Wintour Most Promising Playwright Award after it opened in May 2003. His other work includes *A Bitter Herb* (1998), *Big Nose* (1999), *Blues Brother, Soul Sister* (2001) and *Let There Be Love* (2008).

When *Elmina's Kitchen* transferred to the Garrick Theatre in 2005, Kwei-Armah became the first black Briton to have a play staged in the West End. This was also the moment when it became clear that much of the energy in British new writing was now coming from black writers whose point of view was critical of both established society and the black subcultures within it. Each writer has their own individuality: Kwei-Armah is an ideas man who also delights in human singularity. His exploration of the issues of black British identity pulsates with provocative insights – often expressed through punchy and hilarious one-liners – and glows with a warm humanity, and he bolsters the cast with eccentrics (a bolshie woman who reads books, an old biddy who plays draughts and a black man who dresses in Native American garb). Mixing the fluency of sitcom with a burning sense of injustice and a profound understanding of human tragedy, his plays are usually concerned with how families have weathered the great social storms of the past few decades.

The central theme of *Elmina's Kitchen* is the acute social problem of gun crime and the way young people of West Indian heritage are drawn towards criminality, but this is

contained within a recognisable family drama. Set in an
eatery with a name echoing that of a notorious slaving fort,
Elmina Castle, the play focuses on Deli, a black Briton who has
been in prison, but who is now reformed. His son, nineteen-
year-old rudeboy Ashley, however, is tempted by easy loot
and peer pressure, and falls prey to his father's mate Digger,
a West Indian gangsta. With a couple more characters –
Anastasia (a gutsy woman) and Clifton (Deli's dad) – the brew
begins to bubble. Being a black man in today's Britain,
suggests Kwei-Armah, means trying to live up to the images
of masculine violence that saturate street culture. Typically,
the play also highlights the problem of absent parents,
showing the psychological results on their offspring of Clifton's
poor fathering skills and Elmina's early death. But if the
theme of personal responsibility in a racist society is both
serious and pressing, Kwei-Armah gives it a comic twist with
his choice of theatrical style. He takes elements of the
stomping West Indian comedy, a genre that convulses its
audiences with rude innuendo and sexy suggestiveness, and
seamlessly mixes them with social comment.

The first production, directed by Angus Jackson, boasted a
detailed set by Bunnie Christie which allowed a grungy café
to be transformed into a trendy restaurant in the interval, and
which was lit up by fine performances from Paterson Joseph
as the sincere Deli and Shaun Parkes as the sinister Digger.
The play was immediately recognised as a cry of anguish, an
example of contemporary theatre at its best, which 'urges
people with half-closed minds and averted eyes to confront
the ignored and evaded problems of our time',[4] and was also
appreciated as 'an angry, provocative, vital play, one that
demands change in society while recognising that there are
no easy solutions'.[5] At the same time, its comic brio was also
unmistakable. With lines as sharp as chilli and as fast as a
takeaway, the play is really great entertainment.

Now an Artistic Associate of the National Theatre of Scotland,
Anthony Neilson made his name in the early 1990s as the
creator of pioneering, taboo-breaking new work. He soon
became the master of experiential theatre, which forces the

audience to experience the story shown on stage by feeling the emotions portrayed, and his greatest works include *Normal* (1991), *Penetrator* (1993), *The Censor* (1997) and *Stitching* (2002). Then, in order to avoid what he considers the number one sin of boring his audience, Neilson took a more surrealist or absurdist turn, with plays as deliciously varied as *Edward Gant's Amazing Feats of Loneliness* (2002), *The Wonderful World of Dissocia* (2004) and *God in Ruins* (2007). It is worth noting that he usually directs his own work, and his rehearsal methods aim to bring a blast of fresh – meaning emotionally truthful and physically alive – acting to the stage. A new play by Neilson is always a highly theatrical event.

Realism, which was staged at the Royal Lyceum as part of the Edinburgh International Festival in August 2006, is a great example both of Neilson's sense of comedy and of his thoroughly absurdist sensibility. It shows a day in the life of Stuart McQuarrie, a lonely man whose lover has left him and who spends most of the day sleeping or doing domestic chores. But just as thoughts often seem to run around unbidden inside our heads, Neilson fills the stage with various people that Stuart knows, and dramatises his thoughts through onstage dialogues. Thus, Stuart's internal conversations open out into everyday conflicts, with his friend Paul, his ex-girlfriends Laura and Angie, his mother and father, and even his childhood friend Mullet all joining in. Alive in Stuart's mind is the nagging voice of his mother, regretful thoughts about his former lovers, and both the irritations and consolations of male friendship – even his cat is full of recrimination. At one point, Stuart feels so sorry for himself that he imagines the reactions to his own death.

At all times, the tension between banal appearance and an individual's inner life is highlighted. But *Realism* is also a fun play, which zips along with bizarre fantasies and mundane thoughts in constant tension, and in comic commotion. These interactions are a theatrical technique that, in Neilson's own words, allows him 'to dramatise *contradiction*' – after all, most human beings 'both want and not want' various things, often at the same time. This ambiguity, highlighted throughout the play, is doubtlessly funny – but only from the outside. For each audience member, it must surely remind them of their own internal conflicts. So as well as the comedy of Stuart's masturbatory sexual dreams and his absurdly self-regarding fantasy of appearing, hugely eloquent, on a radio panel discussion about the smoking ban, *Realism* is also concerned with loss, which is one of Neilson's great themes. Typical of this is the moment when Stuart, in his imagination appearing on *Desert Island Discs*, talks about the 'little death' of losing a lover, and 'the accumulated losses of life'. Yes, that's the beating heart that thumps insistently beneath the play's surface surrealism and its outrageous jokes.

Directed by Neilson himself, the original production saw Stuart McQuarrie played by his namesake on a tilted set that showed a domestic environment half-buried in sand and lit up at various points by the light of the sunken television. Despite its innovative form, reviewers had no trouble in understanding the play. It was described variously as a play that 'twitches uneasily between the acutely embarrassing, the wildly fantastical, the endearingly comic and the plain unpleasant'[6] and 'a wild delirious trip in which the conscious and unconscious mind grate against each other like giant tectonic plates'.[7] All agreed that the play's stand-out episode was when Stuart, irritated by a gas bill, performs a song and dance number, complete with politically incorrect Black and White Minstrels. On stage, this was typically hilarious, provocatively offensive and combined inspired silliness with deep sorrow.

The youngest of the playwrights in this volume, Bola Agbaje is one of the most exciting writers to appear in the first decade of this century. According to *The Times*, she arrived at a fast pace: 'Bored with writing stories on the back of receipts, Agbaje typed "young+writers+programme" into Google; two years later, she graduated from the Royal Court's scheme for promising playwrights.' Inspired by a Nigerian play – Ola Rotimi's *The Gods Are Not To Blame*, which she saw performed by black theatre company Tiata Fahodzi – her debut, *Gone Too Far!*, was staged in the small Theatre Upstairs at the Royal Court in February 2007 as part of the Young Writers'

Festival. It was so successful, winning the 2008 Olivier Award
for Outstanding Achievement, that it was restaged on the
Royal Court's main stage in July 2008, confirming her as a
new writer of fine emotional insight and moral intelligence.
Drawing on her own experiences as a London-born teenager
hanging around a Peckham estate, and on the Nigerian
background of her parents, Agbaje explores a community
divided by race and prejudice.

In *Gone Too Far!*, two brothers – eighteen-year-old Ikudayisi
(who has grown up in Nigeria) and sixteen-year-old Yemi
(who has been brought up in Britain) – cross a London council
estate on a simple errand to buy a pint of milk. Along the
way, they encounter an Asian shopkeeper, a nervous old lady,
a couple of racist policemen and a pair of mouthy teenage
girls – Armani and Paris – plus their street-smart friends,
Blazer, Razer and Flamer. As well as being a sharply written,
comic account of two teenage brothers who are just getting to
know each other, this is also a play about the issue of knife
crime and a knowing commentary on black youth which
especially highlights the tensions between those of African
and West Indian origin. But the trouble with black teenagers,
Agbaje suggests, is also the trouble with British society. What
holds back these young people is their poverty, their limited
horizons, their stunted aspirations. And the result of
ignorance is powerlessness, compensated for by inane
posturing. As a newcomer, Ikudayisi sees this clearly. At one
point, he says to Yemi, 'Don't go looking for trouble.' But he
also realises that the root of the problem is identity: 'Do you
know who you are?'

In deliberate defiance of stereotypes, Agbaje presents her
teens in unexpected ways: Blazer, the top gang member, is
shown not only as a feared presence but also as an
intellectual, someone who appreciates both the street values
of respect and the importance of knowing a foreign language,
and who has clearly read and understood books such as Alex
Haley's *Roots*. The picture is beautifully, and amusingly,
complex: in order to impress the girls, Ikudayisi
unsuccessfully acts like an American black man, while at
other times he and Blazer speak Yoruba to each other, and

both can veer between Standard English and a black British youth argot. Indeed, the richness of the language employed in the play is both a comic delight and a comment on how we all enact our identities. For example, the brothers' offstage mother speaks Yoruba to her Nigerian friends, a rhetorical Nigerian English to her boys and a refined middle-class English when she answers the phone. The beauty of the play lies not only in this linguistic complexity, but also in the psychological accuracy of its portrayal of troubled teens. In Scenes Eight and Ten, Armani is clearly provoking her boyfriend Razer into acting more macho than he wants to, and the climactic knife attack is one result of this manipulated and over-assertive masculinity. The girls are equally prone to escalating aggression. The argument between Armani and Paris in Scene Five, which starts off being about Blazer's Nigerian identity and ends up with a shouting match between the two girls, is full of spunky putdowns about skin colour and family heritage. The 'Jamaican' identity of Armani is called into question when it is revealed that she has a white mother and a black father she's never met. Individual identity is shown to be unstable, shifting, something that you can put on and off – like a baseball cap or traditional African attire – or something you can't shake off, like skin colour or the culture of your parents. Here, Agbaje cleverly braids in material about racial identity, cultural history and individual psychology. What is so impressive is the writer's confidence, accuracy and humour in dealing with the social complexity of London today.

This complexity was crystallised in young director Bijan Sheibani's original production, which emphasised the theatricality of the piece by including thumping garage music, dance moves and a highly choreographed fight scene on a tough, bare, dark set. As Agbaje's reviewers rightly noted, 'her humanity and ear for snappy dialogue'[8] were superabundant in an impressive debut that convincingly represented young people and 'through the acutely observed cut and thrust of their chat she explores the hazardous mixture of peer pressure, cultural contradiction and virulent racism that defines and blights their lives'.[9] And, in the brothers' tentative reconciliation at the end of the play, there is a note of hope for a whole generation of young people in Britain's inner cities.

During the 2000s, Simon Stephens emerged as one of the best new writers in Britain, winning the Olivier Award for Best New Play 2005 for *On the Shore of the Wide World*. His back catalogue already reads like a comprehensive account of British working-class life in the new millennium: *Herons* (2001), *Port* (2002), *One Minute* (2003), *Christmas* (2004), *Country Music* (2004) and *Motortown* (2006) together look at life's brutal losers and desperate victims but always with hope, honesty and humour. All of them are trapped, but all manage to rattle the bars of their cages. Like *On the Shore of the Wide World*, Stephens's *Harper Regan* (2008) shifted its gaze onto more middle-class families and their familiar anguish. But as well as being a playwright, Stephens has also been an influential and inspirational teacher. For five years, he was tutor on the Royal Court Young Writers' Programme and then became the National's first ever Resident Dramatist in 2005. His writing blends the great British tradition of naturalism with a much more poetic style. When his characters pause, they allow their imaginations to take flight in highly individual excursions into the odd, the wry and the amazing.

First staged in a German translation in Hanover and Hamburg in 2007, *Pornography* had its British premiere at the Traverse Theatre in Edinburgh in July 2008. The background of the action is the week in July 2005 which began with the Live 8 series of benefit concerts that took place on 2 July up and down Britain, followed by the G8 summit of world leaders in Gleneagles, Scotland, the winning of the bid to stage the 2012 Olympics by the UK on 6 July, and the explosion of the 7/7 bombs in London the day after. Appreciated by the critics as a 'play of grace and terror'[10] with 'humour put at the service of defiance',[11] this masterly and thought-provoking work was seen as 'unmistakably a state of the nation play in the fullest sense'[12] and as 'a fascinatingly up-to-the-minute piece of internal psycho-geography, a London love affair alive with heart and soul'.[13]

The most daring of the works in this volume in terms of its form, *Pornography* has seven scenes or chapters but no specified characters, meaning that it can be performed by casts of different sizes. Stephens's initial stage direction is clear: 'This play can be performed by any number of actors. It can be performed in any order.' The seven scenes are numbered in descending order, beginning with seven and ending with Scene One, like a countdown, but the main thrust is chronological. Some scenes clearly involve conversations, others are monologues. Each one alludes to Shakespeare's idea of the Seven Ages of Man (outlined in a haunting speech, which begins 'All the world's a stage', by Jaques in *As You Like It*). Each also involves a transgression. The first age is infancy and Stephens's first scene is about a woman who has a young baby and who betrays her boss by leaking details of an important business report. The second age, childhood, is about Jason, a schoolboy who has a crush on his teacher. Scene Three, the lover, is enacted by two siblings who have an incestuous reunion. Scene Four, the soldier, focuses on a suicide bomber travelling to London. Next, justice and wisdom is represented ironically by a brief and embarrassing encounter between a university teacher and a student half his age. Old age is an eighty-two-year-old woman who walks home from central London on the day of the 7/7 bombings, and calls uninvited on a suburban barbecue. The final scene is a list of fifty-two mini-biographies, each of which represents one of the real victims of 7/7 (number 43, which is blank, is arguably the saddest). In the first British production, this list was projected onto the back wall of the stage after the curtain call. Apart from this last scene, the rest of the play is purely fictional: significantly, the suicide bomber in Scene Four travels from Manchester not Leeds.

But why is the play called *Pornography*? Because the central transgression in the play is a suicide bombing, Stephens suggests that this kind of action is only possible if the terrorist is able to objectify, to dehumanise, his victims. This vision of a world of objects is alienating and oppressive. Hence, Stephens equates this psychological manoeuvre with the objectification of women by pornographers. In a world of images, human reality is the first casualty of exploitation; the suicide bomber strikes at the heart of our shared identity. But this is not a play about Islamism, or political ideology. It's a play about the disaffection of a young man from British society – and by implication this emphasises the Englishness of the 7/7 bombing. The bombers are us. The play is also a vision of London in all its chaotic glory. Although the scenes can be performed in any order, most productions have used the order in which they appear here, although one memorable production took the idea of transgression even further by having two male actors play the incestuous siblings. It is also possible to use actors to create various new relationships between the various voices in the story, or to chop up each scene and interweave it with other fragments, as in Sean Holmes's stark but redemptive British premiere which fizzed with electric sound and the static of television screens. In the text, coherence is achieved through recurring images, such as quotations from Coldplay's 'Yellow', having a drink of alcohol or getting information from the media; the repeated stage direction 'Images of hell' is a reminder of the horror of 7/7. Typically, Stephens's characters respond to the sense of living in an alienated society by suddenly launching into imaginative speeches, as in Scene Three when one of the siblings does an acidic riff on the 'intellectual Pepto-Bismol' of our times, part of a private war on cliché. Finally, the sheer unexpectedness of the play's structure perfectly reflects the shocking events that characterised that astonishing week in July 2005.

The Methuen Drama Book of Twenty-First Century British Plays showcases five of the most exciting new plays from the first decade of the new millennium. Taken together, they demonstrate the rude health of current playwriting. They also offer a snapshot of a nation obsessed with themes of broken families, absent fathers, masculine rivalry, the lure of transgression and the loneliness of existence. Despite competition from the digital technologies, both the potency of these plays' themes and the exuberance and innovation of their theatricality are a testament to the power of live theatre as an art form.

Aleks Sierz
July 2009

Notes

1 Billington, M., *Guardian*, 14 April 2000.
2 Peter, J., *Sunday Times*, 23 April 2000.
3 Johnson, T., Introduction in *Joe Penhall: Plays 2*, London: Methuen Drama, 2008, p. x.
4 de Jongh, N., *Evening Standard*, 30 May 2003.
5 Costa, M., *Guardian*, 30 May 2003.
6 McMillan, J., *Scotsman*, 16 August 2006.
7 Gardner, L., *Guardian*, 17 August 2006.
8 Halliburton, R., *Time Out*, 14 February 2007.
9 Cavendish, D., *Daily Telegraph*, 10 February 2007.
10 Gardner, L., *Guardian*, 5 August 2008.
11 Cavendish, D., *Daily Telegraph*, 5 August 2008.
12 Chadwick, A., *Metro*, 5 August 2008.
13 Cooper, N., *Herald*, 5 August 2008.

Aleks Sierz is Visiting Research Fellow at Rose Bruford College, and author of *In-Yer-Face Theatre: British Drama Today* (Faber, 2001), *The Theatre of Martin Crimp* (Methuen Drama, 2006) and *John Osborne's Look Back in Anger* (Continuum, 2008). He also works as a journalist, broadcaster, lecturer and theatre critic.

Joe Penhall

Blue/Orange

Joe Penhall lives in London. His plays include *Wild Turkey* (Old Red Lion, Islington); *Some Voices* (Royal Court Theatre Upstairs, 1994), which won a Thames Television Bursary and the John Whiting Award in 1995; *Pale Horse* (Royal Court Theatre Upstairs, 1995), which won the Thames Television Best Play Award; *Love and Understanding* (Bush Theatre, 1997); *The Bullet* (Donmar Warehouse, 1998); *Blue/Orange* (Cottesloe, National Theatre, 2000) which won the *Evening Standard* Best Play Award, the Olivier Award for Best Play 2001 and the Critics' Circle Best New Play 2000; *Dumb Show* (Royal Court Theatre Jerwood Theatre Downstairs, 2004); and *Landscape with Weapon* (Cottesloe, National Theatre, 2007). His film and television work includes the screenplays for *Enduring Love* (produced for FilmFour in 2004), *Deep Water* and *The Road* (both 2009), *The Long Firm*, a four-part serial for the BBC in 2004, *Moodswings* for BBC1 in 2008 and *Moses Jones* for BBC2 in 2009.

For my Dad,
the late, great Brian Penhall (1933–1998)

Blue/Orange was first performed in the Cottesloe auditorium of the National Theatre, London, on 7 April 2000. The cast was as follows:

Christopher	Chiwetel Ejiofor
Bruce	Andrew Lincoln
Robert	Bill Nighy

Directed by Roger Michell
Designed by William Dudley

Michael Codron and Lee Dean transferred the National Theatre production to the Duchess Theatre on 30 April 2001.

Characters

Christopher
Bruce
Robert

Setting

The action takes place over twenty-four hours in a modern
NHS psychiatric hospital in London.

Act One

A consultation room. A transparent water cooler. A round table with a large glass bowl containing three oranges.

Bruce *and* **Christopher** *stand facing each other.*

Christopher Mister Bruce –

Bruce Christopher –

Christopher Mister Bruce –

Bruce How are you doing?

Christopher Brucey Brucey Brucey. How you doing?

Bruce A pleasure as always.

Christopher A pleasure. Yeah, a pleasure. The pleasure's all mine, man.

Bruce Take a seat.

Christopher The pleasure today is mine. D'you know what I mean?

Bruce Plant your arse.

Christopher It's mine! It's my day. Innit. My big day. What can I say . . . ?

Bruce Yes, well, yes – sit down now.

Christopher Gimme some skin.

Bruce Why not.

Bruce *shakes* **Christopher**'s *hand.* **Christopher** *makes it an elaborate one. They punch fists.*

Christopher I'm a free man. D'you know what I mean?

Bruce Well . . . aha ha . . . OK.

Christopher I'm a happy man. Bursting with joy.

Bruce Chris?

Christopher   Oh – hey – oh . . . OK. I'll be good. You're right. I should sit.

Christopher *sits with exaggerated calm.*

Bruce   Relax.

Christopher   I should relax and calm myself.

Bruce   Take a few breaths. Would you like some water?

Christopher (*fidgeting*)   Uh?

Bruce   Would you like a cup of water?

Christopher   Coke.

Bruce   No, you can't have –

Christopher   Ice-cold Coke. The Real Thing.

Bruce   No, you know you can't have Coke –

Christopher   Yeah I can because –

Bruce   What did I tell you about Coke?

Christopher   I'm going home tomorrow.

Bruce   What's wrong with drinking Coke?

Christopher   But I'm going home.

Bruce   Chris? Come on you know this, it's important. What's wrong with Coke?

Pause.

Christopher   It rots your teeth.

Bruce   No – well, yes – and . . . ? What else does it do to you?

Christopher   Makes my head explode.

Bruce   Well – no – no – what does it do to you really?

Christopher   Makes my head explode – oh man – I know – I get you.

Bruce   It's not good for you, is it?

Christopher   No. It's bad.

Bruce   What's the first thing we learnt when you came in here?

Christopher   No coffee no Coke.

Bruce   No coffee no Coke, that's right. Doesn't do us any good at all.

Christopher   Mm.

Bruce   Gets us overexcited.

Christopher   Yeah yeah yeah yeah, makes me jumpy.

Bruce   That's right so — what shall we have instead?

Christopher   I dunno.

Bruce   What would you like?

Christopher   What I'd really like is a Snakebite. D'you know what I mean?

Bruce   A Snakebite. Right, well –

Christopher   Cider and Red Stripe or, you know, or a rum and black or or or . . .

Bruce   Chris, Christopher . . . what's the rule on alcohol now?

Christopher   But –

Bruce   What's the rule on alcohol in here?

Christopher   Alcohol.

Pause.

Oh yeah. Alcohol. Heh heh. D'you know what I mean?

Bruce   What does alcohol do?

Christopher   It makes your blood thin.

Bruce   No . . . well, possibly, but –

Christopher   Makes you see things.

Bruce   Well . . . yes, but –

Christopher   See into the future maybe.

Bruce   Well . . . s . . . sometimes maybe but what does it mostly do?

Christopher   It fucks you up.

Bruce   It fucks you up. Precisely. How about a glass of water. Eh? Some nice cool water? From the, from the thing?

Christopher   Water from the thing. That's cool.

Bruce   Nice cool water, yes. Let me – just hold on . . .

Bruce *gets up and* **Christopher** *suddenly gets up too.*

Bruce   No no – you're all right, I'm just –

Christopher   No, you're all right –

Bruce (*sitting*)   Help yourself –

Christopher (*sitting*)   No no, I'll –

Bruce   I'll – look – this is silly.

Bruce *gestures.*

Christopher   Are you sure?

Bruce   Be my guest.

Christopher *gets up and goes to the water cooler, takes two cups, pours.*

Bruce   Sorted.

Christopher (*drinking shakily*)   Sorted for Es and whiz.

Bruce   . . . Indeed.

Christopher   Sorted, innit. Sorted for Es and whiz.

Bruce   Absolutely.

Christopher (*sitting*)   D'you know what I mean? Heh heh. You must know what I mean? Eh? Eh? *Doctor.*

He puts a cup of water in front of **Bruce** *and sips his own.*

Christopher   D'you know what I mean?

Bruce   Huh. Of course . . .

Christopher   D'you know what I mean?

Bruce   Well . . .

Pause.

No. I don't.

Christopher   Yeah you do.

Bruce *sips his water.*

Christopher   Where's the *drugs*, man?

Bruce   . . . Oh the *drugs*. Of course . . .

Christopher   It's all that, innit. 'Where's the drugs, man? Oh man, these patients giving me massive big headache, man, massive big headache, what have I got in my doctor's bag, gimme some smack, where's some smack? Where's the Tamazie Party? This bad nigga patient I got. This *bad nigga dude* I know. My God! I Can't Take The Pressure!' Innit? Innit. Go home to the old lady – 'Aw I can't take the pressure. Oh no. I can't calm down. Oh no – yes – no – I can't shag until you gimme the smack, darling!' D'you know what I mean? Ha ha ha ha ha. Oh no. Ha ha. It's all that. You with me?

Pause.

Bruce   Well . . .

Christopher   Yeah yeah . . . go on! Typical white doctor. This is how *white* doctors speak: 'Drugs? What drugs? No drugs for *you*, nigga. Cos you'll only enjoy them! These are *my* drugs . . .'

Bruce   It's not quite like that.

Christopher   Deny. It's all you doctors do! Deny, man.

Bruce   Well, I don't think so really . . .

Christopher (*sipping water shakily*)   Bullshit. Bullshit. Why else would you do it? Why else are you here?

Bruce   Well, Christopher, why do you think you're here?

Christopher   Eh?

Bruce   Why are you here? Why do you think you're here?

Christopher   Why am I here?

Bruce   Yes.

Pause.

Christopher   I dunno.

Bruce   And you've been here a while now.

Christopher   Yeah – yes I have . . . that's true.

Bruce   Why do you think that is? If you'd just wanted drugs you wouldn't really be here, would you? You'd be out there. Scoring off somebody and . . . going home. Wouldn't you?

Pause.

I know I would! Eh? Ha ha. Have a smoke. Watch the football.

Pause.

N'ha ha.

Pause.

No. Obviously. I'm not a drug user – OK? You know. But joking aside – it doesn't make sense that anybody would be in here just for drugs as opposed to say, you know, out there *enjoying*, enjoying their drugs. Having some fun. D'you see what I mean?

Pause.

I mean, they are supposed to be recreational.

Pause.

So my point is – and this is one of the things I want to talk to you about today – you're here to get better, aren't you? Because you've been very poorly. Haven't you?

Long pause.

Christopher   I dunno.

Bruce   Ah.

Christopher   What's up? I'm going home. You should be happy.

Bruce   Well, I'm not as happy as you.

Christopher   I been saying all along, there's nothing wrong with me and now you agree with me and, I just, I just, I just . . . I'm going home.

Pause.

I don't know why I'm here.

Pause.

It's mad, innit. It's bonkers. Mad shit. First thing I said when I arrived. When I first come in here. I had a look, I saw all the all the, you know, the others, the other geezers and I thought . . . Fuck This. My God! These people are insane! Ha ha ha ha ha . . . Get Me Outta Here –

Bruce   Ha ha yes –

Christopher   It's a *nut*house, man.

Bruce   I grant you – indeed – there are a fair proportion –

Christopher   A *fair proportion*? You're kidding me.

Bruce   Of quite, quite –

Christopher   They are NUTS!

Bruce   . . . crazy people here . . . yes –

Christopher   Crazies, man! Radio Rental.

Bruce   People with – well – we don't actually use the term 'crazy' . . .

Christopher   You just said it.

Bruce   I know I just said it but – I shouldn't have – I was – humouring – I was, you know – it's a no-no.

Christopher   But you just said it.

Bruce   I know, but – you see my point?

Christopher   You said it first.

Bruce   OK, look . . . there are things we . . . there are terms we use which people used to use all the time, terms which used to be inoffensive but things are a bit different now. Certain words.

Christopher   Certain words, what words?

Bruce   Just . . . terms which aren't even that offensive but –

Christopher   Same as I say, what's offensive about it?

Bruce   Well –

Christopher   It's true!

Bruce   It's not true . . . it's – OK – it's not even that – it's just inaccurate. Some terms are just inaccurate. 'Crazy' is one of them. It's just . . . unhelpful. Woolly.

Christopher   'Woolly'. Oh. OK. I'm sorry.

Bruce   For example, people used to say 'schizophrenic' all the time. 'Such-and-such is schizophrenic.' Because it's two things at once. OK. Used to denote a divided agenda, a dual identity, the analogy of a split personality. Except we know now that schizophrenia doesn't mean that at all. Split personality? Meaningless. OK? So it's an unhelpful term. It's inaccurate. What we call a 'misnomer'. And this is a sensitive subject. We must think carefully, be *specific*. Because it's too . . . you know . . . it's too serious.

Pause.

You were diagnosed with 'Borderline Personality Disorder'. What does that mean?

Pause.

Borderline personality disorder. OK? Key word – *borderline*. Because, clinically speaking, you're on the *border* between neurotic and psychotic.

Christopher   Just . . . on the border.

Bruce   Yes. And that's a very useful term, isn't it? Because if people get the word wrong – if people just get the meaning of the word wrong, how can they get the person right? How can there be any . . . any awareness? People don't know anything about it. They have stupid ideas. You lose out. So we try to 'demystify'. We try to explain.

Pause.

Which is what I wanted to talk to you about today. Your diagnosis. This term, this label, and what it means, because the thing is, I'm beginning to think, now . . . it's . . . well, it's a little inaccurate –

Christopher   YOU'VE MADE YOUR POINT I SAID I'M SORRY WHAT DO YOU WANT – BLOOD?

Bruce   But I'm just saying . . . in the light of recent developments –

Christopher   Developments? What developments. What you on about, man?

Robert, *carrying a cup of coffee also in a plastic cup, appears at the door and just stands there waiting.*

Robert   You wanted to see me.

Bruce   Doctor Smith. Yes, come in. Hi.

Robert   How's tricks?

Bruce   I'm fine. How are you?

Robert   I don't believe I've thanked you for that stupendous spread.

Bruce   Sorry?

Robert   That sumptuous meal on Saturday. After the rugby. The food.

Bruce   Oh. Thanks.

Robert   Hang on to that woman, Bruce.

Bruce   Sure.

Robert   You'll live to a hundred and three.

Bruce   The thing is –

Robert   The only woman I know with the audacity to pull off a fondue. I thought, 'Any minute now she'll be climbing into her caftan.'

Bruce   It was Welsh rarebit.

Robert   Welsh rarebit? The very thing.

Bruce   I know it's not what you're used to –

Robert   On the contrary. It was just the ticket. Miserable and wet. Vanquished by the Frog and foot-sore.

Bruce   Well, it soaked up the booze.

Robert   I couldn't believe that score. Not from the Frogs. Still, at least it wasn't Australia –

Bruce   Doctor Smith –

Robert   Or New Zealand or any of the other hairy colonial outposts.

Bruce   Doctor –

Robert   Welsh rarebit, eh? Took me back to my student days. Tie that woman to the nearest bed and inseminate her at once.

Bruce   Doctor –

Robert   *Breed*. Lots of little Bruces. Have you thought any more about that loft conversion? All the rage when I was a student. Quite the thing for somebody in your circumstances.

Robert *winks at* **Christopher** *conspiratorially and* **Christopher** *just stares back blankly*.

Bruce   Doc –

Robert   That'll set you back a few quid. Still, when you become a consultant . . .

Bruce   D –

Robert   That's where the big bucks are.

Bruce   The thing is –

Robert (*to* **Christopher**)   Hello.

Bruce   You remember Christopher? Chris, do you remember Doctor Smith? Senior Consultant.

Christopher   Warning warning warning! Alien life form approaching, Will Robinson.

Robert   Mm, ha ha ha –

Bruce   Mm, yes –

Robert   Very witty –

Bruce   OK . . . look –

Christopher   Warning warning warning . . . d'you know what I mean?

Bruce   Let's not get too distracted.

Robert   I'm distracting you of course.

Bruce   No no, you –

Robert   I –

Bruce   I want you to –

Robert   Well, of course, you asked me to –

Christopher   D'you know what I mean?

Bruce   I've asked Doctor Smith to sit in today.

Robert   Yes that's right. Just got myself a nice cup of coffee and I'll just lurk in the corner . . .

Christopher (*simultaneously with 'corner'*)   Coffee . . . !

Robert   You won't know I'm here.

Christopher   He's got coffee.

Bruce   There's plenty of water in the –

Christopher   Oh wow!

Bruce   That's not for you.

Christopher (*reaching over and gesturing for coffee*)   Oh come on, man. Coffee!

Bruce   Chris . . . Chris . . . (*To* **Robert**.) Excuse me.

Christopher   I want a cup of coffee.

Bruce   Christopher, hey listen, that's not yours.

Christopher   I'll split it with you.

Bruce   Is that yours or isn't it?

Christopher   Come on, man.

Bruce   Chris . . . Chris, come on! What's the rule on coffee?

Christopher *sits and kisses his teeth.*

Bruce   No Coke no coffee. I'm sorry. You know why.

Christopher   Why?

Bruce   You know why.

Christopher   Yeah, but I get out tomorrow. I'm getting out.

Robert   I think your man has a point.

Bruce *looks at* **Robert**.

Robert *takes out a packet of cigarettes and lights one.*

Robert   Sorry. I'm distracting you.

Robert *gets up to leave but* **Bruce** *gestures for him to sit.*

Bruce   Please, you aren't. Really.

Christopher   You got cigarettes! Gimme a cigarette, Doc, just one, I'm gagging for a puff, d'you know what I mean?

Bruce *nods.*

Robert *sits again and offers the pack to* **Christopher** *who takes a cigarette, then another, then another two, putting one behind his ear, two in his top pocket and one in his mouth.*

Robert *lights the cigarette for him and* **Christopher** *exhales a plume of smoke.*

Robert   Better?

Christopher   It's my nerves. I'm getting out tomorrow. You can't tell me what to do when I get out – when I'm out there – which is in (*checks his watch*) exactly twenty-four hours. I'm not under your . . . it's none of your business then, man. I'm twenty-four hours away from freedom. Out of this hole. D'you know what I mean?

Pause.

Forty-eight hours tops.

Robert   Give him some coffee, he's going home. I haven't touched mine.

Robert *offers the coffee,* **Christopher** *reaches for it but* **Bruce** *is there first and takes the cup, drains it in one and throws it expertly into a waste-paper bin in the corner.*

Christopher   Hey, man –

Bruce   Coffee's got caffeine in it.

Robert   Or a nice cup of tea?

Bruce   So has tea. The water's over there.

Christopher   What did you do that for?

Robert   If this isn't a good time . . . ?

Bruce   No, it's perfect timing. I wanted you to see this.

Robert   See what?

Christopher   I'm already *packed*.

Bruce   You're packed?

Robert   I'll just –

Christopher   Yeah, man. What, you think I'm not in a hurry? (*To* **Robert**.) I could use a coffee to give me a bump. Just to get me on my way, d'you know what I mean?

Bruce   Who said you could pack?

Robert (*half standing, hovering*)   Look, I can just –

Christopher   No one, man, I just did it. I just (no, you stay there), I put my pyjamas in a bag and my toothbrush in on top. (Don't move.) Took a whole five minutes. Shoot me. What, you think I 'pinched the towels' and some stationery?

Bruce   The thing is . . .

Christopher   Cos I'm I'm I'm . . . I'm what?

Robert   I can come back –

Christopher   Because I'm . . . ? (No you're all right.) Cos I'm . . . ?

Bruce   No –

Christopher   I'm –

Bruce   No –

Christopher   No what? You don't even know what I was gonna say. What was I gonna say?

Robert   Or I can stay?

Bruce   No, no I wasn't –

Christopher   Because I'm a Brother?

Pause.

Bruce (*to* **Robert**)   Paranoia. Nihilism. Persecution. Delusion –

Christopher   Cos I'm an 'uppity nigga'.

Bruce   No. You always say that and I always tell you the same thing. No.

Robert   I'll come back, shall I?

Bruce   Doctor Smith –

Christopher   WOULD YOU JUST MAKE UP YOUR MIND BEFORE I GO STARK STARING BANANAS? Bouncing about like Zebedee.

Bruce   Christopher –

Christopher   Don't Christopher me, man . . . (One sip of coffee he thinks he's Batman.)

Bruce   You know that's not the way you talk to the consultants.

Christopher   He's giving me the fear.

Bruce   Calm down. Now you are acting like a –

Christopher   A what? A what. Go on, say it. An 'uppity nigga'.

Christopher *kisses his teeth and starts eyeballing* **Robert**.

Bruce   Well . . . OK, yes, frankly you are and that's not what we do, is it? Eh? And when you get out of here, if you start staring at people like that, what are they going to think?

Christopher   What?

Bruce   What are people going to think? When you get out? When you're ready . . . ?

Christopher   I don't fucking know.

Bruce   Well, what do you think they're gonna think?

Christopher   I don't know.

Bruce   They'll think you're a, a, an 'uppity nigga', that's what they'll think. Kissing your teeth. It's not you. It's silly. It's crazy. You're not a, a, a, some type of '*Yardie*' –

Christopher   Now you're telling me who I am?

Bruce   No, I'm –

Christopher   You're telling me who I am?

Bruce   I'm telling you . . . to be You.

Christopher   That's rum, that is. That's rich. Now I've got an identity crisis. You're a cheeky fucking monkey, you are, aren't you?

Pause.

Robert   Mm. 'Uppity' isn't strictly speaking a term we –

Bruce (*to* **Robert**)   Learned Unresponsiveness? Disorganised Behaviour? Decline in Social Skills? Do you get me?

Robert   So?

Bruce   Eh?

Robert   Look around you. *Who isn't* unresponsive, and disorganised with declining social skills? Eh? Heh heh. It's *normal*.

Pause.

Uh-huh huh huh.

Bruce   Could we have a quiet word?

Christopher *stands abruptly and slams his fist on the desk.*

Christopher   Hey! You! I'm talking to you. When I get out of this place, people won't think *anything* because I'll be gone, boy. I'm going far away where I can get some peace and quiet, no people, no cars, pollution, planes flying overhead like fruit flies, no cities, no fucking TVs, no construction work, no roadworks, no drills, no neighbours squatting on my head, under the floor, through the walls, rowing all day and night. Nothing. No people at all, man, and nobody looking at me funny like they never seen a Brother before except on fucking *Sesame Street*! I'm going far away. (What's he looking at?) Look at you – nervous as a tomcat with big balls.
D'you think I'm gonna eat you?
I might do just to see the look on your face.

Bruce   Nobody's looking at you funny, Chris.

Christopher   He is.

Robert   Well, are you surprised?

Christopher   What?

Robert   Are you surprised? Look at yourself. Now just . . . sit down and . . . relax, would you? Of course people stare at you when you act like this. You know that, you know what it's like.

Christopher *looks from one to another, kisses his teeth.*

Pause.

Bruce (*to* **Robert**)   Overburdened Nervous System. Can't look me in the eye. Thinks we're staring at him.

Robert   We are.

Pause.

Christopher   I'm gone, oh yes. Believe. A place with a desert. And beaches. Palm trees. Somewhere hot. D'you know what I mean?

Bruce   Chris . . . ? Would you mind waiting in the other room for two minutes?

Christopher   What did I say?

Bruce   Nothing at all, we just need to –

Robert   Consult.

Bruce   That's right.

Robert   That's why the badge says 'Consultant'. (I'm not wearing it.)

Bruce   Please. I'd really appreciate it. Just go through that door.

Christopher (*sighs*)   OK. But I hope you know what you're doing, yeah?

Bruce   How do you mean?

Christopher   I hope you're not gonna let him talk you into anything.

Robert   Good God no. No no no no no.

Christopher   Hope you're not gonna go changing your mind on me. Cos my twenty-eight . . .

Bruce   Chris –

Christopher   My twenty-eight days –

Bruce   I know –

Christopher   My twenty-eight days is up. It's up, man. You've had your fun. I'm gone. Believe.

Bruce   Uh-huh, OK . . . thank you.

Christopher *stands, lingers, stares at them both, then goes through a door.*

Silence.

Bruce   Do you think he knows?

Robert   What's there to know? He's a Section 2. His twenty-eight days are up. He's responded to treatment and now he's going home.

Pause.

Am I right?

Bruce   But –

Robert   But what?

Bruce   Well . . . I mean, you know what I'm going to ask you, don't you?

Pause.

Robert   What?

Bruce   I want a Section 3.

Robert   Take a deep breath, and forget you even thought of it.

Bruce   But –

Robert   Let him out. You're doing the right thing.

Bruce   But I'm not.

Robert   Yes, this is right. You are doing what is fair and right and *just* and textbook medically beneficial.

Pause.

And apart from anything else we don't have the beds.

Bruce   I'm really quite concerned –

Robert   Those beds are Prioritised for Emergency Admissions and Level Ones. Otherwise we'll wind up with a hospital full of long-term chronic mental patients hurtling about on *trolleys* – it'll be like the *Wacky Races*.

Bruce   Look –

Robert   There'd be scandal. They'd have my arse out of here faster than his and you'd be next. That's right. I'll never make Professor. You'll never make your Specialist Registrar Training. And how long did you study for that? Six years? What were we saying on Saturday?

Bruce   When?

Robert   After the rugby. What did we talk about?

Bruce   I dunno, what?

Robert   Well, your Specialist Registrar Training. And I said, for the coming year I am prepared to supervise you, I'll be your 'Mentor', I'll teach you 'all I know' . . . but you have to play the game.

Bruce   'Play the game'?

Robert   That's right. I'll push your barrow. I'll feed the scrum but you're going to have to kick the ball into touch once in a while.

Bruce   But –

Robert   Take my advice, if you keep your nose clean and you enjoy psychiatry you'll almost certainly become a consultant. Nevertheless, you don't want to be a consultant for ever. Sooner or later you'll want to become a Senior. You too may one day seek a professorship.

Bruce   If I . . . ?

Robert   But you can't afford to be indecisive about this.

Bruce   But I *am* indecisive.

Robert   You can't afford not to follow my advice is what I mean.

Bruce   Oh, that kind of indecisive.

Robert   They'll close the hospital down and build another Millennium Dome.

Bruce   Nobody's going to close the hospital because of one Section 3. Are they? D'you think . . . ?

Robert   Yes. Perhaps.

Bruce   Really?

Robert   Yes. Perhaps.

Pause.

Follow the Path of Least Resistance.

Bruce   But . . . I can't justify throwing him out on the basis of beds.

Robert   You're not 'throwing him out' . . . you're doing what we are here to do. What *they* are here for us to do – and what everybody *expects* us to do.

Pause.

Eh? You are giving this man his *freedom.*
You are releasing this man into the bosom of the community.
You are giving him back his life.
He's going back to his people.

Bruce   His 'people'? He doesn't have any *people*. He doesn't have a life.

Robert   That's a matter of conjecture.

Bruce   It's true. He's on the White City Estate. It's a predominantly Jamaican community, he didn't grow up there, he doesn't know anybody and he hates it.

Robert   Where did he grow up?

Bruce   All over the place. Peripatetic childhood.

Robert   What about family? He must have a mother.

Bruce   He doesn't seem to be in contact with her any more.

Robert   Are you proposing to section this man again on the basis that he – what – he's lonely?

Bruce   It'll do his head in.

Robert   It'll do his head in if you section him again.

Bruce   He isn't ready to go. You heard him. He's unstable.

Robert   Borderline personality disorder. On the border of neurotic and psychotic.

Bruce   He was highly animated, shouting, staring.

Robert   You'd shout and stare if you were on the border of neurotic and psychotic.

Bruce   The loosening of associations? The paranoia?

Robert   And you can add, reckless, impulsive, prone to extreme behaviour, problems handling personal life, handling money, maintaining a home, family, sex, relationships, alcohol, a fundamental inability to handle practically everything that makes us human – and hey, Some People Are Just *Like* That. Borderline. On the border. Occasionally visits but doesn't live there. See, technically he's not *that* mentally ill. We can't keep him here. It's Ugly but it's Right.

Pause.

Shoot me, those are the rules.

Bruce   'Shoot me'? 'Some people are just like that. Shoot me'? Are you joking?

Robert   Deadly serious. It's what makes it so hard for us. And one day, when you're a consultant like me, and you will be, if you don't fuck this up, when every young clinician is saying exactly the same thing as you, you'll tell them what I'm telling you now. Some People Are Just Like That. Get over it. We hold their hands for twenty-eight days, wait until things have calmed down, the mess has been mopped up and off they trot, back to whatever hell they've just blown in from, usually a little bit happier and maybe even a little bit wiser until the next time.

Pause.

Bruce   Christopher is a schizophrenic.

Pause.

Did you hear me?

Robert   No, he's BPD.

Bruce   If you Section 3 him I can keep him here until he's properly diagnosed.

Robert   No. Absolutely not.

Bruce   He's a Type I Schizophrenic with Positive Symptoms including Paranoid Tendencies. Probably Thought Disorder as well.

Robert   Not Paranoid Schizophrenia?

Bruce   Close but I'd be loath to go that far at this –

Robert   It's another month before we can diagnose Schizophrenia – Paranoid or Disorganised.

Bruce   So resection him.

Robert   Is he delusional?

Bruce   Sometimes.

Robert   Since when?

Bruce   Since he presented.

Robert   How delusional?

Bruce   Give me time and I'll show you.

Robert   You haven't got time. He's been here a month. He's been steadily improving – it's therefore a brief Psychotic Episode associated with BPD. Nothing more insidious.

Bruce   He's paranoid. You heard him.

Robert   How does BPD with Paranoia sound? Stick to the ICD 10 Classification.

Bruce   You love the ICD 10, don't you? All the different euphemisms for 'he's nuts' without actually having to admit he's nuts. It's like your Linus blanket.

Robert   OK. BPD and A Bit Nuts.

Bruce   No. Doctor. Please.

Robert   'Eccentric'.

Bruce   Look –

Robert   Was he squiffy?

Bruce   . . . 'Squiffy'?

Robert   'Squiffy'. Intoxicated. When he was sectioned.

Bruce   . . . Yes . . . I think . . .

Robert   BPD with Alcoholism. It's a movable feast.

Bruce   What? No it's not!

Robert   It's a matter of 'opinion'. And I'd be loath to resection the boy on the basis of a difference of opinion. It's semantics. And right now, Doctor, my semantics are better than yours so I win.

Bruce   I can't live with that diagnosis.

Robert   *You* don't have to.

Bruce   I can't live with the *prognosis*.

Robert   Well, you can't make a new diagnosis safely for at least another month.

Bruce   And I can't keep him another month unless I make a new diagnosis!

Pause.

Robert   But what's he done?

Bruce   He hasn't done anything yet.

Robert   Has he tried to harm himself?

Bruce   No.

Robert   Has he tried to harm anybody else?

Bruce   Of course not.

Robert   Well, you can't section him again until he does something. Is he a danger to himself or to the public is what I'm getting at.

Bruce   You want to wait until he becomes dangerous?

Robert   We have to be sure.

Bruce   But we can't be sure until it's too late.

Robert   And we can't do anything until he does something. It's a conundrum, I know.

Bruce   A 'conundrum'?

Robert   What's the risk factor? Come on. Write it down. Pretend you're running a business.

Bruce   'Pretend I'm . . . running a business'?

Robert   If we don't keep him in here – if we do not make this 'very costly outlay' . . .

Bruce   Well, it is risky.

Robert   How risky?

Bruce   *Very* risky.

Robert   What did he do before?

Bruce   Before when?

Robert   Before he was admitted. What happened?

Bruce   He was . . . he was in the market . . . doing . . . I dunno, something funny.

Robert   He was doing 'something funny' in the market. Which market?

Bruce   Does it matter?

Robert   I'm curious.

Bruce   Shepherd's Bush.

Robert   'Funny' strange or 'funny' ha ha?

Bruce   It's in the file. Read the file.

Robert   Why can't you just tell me?

Bruce   I'd rather not.

Robert   Why not?

Bruce   I'd just rather not.

Pause.

Robert   Why not?

Pause.

Why not, Doctor? What did he do?

Bruce   It's rather delicate.

Robert   Well, if you're going to be coy about it –

Bruce   I just don't think it's relevant.

Robert   We can't keep him in here unless he's dangerous. You know the rules.

Bruce   I think he's becoming depressed.

Robert   *I'm* becoming depressed now.

Pause.

Look.
Doctor. If you keep him here long enough he won't be able to go home because he won't know what home is any more. He won't know how it works any more – he won't know How To Do It. Get him out there now. Assign a community psychiatric nurse and treat him in the home – he's more comfortable, we're more comfortable, it's less of a drain on resources, the Authority is ecstatic.

Bruce   OK. In a perfect world, forgetting about 'resources', forgetting about 'budgetary constraints' – say we've got *unlimited beds* – what would you do?

Robert   In a perfect world I'd send him home with fucking bells on and spread a little happiness. Why the hell not? Now, you have a job to do. If you don't feel you can do that job, you go away and have a think for a while. You know, in the medical wilderness, in your new job proofreading for the fucking *Lancet*; writing Bolshevik columns for *Welsh Doctor Weekly*.

Pause.

Is he still in there? Where is he?

Bruce   He's in there.

Robert   In the . . . the . . .

Bruce   That little room.

Robert   What little room? The cleaners' room?

Bruce   No, the, you know. That little waiting room. That's where they go to wait. It's a new thing.

Pause.

Robert   You know, there is nothing wrong with your patient, Bruce. He may be a bit jumpy, he may be a bit brusque, a bit shouty, a bit OTT – but hey, maybe that's just what you do where he comes from.

Bruce   'Where he comes from'?

Robert   His 'community'.

Bruce   He comes from Shepherd's Bush. What exactly are you trying to say?

Robert   I'm not saying anything.

Bruce   'Where he comes from'? What are you saying?

Robert   I'm not saying anything.

Bruce   Go on. What are you saying?

Robert   Nothing.

Pause.

I'm only saying . . .

Pause.

Maybe . . . maybe, maybe it's just you. Maybe you just make him nervous. Eh?

Bruce   *What?*

Robert   Hear me out, it happens. This is the question we must ask ourselves. As a profession.

Bruce   'Is it me? Do I just make him nervous?'

Robert   Yes.

Bruce   He's a paranoid schizophrenic.

Robert   'Allegedly.'

Bruce   This is ridiculous.

Robert   We spend our lives asking whether or not this or that person is to be judged normal, a 'normal' person, a 'human', and we blithely assume that we know what 'normal' is. What 'human' is. Maybe he's more 'human' than us. Maybe *we're* the sick ones.

Bruce   He's 'more human than us'?

Robert   Yes.

Bruce   And we're the sick ones.

Robert   Maybe.

Pause.

Bruce   *Why?*

Silence.

Robert   OK, I'm being 'whimsical'. I'm being 'capricious'. But maybe, just maybe he's a *right* to be angry and paranoid and depressed and unstable. Maybe it's the only *suitable* response to the human condition.

Bruce What?

Robert The human species is the only species which is innately insane. 'Sanity is a conditioned response to environmental . . .

Bruce I don't believe you're saying this . . .

Robert . . . stimulae.' Maybe – just maybe it's true.

Bruce Maybe it's *utter horseshit.* (*Beat.*) I'm sorry. Doctor Smith. But. Which, which existential novelist said that? I mean, um, you'll be quoting R.D. Laing next.

Robert That was R.D. Laing.

Bruce R.D. Laing was a *madman.* They don't come any fruitier.

Robert I think there's something in it . . .

Bruce You'll be leaping into your tights and spouting Shakespeare next: Hamlet had a Borderline Personality Disorder with Morbidity, Recklessness, Impulsiveness and a propensity for dithering.

Robert He did!

Bruce Should you really be telling me this? Because, when I was at med school, you know, this is not the sort of thing I learnt.

Robert Well, with respect, Doctor, maybe it's time you grew up, eh? Loosen up, calm down, get your head out of your textbooks and learn a little about *humanity.* Humanity, Doctor. Being human. As the poet said, Alan Ginsberg, *Alan Ginsberg* said this, I'll never forget it . . . 'Human is not a noun, it's a *verb.*'

Pause.

Eh? Don't be so *old-fashioned.*

Silence.

Bruce Alan Ginsberg.

Robert   OK, bad example. But listen . . .
The government guidelines clearly state that the community
is the preferred and proper place and it's our duty to
subscribe to that. Otherwise it's no end of trouble.

Bruce   If I let him out he will have a breakdown and
succumb to all the most horrifying symptoms of
schizophrenia undiagnosed, unchecked, unsupervised and
unmedicated.

Robert   Doctor Flaherty –

Bruce   And we can't do anything about it –

Robert   Doctor Flaherty.

Bruce   Because of policy?

Robert   Calm down.

Bruce   I'm sorry. Um, you're right. I'm calm.

Robert   If you detain this man any longer he will become
institutionalised.
He won't get better he'll get worse.
You will make him ill.

Pause.

Bruce   Well, um, I don't believe I will.

Robert *goes to the door, opens it.*

Christopher *comes through the door.*

Robert   You can come back in now. We've finished our
little chat. Sit down, there's a good fellow. Can I get you
anything, a cup of water?

Robert *pours another cup for* **Christopher** *who drinks thirstily.*

Christopher *paces a moment.*

Bruce   Thirsty?

Christopher *nods and holds his cup out for a refill. He drinks it and
goes back to pacing.*

Bruce   That'll be the haloperidol. Are you still stiff?

Christopher   I'm jumping like a leaf. I been walking it off.

Bruce   Try not to.

Christopher   I like walking.

Bruce   I know. And that's how you get lost.

Christopher   I walked to the Hanger Lane Gyratory once.

Bruce   I know. I'm sure it was wonderful.

Robert   Bravo.

Bruce   No, not Bravo, you must try and control it.

Robert   Oh, let him walk if he wants to walk. Goodness gracious. You go ahead and walk to Hanger Lane. Enjoy. Now. When were you planning on leaving us?

Christopher (*pacing*)   Twenty-four hours.

Robert   Morning, evening?

Christopher   After I had my lunch.

Robert   And you have somewhere to go I take it.

Bruce   Council accommodation. White City.

Robert   Marvellous.

Christopher   Only I don't go there.

Robert   Oh.

Christopher   I don't like White City.

Robert   Why not?

Christopher   Cos of the Fuzz.

Robert   The 'Fuzz'.

Christopher   The Filth. The Pigs. The Cops. The 'Old Bill'.

Robert   The police?

Christopher   I get stopped a *lot* in White City.
That's why I was arrested in Shepherd's Bush. Cos they all
talk to each other on their walkie-talkies. They was waiting
for me. They came to get me in the market. Come all the way
from White City for me. Believe. I lost my shit.

Robert   I see, well –

Christopher   Cos they was after me, man.

Robert   And why do you think that is?

Christopher   What? *Why*?

Robert   Yes, why? Why were they 'after you'?

Christopher   Why do you *think*, man?

Robert   I'm asking you.

Christopher   Cos they're *fascists*. It's obvious.

Silence.

Robert   Where would you like to live?

Christopher   Where?

Robert   Would you prefer?

Christopher   Africa.

Robert   Africa.

Pause.

Christopher *sits and stares at* **Robert** *with intensity.*

Robert   Aha ha ha. Yes, very good. And why not?

Christopher   I already told you.

Robert   Yes, but I mean, for the time being.

Christopher   There is no time being. I'm going to Africa.
Central Africa. Where my dad come from.

Robert   Ah. Well . . . when you get out, if you, if things work out for you and you get a . . . have you got a job to go back to?

Christopher   Got a job in Africa.

Robert   O . . . K . . . Somewhere to stay?

Christopher   In Africa. In Uganda.

Silence.

Robert   Friends?

Christopher   In Africa.

Robert (*beat*)   Excellent.

Robert *stands.*

He hands the notes back to **Bruce**.

Robert   Well, I think I've pretty much finished here. Doctor Flaherty?

Bruce   You're finished?

Robert   Quite finished. It's been nice chatting to you, Christopher. I sincerely hope I never clap eyes on you again, e-heh heh heh.

He shakes **Christopher**'s *hand and* **Christopher** *just stares at him.*

Robert   It's a joke.

Bruce   So you're just going now?

Robert   Is that a problem? Unless you want me for anything else?

They all look at each other.

Christopher *is still holding* **Robert**'s *hand.*

Christopher (*to* **Robert**)   What's up with him? (*To* **Bruce**.) What's up your arse, man?

Bruce If you don't mind, I'd like you to stay while I ask Chris a couple more questions.

Robert What sort of questions?

Bruce Routine. My assessment isn't over yet.

Robert *sits reluctantly, taking his hand back.*

Robert Why not? Fire away.

Bruce Because, the thing is, Chris, Doctor Smith here says that you can go if you want to.

Christopher I know. I'm going.

Bruce But I'm wondering if you really want to?

Christopher I want it *bad*, d'you know what I mean?

Bruce And . . . you're *sure* you're ready. Are you sure?

Christopher I'm cool.

Pause.

Bruce OK. Just a couple of questions.

Christopher Shoot.

Bruce What's in the fruit bowl?

Christopher How d'you mean?

Bruce What do you see in the fruit bowl? What type of fruit do you see?

He proffers the bowl full of oranges. **Christopher** *stares at it long and hard.* **Bruce** *takes an orange from the bowl and hands it to* **Christopher** *who stares at it hard.*

He also tosses one to **Robert**.

Bruce What's in the bowl, Chris?

Christopher Oranges.

Bruce Oranges, good, but what sort of oranges?

Christopher   Just oranges.

Bruce   Yes, but they're not *orange* oranges, are they?

Christopher   Nope.

Bruce   What did you tell me yesterday? Can you remember?

Pause.

Christopher   They're blue oranges.

Bruce   Blue oranges. Really?

Christopher   Bright blue.

Bruce   Peel one. See what's inside.

They wait as **Christopher** *peels the orange, holds it up.*

Bruce   What colour is it inside?

Pause.

Chris?

Christopher   It's blue.

Bruce   So the skin is blue – and even underneath the skin it's the same – it's blue?

Christopher   That's correct. Completely blue.

Pause.

It's bad. It's a bad orange. Don't eat it.

Pause.

I mean, my God! Ha ha. What is it? 'Black magic'?

Bruce   Voodoo.

Christopher   Voodoo! Oh no. *Spooky.* D'you know what I mean? It's – it's – it's *nuts.*

Bruce   'Spooky'.

Christopher   Spooky. 'Yikes!'

Bruce 'Yikes' indeed . . .

Christopher 'This bad nigga dude we got doing his voodoo again.'

Pause.

My dad, right, my dad, that's his favourite fruit. Oranges. *Orange* oranges, though. D'you know what I mean?

Bruce Who is your father, Chris? Chris?

Pause.

Christopher *eats a segment of orange.*

Bruce Who is your father?

Christopher How d'you mean?

Bruce What's his name?

Christopher I already told you.

Bruce Tell me again. In front of Robert.

Christopher Why?

Bruce Just . . . please, Chris . . . it's a simple question.

Christopher It's difficult to answer. D'you know what I mean?

Bruce No I don't. Why?

Christopher If I ask you who your father is nobody gives a shit. With me it's front-page news. D'you understand?

Bruce No, I don't understand. Why is it front-page news?

Christopher Cos of who he is.

Robert Who is he?

Christopher I'm not telling you.

Bruce (This is ridiculous.) Look. Please. Help me out here.

Christopher   You want *me* to help *you*? Now you want me to do your job.

Robert   If you can't tell us who he is – it'll be tricky for us to send you home. You will have to stay here. Do you understand?

Bruce   Who's your father, Chris?

Pause.

Christopher   It sounds silly.

Bruce   For Christ's sake –

Christopher   It's embarrassing.

Bruce   Chris!

Christopher   How can I say it, in all honesty, without you thinking I'm off the stick? How do I know it won't incriminate me, d'you know what I'm saying?

Robert   It won't incriminate you. We promise.

Christopher   Oh you 'promise'? Well, in that case, I feel a whole lot better.

Bruce   Please . . . just do this one thing for me. For me.

Pause.

Christopher   My father . . . my dad . . . was a very important man.

Pause.

Believe it or not . . . my dad . . . is former Ugandan President His Excellency Idi Amin.

Bruce   Fabulous –

Christopher   And if he knew where I was now I would not want to be you.

Bruce   Y – Chris –

Christopher   I would not want to be you.
Because The Man Does Not Fuck About, d'you understand
what I'm saying?
He will *digest* you.
He will juice you and squirt you out of his arse like a
motherfucking firehose, into the sewers for the bats and the
fish.
They don't call him 'The Butcher of the Bush' for nothing.
Believe.

Silence.

Robert   Fine . . . OK . . .

Christopher   What else d'you want to know?

Robert   Well –

Christopher   He got forty-three children and a hundred
grandchildren. He's a family man. He's a Muslim. He lives in
Saudi Arabia. In exile. 'Cept when he goes on holiday to
Paris. Every day he takes a delivery of East African oranges
from the airport. Reminds him of old times.
He drives a Chevrolet and has a talent for the accordion. A
lot of exiles drive Mercedes but he don't like to draw
attention to his self.

Robert   I see . . .

Christopher   He kicked my mum out of Uganda cos she's
from Zaire. He kicked out all the foreigners. D'you know
what I mean? I'm not proud of it. It's just the way he was.
Old-fashioned.

Pause.

Robert   'Old . . . fashioned'. Mm . . .

Pause.

Your mother is from Zaire, you say?

Christopher   You don't believe me, do you?

Robert   When was this?

Christopher   1974. Before I was born.

Robert   *Before* you were born?

Christopher   I was *conceived*. That's why she had to go. He couldn't father a foreigner. It's obvious.

Bruce *and* **Robert** *stare at each other.*

Christopher   He's got another wife in Haringay who runs a chippy. Got closed down for bad hygiene, d'you know what I mean?

Bruce   You can go back to your ward now. Chris? I'll see you later.

Christopher   But –

Bruce   It's over now.

Christopher   We finished?

Bruce   We're finished for today, yes.

Christopher   What did I say?

Robert   Absolutely nothing.

Christopher   Did I pass?

Bruce *just smiles.*

Christopher   Now you're not saying anything. That's no good.

Bruce   You have nothing to worry about.

Christopher   I don't, yeah?

Bruce   No. You're going to be fine.

Christopher   I'm still going home, right?

Pause.

I'm still going home, yeah?

Pause.

I'm . . . I'm still going home?

Robert   Shhhh . . . OK? Just relax.

Pause.

Christopher   But . . . I'm –

Robert   Shhh.

Pause.

Christopher   I'm –

Robert (*waving a finger*)   Uh. Uh-uh.

Pause.

Christopher   But I'm still going home, aren't I?

Robert   Of course you are.

Bruce   Chris? I'll speak to you later. Go back to your ward now.

Christopher   But I'm still going home, yeah?

Robert   Yes.

Bruce *takes back the remains of the orange,* **Christopher** *gets up and shuffles out.*

Robert *takes the remains of the orange from* **Bruce** *and eats a segment.*

Robert   Very interesting.

Bruce   Happy?

Robert   'Le Monde est Bleu comme une Orange'.

Bruce   What?

Robert   It's a poem by Paul Eluard. He was a French surrealist.

Bruce   You don't say.

Robert   'The World is as Blue as an Orange'. (*Beat*.) It's an analogy.

Bruce   Classic hallucinatory behaviour.

Robert   Or is it a simile?

Bruce   Already he's building a system of logic around it . . . his '*father*' who loves oranges de da de da de da.

Robert   Hypomania. Brief psychotic episode requiring short-term hospital treatment and a course of antipsychotics when he goes home. Simple.

Bruce   What if it isn't? What if it's just the tip of the iceberg?

Robert   Is he hearing voices? Auditory hallucinations?

Bruce   Not yet.

Robert   Is he seeing things – other than blue oranges?

Bruce   Isn't this enough?

Robert (*shrugs*)   For some reason he wants to see blue instead of orange. Neurotics do it all the time. They see what they want to see, not what they really see. Maybe he knows the poem.

Bruce   You're joking, aren't you?

Robert   Entirely serious. There's a lot of French speakers in Central Africa. His mother could have read it him as a child. It planted an image in his mind. When he's not a hundred per cent that image presents itself.

Bruce   You are joking.

Robert   There's a Tintin book. *Tintin and the Blue Oranges*. It's about a 'mad professor' who invents an orange which will grow in the Sahara. Only trouble is it's bright blue and tastes salty. Tintin was banned in the Belgian Congo. They thought he was a communist. But in colonial Uganda the notoriety no doubt made Tintin a 'must read' for the bourgeoisie. He was

a cultural icon and a symbol of middle-class insurrection. A
delusion waiting to happen.
BPD with Delusion.

Bruce   Are you making this up?

Robert *shakes his head.*

Bruce   Surely, you must agree, there's something terribly
wrong here. Surely we have a responsibility to . . .

Robert   A responsibility to let him out. Level 2. Prescribe
medication, CPN twice weekly.

Bruce   He won't take medication, you know that, they
never do.

Robert   That's what we have CPNs for. Just till he's back
on his feet.

Bruce   They never do because it's dated toxic crud which
will paralyse him from the skull downwards and make his life
a misery. Nobody in their right mind will take those drugs by
choice.

Robert   Precisely.

Bruce   So . . . ?

Robert   New generation antipsychotics. Clozapine,
risperidone, olanzapine. Let him go home.

Bruce   At thirty times the cost? Have you got the resources
or does he have to go private?

Robert   Risperidone and clozapine are now licensed, by
the next budget they'll be cheaper than Mars bars.

Bruce   What?

Robert   Cheaper than hospitals anyway. Do the maths.

Bruce   OK. We'll keep him here until the next budget.
Simple.

Robert   Don't be facetious. It's not a rest home.

Bruce   He needs looking after. You *agreed*, he needs to be on antipsychotics.

Robert   Maybe he does, maybe he doesn't.
Maybe he really does have some connection with Idi Amin. Jesus Christ-on-a-mountain-bike. The man was spawning offspring all over the shop.

Bruce   You can't be serious.

Robert   Maybe I am.

Bruce   Oh for God's sake.

Robert   OK, calm down.

He paces and wipes his hands on his shirt, rubs his hands together, talks with a mouthful.

Now (*clears his throat*) for what it's worth, it's quite possible he's heard some family story, handed down through the generations, some apocryphal story, maybe Idi Amin came to town, to the village, de da de da de da, Chinese whispers, it's just gathered importance, gained in stature and now he believes this. It happens. Read my manuscript.

Bruce   What manuscript?

Robert   It's a continuation of my PhD really. It's not finished. There's a chapter missing – something rather complex and enigmatic – a certain *je ne sais quoi* although I can't think what.
Seriously. I think there's something in it.

Bruce   I think there's something in feng shui, Doctor, but I wouldn't do a PhD in it.

Robert   As your supervisor I wouldn't have it any other way.

Bruce   I read your PhD. 'Cultural Antecedent and Cultural Specificity in Connection with a Delusional Belief System'. Enables us to understand the origins of delusion. African tribesmen develop delusions about sorcerers; Westerners

develop delusions about the Spice Girls and extraterrestrials.
The specifics of Christopher's cultural background are that
his mother once lived in Uganda: he's got a delusion about a
Ugandan dictator she no doubt talked about. You're saying
he's not sick, it's a cultural thing.

Robert I'm saying he's not mad. There's a difference.

Pause.

Do you know what happened to his mother in Uganda? Do
you know whether she was raped by soldiers after the military
coup? By Idi Amin himself? She could have been a journalist
or a cook at State House for all you know. Have you asked
her?

Bruce That's not possible.

Robert Why not?

Bruce I can't trace her. We think she lives in Feltham.

Robert Where in Feltham?

Bruce Nobody seems to have an address.

Robert Find her. It might not all be true – but then again
it might.
Can you imagine the ramifications of that?
This is precisely what I'm getting at in my research.

Bruce What are you talking about? You can't use him for
research.

Robert Why not? Why ever not? Think about it.
There is more mental illness amongst the Afro-Caribbean
population in London than any other ethnic grouping.
Why?
Is it the way we're diagnosing it? Is it us? Is it them? What's
causing it? What's the answer? What's the cure?
There's no 'cure' for schizophrenia.
No 'cure' for psychosis.
Only *palliative drugs*.
But what if it *isn't* psychosis? Wouldn't that be a relief? What

if there is a cure? *Cognitive* therapy. *Minimal* medication.
A 'cure' for 'black psychosis'.
Imagine it.
The Holy Grail.
And imagine if the fucker who found it was . . . us.

Silence.

Bruce   'A Cure for Black Psychosis'.

Robert   Figuratively speaking.

Bruce   You're being 'whimsical' again?

Robert (*shaking his head*)   An end to palliatives. No more
'dated toxic crud'.

Bruce   OK. Say it is true. It's all true. Christopher is Idi
Amin's son. And he's schizophrenic. It's both. Had you
thought of that?

Pause.

Kind of blows your theory out of the water, doesn't it?

Silence.

Robert   OK, look. I'm merely pointing out that sometimes
our analysis is *ethnocentric*: in this case you are evaluating the
situation according to your own specific cultural criteria.

Bruce   'Ethnocentric'?

Robert   Our colonial antecedents are latent and barely
suppressed. We are intuitively suspicious because of our
cultural background.
For example, on the way back from the rugby the other night
we stopped at the off-licence for a bottle of wine. I noticed
that the Hindu gentleman behind the counter said neither
Please nor Thank you. I had to ask myself, is he just *like*
that – is he just *rude*? Or is it because there is no such thing as
Please and Thank you in Urdu – is it not customary in his
culture?

Bruce   What are you talking about? He always says Please and Thank you.

Robert   OK, fine. So perhaps I should ask myself, Is it me? What are *my* cultural expectations?

Bruce   Look, after the rugby, everybody goes in there, all the rugger buggers, pissy drunk and *they* don't say Please and Thank you –

Robert   Nevertheless, we must guard against our ethnocentricity.

Bruce   I don't think I like the direction this is heading.

Robert   The point is, this is my *province*, Doctor.
That's why you asked me here.
Because I know how many beans make five.
I am, as they say, an 'expert'.
I am Senior Consultant and I am here to be 'consulted'.
I am not here to be 'bounced off'.
To 'run it up the flag pole and see who salutes'.
I'm here because 'I know'.

Bruce   But . . . with the greatest respect, Doctor Smith, you don't. He's *my* patient . . . so . . . really . . .

Robert   OK, fine. Whatever. Discharge him. Next case.

Pause.

Bruce   But –

Robert   We can skin this cat as artfully as we like.
However, in the opinion of this highly experienced Department Head, Doctor Flaherty, what we have here is No Beds and, more importantly, a patient who has No Need of a Bed.

Bruce   But I think –

Robert   What I 'think' is that you think too much.
What I think is that you should let me do the thinking.
Now if you don't mind, I'm very busy.

Robert *goes to the door.*

Bruce   But . . . you're saying . . . what you're really saying is Christopher's . . . unable to distinguish between realistic and utterly unrealistic notions because . . . what . . .? Because he's . . . ?

Robert   BPD. Case closed.

Bruce   It's because he's b –

Robert   BPD. Goodbye, Doctor.

Bruce   Because he's black?

Robert *sighs, clenches his teeth. Walks back into the room.*

Robert (*icily*)   I'm saying where he comes from it is almost certainly not an unrealistic notion. Where we come from, it evidently is. Get it?

Bruce   But he comes from Shepherd's Bush.

Robert   He sees himself as African. And we don't say 'black' any more –

Bruce   Yes we do –

Robert   We say 'Afro-Caribbean'.

Bruce   Where does the Caribbean come into it?

Robert   All right, he's 'African'.

Bruce   From Shepherd's Bush.

Robert   I'm not going to quibble over this twaddle.

Bruce   'Twaddle'?

Robert   I'm not going to squabble. His 'origins' are in Africa.

Bruce   How far back are you going?

Robert   And for the last time I'll remind you that you are under my supervision, you are my subordinate, and your tone

is beginning to sound dangerously insubordinate if not
nakedly insulting.

Bruce   I'm sorry . . . but –

Robert   Do you know what most young doctors would do
to have me as Supervisor? I mean, normal ones . . . the smart
ones . . . what they'd do to know they have a future. To have
a shot at becoming Consultant? They'd *lick my anus*.

Silence.

(But that's beside the point . . .)

He goes to the door and looks out.
Comes back. Sits.

Now. Do you want me to recommend your consultancy at
this hospital or don't you?

Bruce   Of course.

Robert   Then act like a professional. Act like a
representative of the Royal College of Psychiatrists.

Bruce   But I'm *not* a –

Robert   Do you want to be? Mm? Now. Pull yourself
together. Try not to be so wet behind the ears. Otherwise I'm
taking you off this case.

Bruce   You can't take me off this case.

Robert   I'll assign a CPN and discharge him myself.

Bruce   If you do I'll appeal to the Authority.

Robert   I am the Authority. (Just between you and me.)

Bruce   I feel very strongly. I feel . . . very strongly . . . that
keeping him in hospital for the time being is the right thing to
do.

Robert   And what if you make him worse?
He starts out as borderline but because of your diagnosis he
stays here indefinitely and disintegrates. The family comes

forward, pillars of the community. Local MPs. Shit will hit
rotor blades.

Pause.

And and and apart from anything else do you really want to
make a schizophrenia diagnosis now? He's twenty-four hours
away from normality. Do you want this man *stigmatised*? For
the rest of his life. Don't you think he has enough problems as
it is?

Pause.

Do you understand the weight of responsibility, lifetime
responsibility that goes with such a diagnosis? No doctor
wants to make that kind of diagnosis. No CPN, no GP, no
consultant. Nobody. Do you understand?

Bruce   Perfectly. But . . . um . . . with respect, it's it's it's it's
what I believe in.

Robert   Well, you know, Doctor, with respect, that isn't
good enough.

Bruce   It's not good enough that I do what I believe is
right?

Robert   That's right. It's naive.

Bruce   *Naive?*

Robert   That's right. You're naive. And you're beginning
to get on my *wick*.

Silence.

Bruce   Why won't you listen to me?

Robert   What? 'Listen to you'? To you? It's not my job to
listen to you. It's your job to . . . oh for goodness' sake . . .

Pause.

OK. All right. Listen.
Let me join up some of the dots for you.
Let me do some of the maths for you:

Schizophrenia is the worst pariah.
One of the last great taboos.
People don't understand it.
They don't want to understand it.
It scares them.
It depresses them.
It is not treatable with glamorous and intriguing wonderdrugs like Prozac or Viagra.
It isn't newsworthy.
It isn't curable.
It isn't heroin or Ecstasy.
It is not the preserve of rock stars and supermodels and hip young authors.
It is not a topic of dinner-party conversation.
Organised crime gets better press.
They make *movies* about junkies and alcoholics and gangsters and men who drink too much, fall over and beat their woman until bubbles come out of her nose, but schizophrenia, my friend, is just not in the phone book.

Bruce   Then we must change that.

Robert   . . . And they . . . *what?*

Bruce   Then we must change that.

Robert   'Change'. Hmm. Well . . . the thing is, you can't change that. D'you see? I can't. Seriously.
The Authority – the rest of the Board, not even me – they will question your expertise. They will wonder why you got so upset about it. They will wonder whether or not this case has a 'deeper personal significance' to you and they will undermine you at every turn and then they will screw you. As sure as eggs are fucking eggs.

Bruce   A 'deeper personal . . .'?

Robert   People will question your mental *wellness.*

Silence.

They'll say you're mad.
And then they'll say *I'm* mad for supervising you and allowing my department to disintegrate so.

Bruce   Well, if you don't want to supervise me . . . if you've changed your mind . . . you only have to say.

Robert   Not at all. This is a 'Teaching Hospital' and I am here to teach.

Bruce   W . . . was it Saturday? Did I say something after the rugby?

Robert   Look. I'm not the big bad wolf. I'm not trying to undermine your decision and I certainly don't want to release Christopher if he isn't ready. I *care*. And I know you care. All I'm saying is sometimes one can care *too much*. One can have too much Empathy – Understanding – an *overweening* Compassion. You try to be all things to all men: Doctor. Friend. A *reasonable* man. We all want to be *reasonable* men. Eh? Bruce? Please. Now. Am I not your friend?

Pause.

Aren't we friends?

Bruce *slowly nods.*

Robert   Sleep on it.
Let me conduct my own assessment. We can reconvene in the morning and all decide together. Eh? I'll talk to him tonight. I promise you I won't be partisan.

Bruce   OK. Fine. Whatever you say.

Robert   Don't look so gloomy. Just wait till you're a consultant. Think of that loft conversion.

Bruce   Robert . . .

Robert   Bruce . . . Bruce . . . Bruce . . .
You have it all to look forward to.
Trust me.
I want what you want. I really do.

I believe in what you believe in.
I'm On Your Side.

Blackout.

Act Two

That night. **Robert** *and* **Christopher** *sit facing each other across the table. A reading light is the only light.*

Robert *takes a cigarette from his pack and lights it.* **Christopher** *takes a cigarette from behind his ear and* **Robert** *lights it. They exhale.*

Robert   Listen listen listen listen.

Pause.

Listen.

Pause.

We all have these thoughts. It's perfectly natural. Even I have them. Yes. Me. Some days I get home from work, from a long night in the hospital, visiting, ward rounds, nothing untoward, nothing terrible, a few cross words with a colleague, some silly argument, I get home and I get in the door and I *slump*. All the life drains out of me. I think . . . Why Am I Doing This? Eh? What's in it for me? A table at the Ivy if I use the right prefix. A seminar in Norway. Some spotty young registrar takes me to the rugby and hangs on my every word. Big deal. And there are times, when I look across at this professor and that professor turning up to work in a new *Jag*, he's just come back from La Rochelle, he's off to play a round of golf at his thousand-pound-a-year golf club, have a drink at his jolly old Mayfair club, posh dinners with drug company reps, knighthoods, appearances on Radio Four n'ha ha ha . . .
And I think . . . How do they do that?
What, are they 'experts' or something?
I Want To Be Professor!
What do they do that I don't?
And the answer is:
Who *cares*? That's *their* life. Nevertheless, I feel small and I think my life adds up to nothing. And I have to keep reminding myself: Why not? Why not think these things? It's

not greedy, it's not covetous. It's *human*. It's me being a
human being. And it applies to us all. And it's my right to do
something about it. It's everybody's right to take steps.
But *killing yourself*?
Christopher?
Why?

Silence.

Everybody Feels Like This. At some point. In their life.
Everybody feels that they've . . . lost out. It's the Human
Condition. The capacity to feel *disappointment*. It's what
distinguishes us from the animals. Our *disappointment*. Mm. It's
true. The capacity to grieve for lost opportunity. For the lives
we *could* have *led*. The men or women we *may* have become. It
has us in an appalling stranglehold.
And sometimes we say, Why Go On? And we want to end it
all. The hell with it. Life's a sham.
That's human too. You don't hear doggies running about
going, 'Oh that this too too solid flesh would melt.' Of course
not. Why not? They're *dogs*! It would be ridiculous. Dogs have
other talents. They can lick their own balls. A talent for
simplicity. N'ha ha ha. Do you see? Learn to cultivate a
Talent for Simplicity.

Pause.

Christopher   Learn to Lick My Balls?
That's your expert advice, yeah?

Robert   N'ha ha ha. N'ha ha ha, well . . . it might work . . .

Christopher   You're a fucking *doctor*, man.

Robert   I know, I'm joking, but you, you, you see my point.
This life is a *gift*. The food we eat, the smells we smell, the
trees, the sky, the *fecundity* of Creation . . . It's a *really lovely* gift,
and if for whatever reason you cannot see that right now,
then I'm here to Heal Your Vision. To help you. See. I
promise you, I plead with you, I *entreat* you. Take a few deep
breaths. Calm down. Think about this. You're not 'suicidal'.
It's ridiculous.

Silence.

Christopher   I don't want to go home.

Pause.

I changed my mind. I'm not going.

Robert   Christopher . . .

Christopher   I . . . I . . . I don't have a home. I'm not . . .
I'm not ready.

Robert   What happens to you when you go home?

Christopher   I told you about the Fuzz.

Robert   OK. Fine. But apart from . . . the 'Fuzz'. What else
happens to you?

Pause.

Chris?

Pause.

Christopher   People stare at me. Like they know . . . like
they know about me.
Like they know something about me that I don't know.

Robert   Such as?

Christopher   Eh?

Robert   What could they know that you don't know?

Christopher   I don't know. They hate me. They think I'm
bad.

Robert   Which people?

Christopher   Eh?

Robert   Who are these people who . . . think you're bad?

Christopher   I hear noises. At night. Outside my window.
Sometimes I hear . . . talking. People talking about me.

Robert   Talking about you?

Christopher   Laughing sometimes.

Robert   And you've no idea who it is?

Christopher   No idea. Sometimes I hear machinery. Whirring. Like a . . . a strange droning noise. And beeping. A strange beeping noise. Very loud.

Robert   It's the dustbin men.

Christopher   On Saturdays and Sundays?

Robert   Builders. OK? We're in the midst of a property boom. Interest rates are low, people are buying and building and renovating – people want more of the life gifted them. Life is Rich. People are greedy for Life.

Christopher   Not in White City they're not. 'White City'. 'South Africa Road'. Even the names are a fucking wind-up.

Robert   But you have your friends. Your *community*. People who care.

Christopher   I don't have any friends.
I try to make friends with people but it's not easy. I try to make conversation but it's not easy. Sometimes I say the wrong thing.
Actually I always say the wrong thing. I don't have a girlfriend. Who'd want me?

Pause.

Robert   Well. You'll make new friends when you get out.

Christopher   I made friends with Bruce.

Robert   You won't be alone in all this. I'll make sure of that.

Christopher   Yeah but I want double glazing. Don't talk to me about the fucking property boom. It's like living in a biscuit tin.

Pause.

Robert   Well, you know, Chris, I can't provide you with double glazing. It's not part of my remit. If you want double glazing . . .
Go to the Council. See your housing officer.

Christopher   You said you would help me.

Robert   I know, but –

Christopher   So help me –

Robert   It's –

Christopher   Help me –

Robert   It's not my job! N'ha ha ha. D'you see?

Christopher   Yeah, but what I thought was, if I moved somewhere else –

Robert   OK. There's a procedure for that. The Council will have a procedure for transferring you.

Christopher   Yeah, but I wanna go to Africa.

Robert   You want to go to Africa.

Christopher   I want to go to Africa.

Robert   Back to your roots.

Christopher   My 'roots'?

Robert   You feel you 'belong' there?

Christopher   *No*, man. I already told you. It's nice there. And and and you know I told you about my dad.

Robert   Idi Amin.

Christopher   Idi Amin Dada. That's his proper name. Idi Amin Dada.

Robert   O . . . K . . .

Pause.

Tell me about your mother. What did she do in Uganda?

Christopher   She was a barmaid.

Robert   A 'barmaid'. Really? In a pub?

Christopher   No, in a shoe shop, innit.

Robert   Where the soldiers drank?

Christopher   Eh?

Robert   Did many soldiers drink there?

Christopher   I don't know.

Robert   What I'm getting at is . . . how . . . how did your mum actually meet President Amin?

Silence.

Christopher *stares into space.*

Robert   Christopher?

Christopher   You wouldn't understand.

Robert   Why wouldn't I understand?

Christopher   You wouldn't understand.

Silence.

Robert   Try me.

Christopher   She was a student. He closed down the university for political reasons.

Robert   She told you this?

Christopher   She never talks about it – d'you know what I mean? It's personal.

Pause.

She gets upset.

Robert   What did she read?

Christopher   How d'you mean?

Robert   What was her subject? English literature?

Christopher   How d'you mean?

Robert   What I'm getting at is, well, does she read you poetry, for example? Or plays?

Christopher   No.

Robert   What about at school? Did you read poetry at school?

Christopher   No.

Robert   Oh. OK. Fine.

Pause.

What about books? Children's books? Comics? *Tintin? Asterix?* She must have given you books.

Christopher   No.

Robert   Do you still see her? Christopher? D'you know where she lives?

Pause.

Chris?

Christopher   She lives in Feltham.

Robert   Do you know her address? Do you want to tell me?

Pause.

You don't want to tell me where she lives?
Why should I believe you if you can't even tell me your mother's address?

Christopher   Bruce don't believe me either but I can prove it.

Robert   You can 'prove it'?

Christopher   Yeah, man.

Robert   How?

Christopher   Why should I tell you?

Robert   Well . . . because I'm asking you to . . .

Christopher   What if I don't trust you?

Robert   Well . . . then . . . that would be a great shame.

Christopher   A shame? (*Beat.*) You think it'd be a shame, yeah?

Robert   Yeah.

Christopher   Oh.

Christopher *weighs it up.*
He produces a wallet from his pocket.
From the wallet he produces a tightly folded up newspaper article.
He unfolds it and holds it out to **Robert**.
Robert *hesitates, then takes it and reads.*
Christopher *reads over his shoulder.*

Robert (*reading*)   'A delivery of East African oranges from the airport . . . the Butcher of the Bush . . . talent for the accordion blah blah blah . . . Forty-three children by four wives . . .'

Christopher   Five wives.

Robert   Eh?

Christopher   Five wives really. There's a fifth. A secret one.

Robert   A . . . a . . . where?

Christopher (*pointing*)   Not the one who runs a chippy. Another one. Common-law wife. Living in 'penury'.

Robert (*reading*)   'Living in . . . in Feltham.'

Christopher   In 'penury'.

Robert   'In penury . . . in Feltham.' Bugger me. How long have you had this?

Christopher   My mother gave it to me.

Robert   Bugger me.

They look at each other.

Silence.

Robert *puts his fingertips to his temples momentarily, thinking hard.*

Christopher (*pointing*)   Look. That's his photo.

Robert (*holding the article*)   Can I keep this?

Christopher   No you cannot keep that.

Robert   Please. Christopher . . . listen . . .

Christopher *snatches the article back, folds it, puts it away as he speaks.*

Christopher   I am being *harassed*. I'm in fear of my *life*. I live in *fear*. They Know Who I Am.

Robert   Who does?

Christopher   The men. Where I live. The noises. The . . . the police. It all makes sense.

Robert   They're . . . look . . . it's . . . they're just ordinary *men*. *Work* men . . . *police* men.

Christopher   Other men too. Another man. He throws bananas at me.

Robert   Bananas . . . ?

Christopher   When I'm at work. Even at work – d'you know what I mean! Big bloke with a little pointy head. Long thin arms trailing along the ground. A real knuckle-dragger. Very white skin. Hideous-looking bastard. He's the ring-leader. I see him at night. He bangs on my door. Says he's coming to get me. He says he'll do me and nobody would even notice and I believe him. There's a whole family of them. A tribe. I don't like them at all. They're a race apart. *Zombies*! The undead. Monsters!
QPR supporters.

Pause.

Robert   Football hooligans?

Christopher   On Saturdays, I seem 'em in the crowds at
Loftus Road.
They come after the game. And before the game. With
bananas.
With . . . with shit smeared through the letter box, not dog
shit – real shit. Pissing through the letter box, fires,
firestarting on the front step. It's a disgrace. They call me
'Jungle Boy'. If my dad was here he'd kill them dead.
He'd monster them.
Believe.

Silence.

It's their appearance that spooks me the most. Those tiny,
bony, shrunken heads. All shaved. Ugly.

Robert   D'you mean . . . Skinheads?

Christopher   *Zombies.*

Robert   What makes you think these people are . . . 'the
undead'?

Christopher   They look *half* dead. It's that ghostly white
skin, looks like tapioca, d'you know what I mean?

Robert   Christopher –

Christopher   Baldies. 'Baldy-Heads', that's what I call
them. Baldy-Heads.

Robert   'Baldy-Heads'. I see. But . . . they're not really . . .
'Zombies', now are they? Chris? Which is it, 'Zombies' or
'Baldy-Heads'?

Pause.

There is a difference.

Christopher   D'you think it's funny?

Robert   Not in the least. It could be the difference between
you staying here or you going home.

Christopher   They're *dangerous*, man. Believe. They're spooky. I could be dead tomorrow.

Robert *rubs his eyes and sighs.*

Christopher   You know the average life expectancy of the modern black male? Sixty-four years old. That's how long we got. What age do we get the pension? *Sixty-five!* It's a fucking *rip-off*, man! D'you know what I mean?

Robert   So . . . fundamentally, you don't think you're sick? Am I right?

Christopher   Yeah I'm sick. Sick and tired, man. Sick of everything. I got problems. D'you know what I'm saying?

Robert   Do you keep a diary?

Christopher   A diary? No. Do you?

Robert   You should start keeping a diary.

Christopher   I never go out.

Robert   No, a diary of what *happens*.

Christopher   Nothing ever happens, man. All day every day, nothing.

Robert   I meant, things on the estate. Concerning the letter box . . . ? OK?
Then you go to the Council, you ask to see your housing officer and you show her the diary. She can have you transferred to a different estate.

Christopher   It gets a bit lonely sometimes but –

Robert   Yes I know and that's OK. That's normal. That's human. And I'll tell you something else –

Christopher   Sometimes people scare me.

Robert   I know they do. And you know what you do when they do these things?

Christopher   What?

Robert   You laugh.

Christopher   Laugh?

Robert   When somebody hurts you, just laugh at them. You don't care. They'll soon get the message.

Pause.

Christopher   Laugh, yeah?

Robert   It drives them crazy. Really, it's a good trick.

Christopher   Oh I get you. Laugh. Really.
HA HA HA HA HA. HA HA HA HA HA. 'Laugh and the whole world laughs with you.'
AND THEN THEY LOCK YOU UP!
What the fuck are you on about, man? D'you know what I mean? Pull yourself together!

Robert   OK. Cry. Do handstands. Express Yourself. Just Don't Take It Personally.

Christopher   'Express myself'. And who are you: 'Professor Groovy'?

Robert   Strictly speaking it's 'Doctor Groovy'. N'ha ha ha ha. N'ha ha ha. See? You can do it.

Silence.

No. You're quite right. I'm sorry. But, you see, the thing is, Chris, I don't think that you are ill and I want you to try to settle down somewhere.

Christopher   What I'm saying is, Doctor, I been unlucky where I been housed, yeah?

Robert   Well then . . . you need to be rehoused not locked up.

Christopher   I get scared out there.

Robert   I know, I know. And, look, I'll let you into a secret. Are you listening? I get scared too.

Christopher   What are you scared of?

Robert   Eh?

Christopher   What are you scared of?

Robert   Everything. My life. Academia.

Pause.

I'm lonely too. Everybody –

Christopher   Why are you lonely?

Robert   Supposing I don't measure up.
Supposing my research is less well received than anticipated and then I have no friends.
Supposing I never make Professor.
Supposing nobody wants to hear my ideas.
Nobody wants to talk to me.
And and and even when they *do* talk to me, is it the real *me* they're talking to? Or is it Somebody Up There in the . . . Academic Firmament. Some Great Illustrious Thinker.
Mister Big Cheese Head of Department. Somebody I'm Just Not. You see?

Pause.

Everybody's scared. Everybody's lonely.

Christopher   I think Bruce is right. I'm not ready. I don't wanna go.

Robert   OK . . . well . . . did he actually say that to you, did he?

Christopher   He asked me if I was sure.

Robert   And you said you were, didn't you?

Christopher   Yeah, but I was lying. D'you know what I mean?

Pause.

Robert   You were *lying*.

Christopher   I was lying.

Robert   Why?

Christopher   Cos I wanted to get out of this place.

Robert   Aha! 'The truth will out.' You 'wanted to get out of this place'. You did. It's true.

Christopher   But now I don't.

Robert   Yes you do.

Christopher   No I don't.

Robert   I think you do.

Christopher   I fucking don't, man.

Robert   You do and I'm going to continue to suggest to you that you do whether your conscious mind likes it or not.

Pause.

You see, until your *conscious* mind catches up with what your *subconscious* mind wants . . . and *knows,* which is that you, quote, 'want to get out of here', unquote, you're never going to get better. And you're never going to get out of here.

Christopher   I'm never . . . ?

Robert   Nope. Never. You'll be in hospital – this hospital or some other hospital somewhere – in and out of hospital for the rest of your life.
For the rest of your life.

Pause.

Christopher   Now I'm scared.

Robert   Sure. Of course you are. And I think that that's right. I think if you weren't nervous, you wouldn't be human.

Christopher   I didn't say I was nervous.

Robert   Well . . . I think you are.

Christopher   Oh man. What am I gonna do?

Robert   I've just told you what to do.

Christopher   Uh?

Robert   I just told you what you should do.

Christopher *stares into space.*

Robert   Chris . . . ? The Council . . . ? Your housing officer –

Christopher   He said I could stay. Doctor Flaherty said –

Robert   You know what I think? I think that you think you are scared. And that's all it is, a thought. And I think that it's not your thought.

Christopher   What d'you mean?

Robert   I think that someone else's thoughts have scared you.

Christopher   You think . . . I'm thinking someone else's thoughts?

Pause.

Whose thoughts?

Robert   I'm saying . . . look . . . Maybe Doctor Flaherty 'projected' his fears of letting you go home on to you and now they're *your* fears.
I'm saying maybe, just maybe Doctor Flaherty . . . unconsciously put his thoughts in your head.

Christopher   He put his thoughts in my head. In my head . . . ?

Robert   Look, this morning, you were ready to go home. You were so excited. You couldn't wait. You wanted coffee, you had your bags packed, wahey, it was all happening for you. Remember?

Christopher   Mm . . .

Robert   So what's changed? What's new, my friend? Eh?

Pause.

Nothing. You had your bags packed.

Pause.

Nothing has changed. You're going home. Stop thinking about it. Just do it.

Christopher   But, see, the thing is, I got the impression, I got the impression from Doctor Flaherty –

Robert   What? Did he say something? What did he say?

Christopher   No, but I got the impression –

Robert   Well, did you read his mind?

Christopher *stares.*

Silence.

Robert   OK, forget that, bad idea. But but but . . . what I'm saying is How Do You Know? Because really: he *wants* you to go too. He wants rid of you. I should know.

Christopher   He wants rid of me?

Robert   Yes. He's had enough of you, my friend, we all have, don't jolly well . . . outstay your welcome! N'huh huh huh. Go. Be free.

Pause.

N'huh huh huh. D'you see?

Pause.

I'm trying to help you.

Christopher   I read his mind?

Robert   I said to forget that.

Christopher   He wants rid of me?

Robert   I'm joking. It's a joke!

Christopher   The oranges are blue.

Silence.

Remember he asked me what colour the orange was?

Robert   Mm.

Christopher   And I said it was blue. It was. I *saw* that.

Pause.

Bright blue. Virtually glowing.

Robert   You've had a psychotic episode. Things will be a bit strange for a while. Nothing more insidious.

Christopher   'A bit strange'? They were blue.

Robert   We will give you medication for that.

Christopher   I'm seeing things.

Robert   OK OK OK, look. You're not.

Christopher   What?

Robert   You're not seeing things. I think . . . all right . . . I think you wanted so badly to stay here, subconsciously, that you thought you saw things, or you said you saw things . . .

Christopher   You saying I was lying? *Me?*

Robert   N . . . I'm saying you were lying. Yes.

Christopher   Well, I think *you're* lying.

Robert   Because you wanted to stay here. But, you see, if you do stay here, if we give you what we call a Section 3, you will stay here Indefinitely.

Christopher   How d'you mean?

Robert   We can keep you for up to six months. We can keep you, more or less, for as long as we like.

Pause.

Christopher   You're prolly not even a proper doctor.

Robert   Well . . . n'ha . . . I can assure you, Chris, I am a 'proper doctor'.

Christopher   Prove it.

Robert   I don't have to prove it.

Christopher   Well, that's not fair, is it? What about my job? D'you know what I mean? I got a job to go to. On a fruit stall. In the market. I *sell* oranges.

Pause.

Robert   You sell oranges? (I didn't know that . . .)

Christopher   It's true. What am I supposed to tell the customers? I'm in no condition to sell fruit, d'you know what I'm saying? Same as I say, I got problems.

Pause.

Robert   Well. OK. In fact, as I remember, and correct me if I'm wrong: *First*, Doctor Flaherty *told* you it wasn't orange. The first thing he said was: 'It's not an orange orange.' What does that tell you?
You spontaneously made what's called a 'common association'. You may just have easily said Red.
It's harmless.

Christopher   It means something.

Robert   What does it mean?

Christopher   It's a sign. Cos nobody believes me but I think it proves it.
He likes oranges. Every day a shipment from Nairobi. I just *proved* that. I come in here, first thing I see, oranges! They turn blue. A *signal*.

Pause.

Robert   OK, look . . . we don't have to concern ourselves with these things now.

Christopher   Yeah, but I'm worried now. I got the fear.

Robert   There's nothing to be afraid of.

Christopher   You don't know that.

Robert   I do, yes, I do. Because. Two reasons. I'll tell you then you'll promise to stop fretting about them, OK? Two things.
One: We can sort these things out when you get home. It's unfair for you to be here while we answer those questions.
They are not life-threatening.
They are not a danger to you.
You are not a danger to yourself.
You'll be seeing me once a month and you'll be quite safe and so now I want you to forget all about it.

Christopher   Seeing *you?*

Robert   If I take over your case, yes. That might happen.

Christopher   Why should I see you?

Robert   Because it's what I think is best. Because . . . it would be a 'shame' if you didn't.

Pause.

Christopher   Yeah, but I wanna see Doctor Flaherty.

Robert   I'd be better.

Christopher   Uh-huh.

Pause.

What's the other thing? You said there was two.

Robert   The *second* thing is . . .

Pause.

Doctor Flaherty . . .
Bruce . . . is somewhat *unorthodox* in his approach. What he's suggesting by keeping you in here is, you have to understand, a little unorthodox. We don't do that any more if we can help it. We want you out there.
We want you to go *home.* D'you see?

Christopher   Yeah, but he's worried, that's all.

Robert   I know, and that's because, you see, Bruce, Bruce, see, Bruce is a little, as we say in the trade, He's a Tee-Pee and a Wig-Wam.

Pause.

He's Too Tense.

Pause.

Heh heh. No I'm kidding. But he is . . . you know, he's just a, you know, *I'm* the Head of Department. I'm the Boss. I'm the Big Cheese.

Pause.

The Top Banana.

Pause.

OK, this is very delicate. It's not something we know an awful lot about. But it's my specific field of research, I'm writing a book on it as a matter of fact.

Christopher   You're writing a book? Really? You're really writing a book?

Robert   Well . . . I blush to the toes of my shoes to admit but . . .

Christopher   What's it about?

Robert   Well . . . it's about . . . it's about psychosis diagnosis. In . . . people like you.

Christopher   People like me, yeah?

Robert   You see, I believe there may be a cognitive therapy which we can substitute for the drug palliatives normally associated with psychosis.
My 'assertion' is this:
There is a Cultural Specificity to the apparently delusionary nature of some of your beliefs.
There are Antecedents for some of the beliefs you hold.

'Cultural Specificity and Cultural Antecedent or
Schizophrenia'.
You see? '*Or* Schizophrenia'. Not 'And'. That's what it's
called.

Pause.

Christopher   What does Doctor Flaherty think about it?

Robert   Well . . . uh . . . he hasn't read it yet.

Christopher   I meant about me seeing you.

Robert   Oh well . . . OK . . . well, the thing is . . . see . . .

Pause.

Doctor Flaherty isn't in possession of the full facts.

Christopher   Why not?

Robert   Because he's not an authority. I'm an authority.
He isn't.

Pause.

Because there are things you do and things you believe which
he, within his culture, can only recognise as Insanity.

Pause.

Which I personally believe, for what it's worth, is rather
narrow-minded . . . it's what some people call 'Culturally
Oppressive'.

Christopher   Insanity.

Robert   It means he has a tendency to overlook, in our
discussions at any rate, your cultural identity.

Pause.

It's nothing . . . it's no big deal . . . it's an oversight, that's all.
It's a vastly complex subject. People get things wrong.

Christopher   What did he say?

Robert   OK, look. I don't want you to take this the wrong way because I don't think he meant it in a pejorative sense ... I'm quite sure ... but it indicates a gap in his knowledge which I'm trying to *redress.*

Christopher   What did he say?

Robert   Well ... well ... since you asked ... I think he has a very real fear that ... our response to you is weighted by our response to your colour. I personally feel that *should* be the case; it *should* be a factor in your treatment and that we shouldn't overlook such a thing. Otherwise what happens, in institutions such as this, there develops what's termed 'ethnocentricity'; which ordinarily is fairly harmless but in certain instances is not far off ... well ... it is the progenitor of 'cultural oppression', which in turn leads to what we call 'institutionalised racism'.

Christopher   Racism?

Robert   Yes. And the danger is that in a sense you maybe end up, in a sense, being 'punished' for the colour of your skin. (*Beat.*) For your ethnicity and your attendant cultural beliefs. (*Beat.*) You are sectioned and locked up when you shouldn't be. (*Beat.*) Because you're 'black'.

Silence.

Christopher   I'm being *punished?*

Robert   Maybe that's too strong a term but but but –

Christopher   Because I'm *black?*

Robert   Well, you see, the system is *flawed.* People of ethnic minority are not well catered for, it's a well-known fact. I've just expressed it clumsily –

Christopher   He said that? I'm locked up because I'm black?

Christopher *stands abruptly.*

Robert   No, that's not what was said. Let me finish –

Christopher   Where is he?

Robert   OK, calm down.

Christopher   The fuck does that mean?

Robert   Chris Chris Chris Chris –

Christopher   He really said that? It's cos I'm black?

Christopher *heads for the door and* **Robert** *rushes around and blocks his way, trying to hold him back.*

Robert (*struggling with him*)   Look, listen, look, listen, look, listen, look, listen, look, listen . . .

Pause.

Chris, my dear dear fellow, just sit down and listen for one moment please.
Our colonial antecedents are latent and barely suppressed –

Christopher   What shit!

He paces angrily.

Robert   This really is a storm in a teacup.

Christopher   Punished by who?

Robert   Chris, please, sit down. Sit down. Come on now. I implore you.

Christopher *sits and thinks, stares, quiet.*

Christopher   Who am I being punished by?

Robert   Well, by, by, by the *system*. The system tends to punish without meaning to.

Christopher   That's why I see things? I'm being punished?

Robert   No . . . Chris –

Christopher   That's why I hear things? These *mental . . . fucking* . . . the noises I hear . . . the *fear –*

Robert   What he said was –

Christopher   You said I'm not thinking my own thoughts –

Robert   No –

Christopher   Well, whose thoughts am I thinking?

Robert   Nobody –

Christopher   Doctor Flaherty's . . . ?

Robert   OK, let's not get off the track –

Christopher   He smokes too much *drugs*, man, d'you know what I mean? He likes his puff. I can tell.

Silence.

Robert   Sorry . . . you said? About . . . dr . . . ?

Christopher   He *told* me I should go back out there and *score* some puff, man. Why did he say that? Because I'm black?

Robert   O . . . K . . . but . . . I'm sure . . .

Pause.

'Puff'. For *him* . . . ? Or . . . for . . . ?

Christopher   He goes he goes he goes, If I was only in here to get drugs I'd come to the wrong place. He said the drugs out there, right, were more *fun*.

Robert   I see, well . . . I see . . . well. (*Beat.*) When was this?

Christopher   Earlier. Before you got here.

Robert   Just before or . . . some time before?

Christopher   Just before. This morning.

Robert   Oh.

Pause.

What else did he say?

Christopher   He said it was 'voodoo'. That's why I'm here. Voodoo. Remember?

Robert   W . . . ell . . .

Christopher   And he lied to me. He said he was letting me out when he was just gonna keep me in here longer just like you said, man. He lied to me.

Pause.

And and and he keeps looking at me funny.

Pause.

Can I have a cup of coffee now?

Blackout.

Act Three

Next afternoon. **Bruce** *and* **Christopher** *sit facing each other; the bowl of oranges is on the table between them.*

Bruce *has a report in front of him and is reading from it.*

Christopher *is smoking a cigarette and staring into space.*

Bruce 'He ordered the patient to peel the orange . . .' I didn't *order* you.

He reads.

'. . . establishing that it was the same under the skin. That the flesh was the same colour as the skin.'
OK, I *suggested*, Chris, I *prompted*, and maybe I shouldn't have but, you know, it's not as if this was the first time, was it? You don't need my help to start . . . *(reading)* seeing things . . .

He reads.

Pause.

Do you really believe this? Do you really think I . . . what? I'm . . . 'Provocative, unorthodox, patronising . . .'? And . . . 'Possibly *on drugs* . . .'? I mean, this is . . . this just . . . I've never heard anything so ridiculous in my life!

He reads.

'He snatched away a cup of coffee given to the patient by the consultant . . . He used the pejorative epithet "nigger".'

Silence.

I did not, um, my God, I didn't use the epithet . . . nnn . . .

He stares.

I did not call you a . . . um, um, um, a . . . I didn't say that.

Christopher Say what?

Bruce   Would you please put that out? Christopher? The cigarette.

Christopher *mashes out the cigarette on the table.*

Bruce   I, I, I, didn't call you a, a, a, um, a . . . a . . . (*beat*) 'nigger'.

Christopher   You said 'uppity nigga'. You did. Deny.

Bruce   Only because *you* did. My God! It was a quote!

Christopher   Yeah, but you shouldn'ta said it.

Bruce   Oh, so so so only you can say it?

Christopher   It's not polite.

Bruce   I know it isn't and, um . . .
I'm sorry, excuse me . . .
I feel sick . . .

He steadies himself.

Pause.

Do, do you really think I meant it? Do you really think I meant to 'provoke' you? I was giving vent to 'racist' proclivities?

Christopher   Look. I don't know. I don't know. I just want to go home.

Bruce   What is wrong with you?
Are you out of your mind?
Have you been drinking?

Robert *appears in the doorway, listening.*
He enters and sits down.

Robert   You asked to see me.

Bruce   We have a meeting.

Pause.

We agreed to meet today. The three of us. Unless you know of something that could have happened to change that.

Robert   I'm on the Authority, Doctor Flaherty, of course I know.

Pause.

There was a Management Hearing this morning.

Bruce   Yes I know. How convenient.

Robert *shrugs.*

Bruce   So. Where do we go from here?

Robert   Well, you know, actually, what I think is that you and I need to be alone together.

Bruce   OK. Uh. Christopher, would you mind coming back in . . . ?

He checks his watch.

Christopher   But I've just packed.

Bruce   That's all right. Just go back to your ward and I'll send for you.

Christopher   But I've just –

Bruce   Please, Chris.

Christopher   But we –

Bruce   Please?

Christopher   But . . . I'm getting out today. My twenty-eight –

Bruce   OK, look –

Christopher   My twenty-eight –

Bruce   Chris –

Christopher   My twenty –

Bruce   I know but –

Christopher My –

Bruce All right!

Pause.

Not now. *Later.* I'll send for you.

Christopher I already packed.

Bruce I know.

Christopher *stands and exits.*

Robert I know exactly what you're thinking and before you say anything I want you to know it was nothing to do with me. (*Beat.*) I mean, whatever he said to the *rest* of the Authority . . . (*Beat.*) I had no idea that he'd done this when I went into that Management Hearing this morning. I knew he wanted to make a complaint to the Authority – I tried to talk him out of it. That's the last I knew of it.

Bruce But you 'are the Authority'.

Robert OK . . . I'm a *representative* at *Management Hearings.* One of many.

Bruce But yesterday you said you 'are the Authority'.

Robert Only sometimes . . . sometimes it's me, yes, who . . . whoever is . . . *everybody* runs it. It's a different person each week depending on . . . it's more of a *committee* than a, than a . . .

Bruce The point is . . . have you read this?

Pause.

Robert Of course I've read it.

Bruce Don't tell me. You've read it because: you wrote it?

Robert Of course I didn't write it. What kind of bastard do you take me for?

Pause.

Bruce (*reading*)   'After some initial difficulty following the patient's interpretation of events, the Authority reached a consensus that if the said orange was indeed to be viewed as blue for the purposes of the analogy . . .' For the purposes of . . . ?

He gives **Robert** *a look.*

Bruce   '. . . then clearly as a blue-skinned orange it was indeed in the minority given that other citruses are ordinarily orange, yellow or . . .'

He gives **Robert** *a look.*

Bruce   'By asking the patient to peel the "minority" orange . . . and declaring the insides of the orange to be of equally unusual colouring, the house officer seems to have implied . . .'
What did you *say* to him?

Robert   I didn't say anything.

Bruce *reads.*

Bruce   'The Authority reached a consensus.' How?
Did everybody think of the the the stupidest things they could think of and then put them all in a hat?
By playing a drinking game?
Small children wouldn't come up with this.
Monkeys could do better using *sign language.*
For God's sake!

Robert   'Monkeys'.

Bruce   Yes.

Robert   Is that another analogy?

Bruce *stares.*

Robert   It's too easy to misinterpret, Bruce. You really have to be more careful.

Bruce   Well. Do you agree with 'the Authority'?

Robert   I rather think I should remain impartial on this one. Besides, they're more interested in your side of the story. Give me a statement and they'll probably leave you alone.

Bruce   Give you a 'statement'. But I haven't done anything! I can't . . . believe . . . has it really gone that far? Can't you . . . can't I just talk to them?

Robert   Well . . . not really. There's a Procedure.

Pause.

Bruce *reads.*

Bruce   'The Authority recommends that a senior consultant confers treatment with an outpatient programme.'

Robert   I think it's a good idea.

Bruce   Why?

Robert   I'm a senior consultant. He already knows me.

Bruce   What do you get out of it?

Robert   I don't 'get' anything. It's just expediency.

Bruce   'Expediency'. The Path of Least Resistance.

Robert   Absolutely.

Bruce   OK. So. You want to take over the case. And . . .

Pause.

Then you can continue Your Research?

Pause.

And Then You Can Finish Your Book. Is it a good book? It must be, you'll go to any lengths to finish it . . .

Robert   You're on very thin ice here, Flaherty.

Bruce   'The Search for the Holy Grail'.
What a chapter heading that would make.
'A Cure For Black Psychosis'.
Imagine. No more bed crises. No more hospitals.

We'd save a bundle on Care in the Community.
You'd become Professor overnight.

Robert   I *beg* your pardon!

Bruce   You heard.

Robert   Are you out of your mind?

Bruce   You'll be the toast of Academia the World Over.
Imagine! A golden opportunity to distinguish yourself from all
the other boffins; To be the Eggiest Egg Head of them all; to
be *different* from all the other odious little careerists on the
gravy train kissing management arse. To be Up There with
all the other Cambridge wonderboys in their bow ties and
tweed, flapping about the 'corridors of power' with their
pricks in each other's pockets. What's wrong with just *doing
your job*?

Pause.

Robert   It's the Maudsley actually.

Bruce   I'm sorry?

Robert   I read Psychiatry at the Institute of Psychiatry at
the Maudsley Hospital in Dulwich. Not Cambridge.

Bruce   Oh, the Maudsley, big difference.

Robert   I really recommend you go there. I think you need
to go there. And I don't mean for training.

Pause.

You're already the subject of an inquiry. If the Authority asks
for a Psychiatric Report I'll be in a very awkward position.

Silence.

Bruce   OK. OK. Look . . . have you never heard . . . listen,
uh, Doctor . . . did you hear Christopher refer to himself,
somewhat effacingly, somewhat ironically as a, quote, 'uppity
nigger'? Did you hear him say that?

Robert   It was unmistakable.

Bruce   And presumably you heard me quoting him, also, I offer, somewhat ironically?

Robert   I'd steer clear of irony if I were you. You're not Lenny Bruce.

Bruce   It was . . . it was a *nuance*. It was . . . the way I said it . . . with a note of familiarity . . . because I know him . . . and –

Robert   It's not for me to characterise your 'nuances', Doctor. And if you ask me, yes, perhaps it was somewhat 'provocative and unorthodox'.

Bruce   Only to you.

Robert   How do you mean?

Bruce   It was provocative and unorthodox to you because, well, frankly, it would be, wouldn't it? Perhaps you don't get out enough.

Robert   You're doing it again: you're being provocative.

Pause.

I'm sorry, Doctor. It's pejorative whichever way you say it and these days racial epithets just don't wash.

Bruce   'These days'. I see. Did they use to?

Pause.

Robert   You know what I mean.

Bruce *seizes the report and tears it into bits.*

Robert   May I . . . ?

He produces a mobile phone and dials.

This is Doctor Robert Smith, can somebody send Christopher over here immediately please . . . upstairs . . . yes . . . no, I'm in the consultation room with Doctor Flaherty . . . no, he's my . . . no, he was but . . . he . . . n . . . I understand but . . . well he's my patient now.

He puts the phone away.

Bruce   What did you tell him?

Robert   Bruce –

Bruce   What have you done?

Robert   It's his complaint; why don't you ask him?

Bruce   I intend to. (Just as soon as you've slithered off.)

Robert   Actually, that's not possible, I'm afraid. Not until I've briefed the patient.

Bruce   . . . What?

Robert   That's the procedure. I can't allow you to be alone with him. It's a question of Seniority as much as anything else. Perhaps if you'd shown some respect for Seniority in the first place; if you'd listened to Somebody Who Knew, we wouldn't be in this mess.

Bruce   So I'm not allowed to see Chris any more without you being present?

Robert   Anything you want to ask you must ask the Authority.

Bruce   I just *asked* 'the Authority' and I think 'the Authority' is *lying*.

Robert   I'm presenting you with the opportunity to defend yourself. That's the Procedure. What more do you want?

Bruce   Christ, it's so transparent.

Robert   Oh, do stop whining, Bruce. Before somebody nails you to a cross.

Pause.

Oh. While I'm here I should mention that I've been keeping a diary.

Bruce   A *diary?*

Robert   A diary of my research, but there are things in it which might be relevant to your case.

He produces a diary from his jacket pocket.

Now you've stopped blustering I should read you some things before my patient returns.

Bruce   You just happened to have it on you.

Robert (*reading*)   'Twenty-sixth of October: Mention Antecedent Programme to Doctor Flaherty and he laughs. Not interested in providing African-Caribbean and African patients for research purposes.'

Bruce   I didn't laugh . . . I . . . this is silly . . .

Robert   Which suggests you have been obstructive towards me from the off. I'm your *supervisor*. You don't turn down a request like that unless you have a very good reason.

Bruce   I . . . look . . . I have professional reservations . . . ethical reservations about –

Robert   About what?

Bruce   About using patients as, as guinea pigs in, in, in –

Robert   'Guinea pigs'? Honestly, Bruce. 'Monkeys, guinea pigs, voodoo . . .' You've an entire menagerie of piccaninny slurs to unleash.

Bruce   *What?*

Robert   Can you not see how this could be *interpreted* – by the Authority, for example? You have to admit it doesn't look good.

Bruce   Then don't show it to the Authority.

Robert   I beg your pardon.

Bruce   I said, don't . . . show . . . Doctor Smith . . . please . . . it's . . . it's . . . do we have to show them this?

Robert   We'll pretend you didn't say that, shall we?

Silence.

Bruce *just stares.*

Robert *flips over a few pages.*

Robert 'Twenty-fourth of October: Flaherty implies research funds being used to keep me in, quote, "dickie bows and putters".'

Bruce We were *drunk*. After the rugby.

Robert *You* were drunk.

Bruce And and and you *agreed* with me. It was a joke!

Robert You invite me to watch the rugby with you and then you insult me. You drag me home for a chunk of rancid cheese on toast, get pissy-drunk on Bulgarian hock and start haranguing me about iniquity in the medical profession like some kind of mildly retarded student activist, then you expect the Nobel Peace Prize for Services to Psychiatry.
Why are you so threatened by my ideas?

Bruce Because . . .

Pause.

Because they're *shit*, Doctor.
The research is banal and it's all been done before *anyway*. It's Old News. It's *R.D. Laing* in a gorilla suit.
It isn't empirical.
And it isn't a PhD.
It isn't a Book.
A *cookbook* would be more ground-breaking.
It's a waste of resources and money and everybody's time and you know it.

Robert What are you implying?

Pause.

You see, this is just the type of verbiage –

Bruce Verbiage?

Robert   Which people find so highly offensive about you, Bruce. This is how you wind up under investigation.

Christopher *walks in carrying a large holdall and sits down.*

Christopher   Hope I'm not interrupting.

Robert   Hello again, Christopher. I'm so sorry to send you away like that. We've concluded our meeting now and as soon as the doctor has asked you one or two more questions you'll be on your way.

Christopher   I'm going home now?

Robert   You're going home.

Christopher   Oh boy. Oh man. I'm going home.

Bruce   Chris, have I upset you in any way?

Robert   You can't ask that question.

Bruce   Why – because he might answer it?

Robert   Jurisprudence dictates.

Bruce   Are there 'charges pending'?

Robert   You are Under Investigation, yes. If there are charges to be answered then you will be suspended pending the inquiry.

Bruce   What charges?

Robert   Negligence.

Bruce   'Negligence'?

Robert   Racial harassment.

Bruce   What else? I'm intrigued.

Robert   Abuse.

Bruce   'Abuse'. Well. I was waiting for that. 'Abuse'. Mm. You know what I think? I think people abuse the term 'abuse'.

Robert   Excuse us a moment please, Christopher.

He takes **Bruce** *by the elbow and marches him to a far corner of the room.*

Robert   Doctor Flaherty, if Christopher stays in here indefinitely under a Section 3 and is diagnosed with paranoid schizophrenia, the rest of his life will be ruined.

Bruce   He won't get the help he needs without that diagnosis.

Robert   It would be negligent.

Bruce   Please, Doctor Smith, yours is an *arbitrary diagnosis.* You've observed him in one interview. It's my word against yours.

Robert   Two interviews.

Bruce   And you saw something entirely different to what I've seen.

Robert   That's the ICD 10 for you. Observation and interview.

Bruce   I think . . . look, I think he's suicidal.

Robert   He's not suicidal. He's just depressed.

Bruce   He's depressed because he's schizophrenic.

Robert   He's depressed because he's *here.* Exactly how old is Christopher?

Bruce   Twenty-four.

Robert   Twenty-four. And how do you think it feels for Christopher – a bright, fun, charismatic young man – to be locked up with chronic, dysfunctional mental patients twice his age?
People with a history of institutionalised behaviour.
People who harm themselves.
People with drug problems, who are suicidally depressed, who scream and laugh and cry routinely for no apparent

reason – when they're not *catatonic*.
Have you thought about how intimidating and frightening
that must be for him? Night after night after night, with no
let-up.
Have you thought about what that does to a young man?
It's Like Going To Prison.
It's *cruel*.

Silence.

Now.
I have examined the patient in depth.
I have consulted with a social worker and a CPN.

Bruce   When?

Robert   In this morning's Management Hearing.
And we believe this patient will receive the treatment he
needs in the community.
We concur that the community is the right and proper place
for him.
We believe that we would be failing him by keeping him.

Bruce   So . . . it's all been settled then. I'm being overruled.

Robert   To say the fucking least, Doctor.

Bruce   So why have an inquiry.

Robert   Well, you see, for what it's worth, we're beginning
to wonder whether this patient should ever have been
sectioned in the first place.

Bruce   The, the, the police sectioned him with a 136.

Robert   Well perhaps they were being 'ethnocentric'.
He was drinking.
He was depressed.
The hospitals are full of men like Christopher.
The prisons are full of men like Christopher.
Ordinary men whose lives have flown apart and they've
found themselves in a market one day 'acting funny'. Next
day they've been locked up and a week later they're on the

coast of a crack-up. Don't you think it's time we did something about it?

Pause.

Look at him! He's a mess. Well? What have you got to say for yourself?

Pause.

(*To* **Christopher**.) I'm sorry, Chris.

Christopher   No, you just talk amongst yourselves. D'you know what I mean?

Bruce *stares into space.*

Silence.

Bruce   You're not going to show me any support here, are you? As my supervisor? As a mentor? A friend?

Robert   That would be highly inappropriate.

Bruce   You've made up your mind. You support this allegation.

Robert   Not the allegation, just the inquiry. I'm afraid so.

Bruce   Golly. Just wait till I tell my wife.

Pause.

Maybe *you'd* like to tell her. Next time we invite you for dinner. Next time she slaves over a hot stove to put food in your mouth.

Robert   I'd hardly call Welsh rarebit 'slavery'.

Bruce   Next time I buy you a ticket for the rugby.

Robert   If you'd let me buy them we'd have sat in the members' stand.

Bruce   I don't even *like* fucking rugby. Bunch of hairy twats running about biting each other's ears off.

Pause.

Robert   Bruce, I'm simply asking you to give me a statement. Give the Authority your side of the story. Now. Have you got a lawyer?

Bruce   Why should *I* get a lawyer? *You* get a lawyer. *Prove* this. I can't believe this is even happening!

Robert   I really don't understand why you're taking it so personally. Why are you so angry?

Bruce   Because it *is* personal. You're somebody I trusted. I confided in. I thought you were on my side. I thought you and me could make a difference. Which is why I invited you over. My wife cooked. Nourished you. I should have choked you.

Robert   Bruce. You wanted me for your supervisor. Your mentor. You expect me to recommend your consultancy one day.

Bruce   And why did you agree – if not to get research material out of me? To finish your book. To . . . to . . . Doctor Sm . . . please . . . I don't know why . . .

Robert   I agreed because I liked you.
I thought you had promise.
I thought, such is my vanity, that you could learn something from me. Is that so difficult to believe?
Are you really so insecure?

Silence.

They stare at each other.

Christopher   You got any jelly babies?

Bruce (*to* **Christopher**)   Did I upset you yesterday? When I asked you to peel that orange?

Bruce *tosses* **Christopher** *an orange from the bowl and he catches it.*

Robert   I really don't think this is a good idea.

Bruce   Did that upset you?

Christopher *looks at* **Robert**.

Bruce   No, don't look at him, look at me.

Christopher   D'you know what I mean? I'm thirsty. I need a Coke.

Bruce   You'll get a Coke if you answer my question.

Robert   Doctor Flaherty.

Bruce   Did that upset you when you peeled the orange?

Christopher   No.

Bruce   Later, when you got to thinking about it, were you upset?

Christopher   No. It interested me.

Robert   You're pushing your luck, Flaherty.

Bruce   'No'? Oh, OK. Why do you think I asked you to peel the orange?

Christopher   To see what colour it was inside.

Bruce   And what colour was it? In your own words. Without any help from me.

Christopher   In my own words. Blue.

Bruce   Peel another one. See if it's still blue.

Robert   I really don't recommend this.

Bruce   Go ahead, Christopher. Why not? I'll even let you eat it.

Pause.

Christopher *peels the orange.*

Pause.

He begins eating it suspiciously.

Bruce   What colour is the orange, Chris?

Christopher   Blue.

Bruce   OK. And what do you think that means?

Pause.

Christopher   Something to do with my dad.

Robert   OK, that's enough.

Bruce   Something to do with your dad? OK.

Robert   I said –

Bruce   And what do you think I think it means?

Robert   Enough!

Bruce   What do *I* think it *represents*?

Christopher   S . . . omething to do with my dad?

Robert   This is not the time or the –

Bruce   Any idea what?

Robert   . . . Place.

Christopher   Nope. No idea, man.

Bruce   Well, I have no idea either.

Christopher   Maybe it's a signal.

Robert   . . . I must insist –

Bruce   Or a coincidence?

Christopher   No, it ain't a coincidence.

Bruce   What's it a signal of then?

Christopher *produces the crumpled newspaper cutting from his pocket and smooths it out, shows it to* **Bruce** *who shakes his head slowly.*

Christopher   Idi Amin Dada. See? '*Da-da.*' That's another signal.

Bruce   No, Chris . . . I'm sorry . . . please.

He touches **Christopher** *on the arm.*

Bruce   Put it away now. Concentrate.

Robert   Don't you think you're being a bit arbitrary?

Bruce   What?

Robert   Why should he put it away?

Bruce   'Why'?

Robert   Yes. He's not a child. Why should he?

Pause.

Bruce   Because he cut it out of the newspaper.

Robert   'Because he cu –' Really?

Pause.

And and and what makes you think that?

Robert *snatches the article from* **Christopher** *and examines it.*

Bruce   It's just a hunch.

Robert   Well, my hunch is that he didn't. My hunch is that his mother gave it to him. What is it about this particular disclosure that makes you so uncomfortable, Bruce?

Bruce   What makes me uncomfortable is that this morning he told me his father was Muhammad Ali. He'd seen him on breakfast television winning Sports Personality of the Century.

Silence.

Robert (*to* **Christopher**)   Is this true?

Christopher   1974. *Zaire*. *Think* about it, man.

Robert (*to* **Bruce**)   Why didn't you tell me this before?

Bruce   Before when?

Robert   Before . . . *now.*

Pause.

You told me about his mother in Feltham, blue oranges and
the Chevrolet but the Rumble in the Sodding Jungle you
didn't deem appropriate! Jesus wept!

Silence.

OK. Now. OK, what have we got here? One of the most
feared men in history and one of the most loved. Both
immensely powerful. Both role models. Both of African
origins.

Christopher   Both Muslim Fundamentalists.

Bruce   Abso-fucking-lutely! Christopher, please. I want you
to concentrate on the orange –

Robert   I am warning you, Doctor –

Bruce   What does it represent now?

Robert   It was stipulated at the Management Hearing that
you have no further contact –

Bruce   What do you think Doctor Smith thinks it
represents?

Robert   Listen . . . Christopher –

Christopher   That's easy –

Robert   Chris . . . ? Bruce –

Bruce (*to* **Robert**)   Grant me this one favour, please: listen
to your patient. Chris?

Christopher   He says it's a *person.*

Robert   I never –

Bruce   A person. What kind of person?

Robert   – said anything of the –

Christopher   A Brother.

Robert   No. That's enough.

Bruce   And do you agree with that?

Christopher   I don't know.

Robert   What I said was . . . what I meant was . . . and you obviously completely misunderstood me . . . was –

Christopher   You did –

Robert   Enough! Let me finish –

Christopher   You said it was *me*.

Robert   OK, OK, OK, OK, OK, OK, OK . . . OK . . . Now . . . I commented, I merely *commented* that . . . I *suggested* that it was an unfortunate demonstration which could potentially be viewed . . . by *somebody* very vulnerable . . . by a patient . . . as an 'analogy'.

Bruce   But it wasn't an analogy.

Robert   All right . . . nevertheless . . . it could be 'taken the wrong way'. It could 'cause offence' . . .

Bruce   But it didn't cause offence –

Robert   Well . . . in hindsight –

Bruce   In whose hindsight?

Robert   OK, all right, whatever the *fucking semantics*, it was an unfortunate incident –

Bruce   It wasn't an incident –

Robert   All right, it was very, very . . . it was *upsetting*. He was upset by it, that's all and so, so, so I brought it up in the Management Hearing –

Bruce   Oh, *you* brought it up in the Management Hearing?

Robert   What?

Bruce   You said *you* brought it up. You just said that. You said you brought it up at the Management Hearing this morning.

Silence.

Christopher   And he said I should learn to lick my own balls. He did. Ridiculous but true.

They all stare at each other.

Robert *rubs his eyes.*

Christopher   (Do I look like a contortionist?)

Bruce   So . . . Doctor . . . *you* made the Complaint. *You* lodged this complaint with the Authority.

Robert   The patient was very upset. He was in no state to –

Bruce   Were you upset, Christopher?

Christopher   What? When?

Robert   He was. Take my word for it.

Bruce (*to* **Christopher**)   Are you upset now?

Robert   I'm going to go berserk in a minute. I am trying to straighten this out for you! I am trying to help.

He takes out his packet of cigarettes shakily.

(*Lighting up.*) Give you the benefit of my . . . erudition . . . and experience . . . as a Senior . . . as Senior . . . *Senior* Consultant . . . *Head* of Department . . .

Christopher *takes a cigarette and the lighter and lights it, also shakily.*

Bruce   Christopher, if I upset you, I apologise. Sincerely. I didn't mean to upset you. Did I say anything else that upset you?

Pause.

Chris?

Christopher   You put thoughts in my head.

Bruce   What kind of thoughts?

Christopher   Just thoughts.

Robert   I have to insist this stops right now.

Bruce   Shut up. Chris . . . ?

Robert   Christopher. Not another word.

Bruce   Can you think of anything specific?

Christopher *stares at* **Bruce**.
Christopher *spits the orange out and stares at the remaining segments in his hand.*

Christopher   The thoughts I have are not my thoughts. He said that I think your thoughts.

Bruce   *Doctor Smith* said?

Christopher   And that's why I have to get out of here.

Robert   That's not what I said.

Christopher   I've gotta get outta here cos of you, man!

Robert   Look . . .

Christopher   Cos you're *bad*.

Robert   OK . . . Christopher –

Christopher   And now I don't, I don't, I don't know what to think! I don't know what to think any more.
When I do think, it's not my thoughts, it's not my voice when I talk. You tell me who I am.
Who I'm not. I don't know who I am any more!
I don't know who I am!

Robert   Chris –

Bruce   Chris –

Robert   It's being here that's doing this to you. This place –

Bruce   You're still very confused –

Robert   You can't think straight in this place. How can you . . . ?

Bruce   You're safe here, OK? It's quiet –

Robert   Apart from the bloodcurdling screams of all the other mental patients –

Bruce   Chris, you need to do this, you must try and stay a little longer –

Robert   You can leave now if you want to leave now –

Bruce   Chris –

Robert   But you have to want to.

Christopher   I do want to!

Bruce   Are you sure you're ready?

Christopher   No, man, I'm not sure of anything!

Robert   Christopher –

Bruce   Chris –

Robert   Listen . . . list –

Bruce   Chris –

Robert   Chris –

Christopher   OK OK OK JUST SHUT UP JUST SHUT THE FUCK UP FOR ONE MOMENT FOR GOD'S SAKE YOU ARE DRIVING ME AROUND THE BEND!

Silence.

Bruce   OK, look . . . (*To* **Robert**.) Could we have a minute alone please?

Robert   Absolutely not.

Bruce   I don't think you're in a position to argue any more.

Robert   You're only making it worse.

Bruce   Nevertheless. I think you should.

Robert   OK! OK! It's *your funeral*.

Robert *exits.*

Silence.

Christopher   What the fuck do you want, Bruce?

Bruce   Well, um, well, um, I'd like you to understand that this is a very serious situation.

Christopher   Yeah, but the thing is, like he said, I don't think you should take it so personally, d'you know what I mean?

Pause.

Bruce   Well. You know. Um. I know. Yes. I'm trying.

Christopher   When somebody does something you don't like, you should just learn to laugh. D'you understand?

Bruce   Y – OK – OK. The thing is, Chris . . . see . . . I'm not very good at this. I'm not very good at . . . Not Taking Things Personally.
That's all. I like to . . . Get to the Bottom of Things.

Christopher   You don't say.

Bruce   No, I'm not being funny. Things here at the hospital, at work, I take personally sometimes. I'm ever-mindful of the way one's *professional* life impacts upon one *personally.* Just as what happens to *you* here impacts upon your personal, private life. It's all related. So you see, when you took your complaint to the Authority one of the things they concluded was that I had been 'unprofessional'. Which is in their jurisdiction to decide – they are generally more venerable – more experienced, judicious beings than I. However, the upshot is that depending on what happens now . . . I could possibly be sacked in the *first month* of my training! It isn't your fault. And I am not taking that personally. But what I would like to point out to you is that, that could well affect *both* our personal, private lives in a, in a *terrible, disastrous* way. OK? Do you understand now?

Christopher   Don't patronise me.

He eyeballs **Bruce**.

Pause.

Christopher   I had a life before this. I had a job. On a stall in the market.

Bruce   That's what I'm saying.

Christopher   I got stuff to go back to. I've got my mum.

Bruce   Your mum can't help you just now.

Christopher   She needs me. She gets lonely. I miss her.

Pause.

Bruce (*gently*)   Chris . . . you don't know where she is, do you?

Pause.

You see, my point is, when they let you out this afternoon, the theory is that you'll go back to your family. To your community. But you don't have any family, do you? Not any more. Not so far as we know. And, the thing is, should you come back, should you ever need to return and ask for my help, I might not be here.

Christopher   I'll see Doctor Smith.

Bruce   I . . . I know. But, um . . . you can see him *anyway*.

Christopher   How d'you mean?

Bruce   There's no need for you to press ahead with this complaint. If you no longer want me to treat you, I won't.

Christopher   I don't.

Bruce   Then I won't. Fine.

Christopher   Cos you put your thoughts in my head.

Bruce   OK, well . . . you know, Chris, I really didn't mean to. Maybe other people have put thoughts in your head too but they're not going to be birched for it. Do you, do you, do you see what I mean?

Christopher No.

Bruce I'm saying . . . look . . . I don't know what Doctor Smith said to you yesterday evening, OK, I have no idea – actually, I have a pretty good idea and I think . . . I'll be honest with you. I think Doctor Smith 'coached' you in what you had to say to the Authority.

Pause.

I think he put words in your mouth.

Christopher He put words in my *mouth*?

Bruce Yes. Not literally. Figuratively. OK . . . don't get excited.

Christopher No, *you* put words in my mouth. When I said I wanted to stay and I was scared, that was you. That's why I'm here now! Cos of *you*!

Bruce No. OK? Now . . . no. Just . . . No. Just let me read you something.

He takes a pamphlet from **Christopher**'s *file.*

I'm going to give you this to take with you. Whether you stay or go. This is what the World Health Organisation has to say about schizophrenia. I don't want to alarm you, but I want to explain to you what you've just said. I want to 'demystify'.

He reads.

'The most intimate thoughts . . . are often felt to be known or shared by others and explanatory delusions may develop, to the effect that natural or supernatural forces are at work to influence the individual's thoughts and actions in ways that are often bizarre.'
Sound familiar?

Long pause.

Christopher *snatches the pamphlet, screws it up, throws it on the floor.*

Christopher   You're just trying to get off the hook now.

Bruce   Just listen to me. You don't know what you're talking about.

Christopher   Why? Cos I'm an 'uppity nigga'?

Bruce   Look. Shut up a minute.

Christopher   Oh, that's very nice, that's lovely. It's all coming out now.

Bruce *slams his fist on the table.*

Bruce   This isn't a game! My career is on the line!

Christopher   Your 'career'?

Bruce   And your . . . your . . . you have got so much to *lose*! We both have, don't you see this?

Christopher *kisses his teeth.*

Bruce   Chris . . . please, for God's sake. Can you remember what you did in the market with the orange? Can you see how that could get you into a lot of trouble? If you were doing that . . . on the estate, for example, I don't know what could happen . . .

Christopher   I never trusted you. Mm-mm. I liked you, but I never trusted you.

Bruce   What . . . ?

Christopher   You told me I could have a Coke, yeah? In front of a witness you said I could have a Coke if I answered your questions and I answered your questions so where is it? D'you think I'm thick or something?
D'you think I'm thick?
You told me you were letting me out and now you're not. What's going on, Bruce?

Bruce   I am, Christopher, I will.

Christopher   When?

Bruce   Soon.

Christopher   Oh 'soon'.

Bruce   When you've been diagnosed properly. You must try and be patient.

Christopher   I don't *believe* you. You call me nigga. You say it's voodoo.

Bruce   It was a joke!

Christopher   Oh funny joke. Do you see me laughing?
I've got one for you. I'm gonna Lay Charges.
Cos I ain't staying here, man.
You'll never keep me locked up, white man. This is one nigga you don't get to keep, white man. Cos I'm gonna bark every time you come near. D'you understand?

Bruce   Is this you or is it . . . someone else? Is this the *illness* or is it . . .

Pause.

Maybe you're just *like* this.
Maybe you're just . . . A Wanker.
I mean . . . why do you say these things?

Christopher   Cos you ruined my life!
Cos you're Evil.
And you're a Fascist.

Bruce   How dare you!

Bruce *stands.*

Christopher *stands.*

Bruce   You fucking idiot . . . What Have You *Done*?

Christopher *starts to laugh.*

Bruce   What's funny? Stop laughing! Shut up! You stupid fucker. What are you laughing at?

Robert *is standing in the doorway, unseen.*

Bruce   Shut up! For fuck's sake!

Christopher   The look on your face, boy!

Bruce   You won't be laughing when you get home. You won't be laughing when you start losing your marbles all over again and hearing voices and jabbering like a lunatic and shitting yourself because you think your fucking zombie neighbours are coming to eat your brains, you mad bastard! You *idiot*!

Christopher   'Love Thy Neighbour' it says. How can I love my neighbour when my neighbour is fascist?

Bruce   They're black! All your neighbours are. It's a *black neighbourhood*. You you you *moron*. You stupid *fool*. Are you *retarded*? Jesus! This is the thanks I get for *rotting* in this stinking hellhole, pushing shit uphill, watching what I say, tiptoeing around, treading on eggshells, *kissing arse* while you sit around laughing and squawking and barking like a freak. You didn't know if you were Arthur or Martha when you came in here and this is the thanks I get. Now you're upset. *Now* I've upset you. Good. *Good*. See how much you like it.

He sees **Robert** *standing in the doorway and stares.*

Robert   When you use the term 'neighbour', do you mean it rhetorically or 'generically'?

He comes into the room, takes an orange from the bowl, sits and peels it as he talks.

Because it's just occurred to me that when Chris talks about his 'neighbour', he might not mean literally 'the people next door'. Do you, Chris? Nor would you mean 'sibling' should you allude to a 'Brother'. (*Eating.*) Neighbours is Everybody, isn't it? People in the street giving you a wide berth. Women on escalators holding their handbags that little bit tighter as you pass. People looking straight through you as if you're not even there. Football hooligans. Skinheads. Throwing bananas. Your workmates. Bruce and I can only *guess* at the horror of suffering from acute paranoia *and* being one of a culturally oppressed minority. What a combination.

Pause.

And we ask each other, Why are our mental hospitals full of young men like this? Why do you *think*?

Pause.

Bruce   Robert-Robert-Robert-Robert-Robert-Robert-Robert . . .

Pause.

Doctor . . .

Robert *produces a prescription pad from his pocket and writes a prescription.*

Robert   Why don't you report to outpatients and they'll organise you a car.

Pause.

Chris? Then you can go home.

Christopher   Do you think I should?

Robert   Yes. You must.

Christopher   Do you think I'm ready? Really?

Robert   Yes. You're ready. You can't stay in here for ever. (*To* **Bruce**.) Can he?

Bruce   I . . . what . . . ?

Robert   Do you want to get better?

Christopher   Yeah . . . I want to.

Robert   Then you must do what you must do. Be brave.

Christopher   Uh?

Robert   Be brave.

Christopher   'Be brave'?

Robert   Yes. Because you are brave. You're a very brave young man and you've done really well. This is your prescription.

He hands **Christopher** *the prescription.*

Christopher   Did you hear what he said?

Bruce   I'm sorry. I didn't mean it.

Christopher   Why d'you say those things, man?

Bruce   I really am sorry.

Christopher   My God. It really is a game of two halves with you, d'you know what I mean?

Bruce   Are you all right?

Christopher   What? *No.* That *hurt*, man. I can't stay in here if you're gonna say shit like that. D'you know what I mean? Running your mouth. It's *rude.*

Bruce   I know.

Christopher   It's *weird.*

Bruce   Sure.

Christopher   How would you like it?

Bruce   I know . . . I'm sorry.

Christopher   No, you don't know. How would you like it?

Robert   If you'd like to make another complaint –

Christopher   I *am* complaining. I'm complaining to *him* and he's not even listening.

Bruce   I . . . I think I need to sit down.

Robert   Would you like to lodge a complaint with the Authority?

Christopher   No. I'm OK.

Robert   It's really no trouble.

Christopher   I'm all right now.

Bruce *sits.*
He stares.
They regard him as he picks up a piece of orange peel, examines it, bites into it.

Robert   I'll get one of the nurses to book your first outpatient appointment.

Christopher   Thanks.

Robert   Don't mention it.

Christopher   No really, safe, man. I appreciate it.

Robert   It was the least I could do.

Christopher   Thank you.

Robert *offers his hand and they shake hands.*
Bruce *just stares from one to the other.*
Christopher *goes to* **Bruce***, suddenly staring oddly.*

Silence. **Christopher** *picks up an orange.*

Christopher   Have you ever stuck your dick in one of these?

Bruce *looks at him a little nervously.*

Christopher   One time I tried it with a grapefruit. At Christmas. It's OK but it chafes a bit. The juice stings. On the ward I seen one boy do it with bugs. Straight up. Puts a bug on the end of his willy. A cockroach. Just on the tip. He likes the way it wiggles. You think there's bugs in this?

Bruce   I'm . . . sorry . . . ?

Christopher   Is there bugs in this?

Bruce   Chris . . . please . . .

Christopher   I need a girlfriend, man. D'you know what I mean? That's all I ever wanted. I just wanted somebody nice to be with. A lady.

Silence.

Robert   Take it with you if you like.

Christopher   Uh?

Robert   Take it. Be my guest.

Pause.

It's a gift. It's time to go home.

Christopher   What have you done to it?
What have you put in it?
What are you staring at?

Christopher *ignores the orange.*
He stares from **Robert** *to* **Bruce** *suspiciously.*
He moves a few steps towards the door, then stops.

Robert   That's right. Off you go. Go home and listen to
some reggae music.

Christopher *stares at* **Robert** *for some time.*
Robert *eventually smiles and indicates the door.*
Christopher *goes.*
Robert *looks at* **Bruce**, *shakes his head, 'tuts' at length.*

Bruce   'Reggae music'?

Robert   What is it in Africa, 'jungle'? N'ha ha ha. (*Snorts.*)

Bruce *picks up an orange.*

Bruce   Well. That's that, then.

Robert   How do you mean 'That's that'?

Bruce   I've fucked it up, haven't I?

Robert   Oh, I see what you mean. Well . . . yes.

Bruce   I'll never make Consultant.

Robert   You still want to?

Bruce   Well . . . of course . . . but . . UNIVERSITY OF WINCHESTER
LIBRARY

Robert   Oh.

Long Silence.

Bruce   Unless . . .

Robert   What's that?

Bruce   We . . . don't really have to pursue this . . . now . . .
do we?

Robert   Well, I can tell you, I'm in no hurry to have the
good name of my department dragged through the mud.
Thank you very much.

Bruce   No . . .

Pause.

Not to mention . . . not to mention your Professorship.

Robert   My Professorship? How does it affect that?

Bruce   Well . . . it doesn't.

*He retrieves and carefully unfurls the remains of the screwed-up, torn
report.*

So . . . where do we go from here?

Pause.

I mean . . . what's the procedure? We were getting on quite
well. Until . . . this . . . disagreement.

Robert   It's a little more than that.

Bruce   But it's . . . I mean . . . uh . . . you're a good
supervisor.
And a valuable mentor.

Pause.

I'm pr . . . I'm privileged. I'm grateful to you.

Pause.

For . . . putting me straight.

Pause.

One could have made a dreadful mistake.

Pause.

Perhaps . . . I could . . . buy you a drink . . . to express my gratitude.
Debrief.
I could read your manuscript.

Pause.

Robert   No. I don't think we'll do that.

Bruce   W . . . why not?

Robert   Well. The thing is . . . I'll tell you something.

He takes the report from **Bruce** *and smoothes it out.*

Robert   I don't like you, Bruce.
You talk too much.
You get in the way.

Silence.

You see, sick people come to me.
All creeds and colours.
They are suffering.
They go away again and they no longer suffer.
Because of me.
All because of me.
And there's nothing wrong with that.
Is there?

Bruce   Who do you think you are? God?

Robert   How does Archbishop of Canterbury sound? N'ha ha ha.
You will not be employed by this Authority again. We made a mistake. It's a little Darwinian, I admit, nevertheless.
Goodbye.

He hands **Bruce** *the orange.*

You can eat it on the train.

Bruce *stares at the orange in his hand.*
He slumps in his chair.
He peels the orange.
He stares at **Robert**.
Robert *goes.*

Bruce　I want to make a complaint.

Robert *stops.*

Bruce　I'd like to lodge a complaint with the Authority.

Robert　Sorry?

Bruce　I'm ready to give you a statement.
What's the procedure for that?

Bruce *bites into the orange. They stare at each other.*

Blackout.

Kwame Kwei-Armah

Elmina's Kitchen

Kwame Kwei-Armah won the Peggy Ramsay award for his first play, *Bitter Herb* (1998), which was subsequently put on by the Bristol Old Vic, where he also became Writer-in-Residence. He followed this up with the musical *Blues Brother, Soul Sister* which toured the UK in 2001. He co-wrote the musical *Big Nose* (an adaptation of *Cyrano*) which was performed at the Belgrade Theatre, Coventry, in 1999. In 2003 the National Theatre produced the critically acclaimed *Elmina's Kitchen* for which in 2004 he won the *Evening Standard* Charles Wintour Award for Most Promising Playwright, and was nominated for a Laurence Olivier Award for Best New Play 2003. *Elmina's Kitchen* has since been produced and aired on Radio 3 and BBC4. His next two plays, *Fix Up* and *Statement of Regret*, were produced by the National Theatre in 2004 and 2007. He directed his play, *Let There Be Love*, when it premiered at the Tricycle Theatre, London, in 2008. He received an honorary doctorate from the Open University in 2008. His latest play was *Seize the Day* (Tricycle Theatre, 2009, part of their *Not Black and White* season).

Elmina's Kitchen was first presented in the Cottesloe auditorium of the National Theatre, London, on 29 May 2003. The cast was as follows:

Digger   Shaun Parkes
Deli   Paterson Joseph
Anastasia   Dona Croll
Ashley   Emmanuel Idowu
Baygee   Oscar James
Clifton   George Harris

Director Angus Jackson
Designer Bunny Christie
Lighting Designer Hartley T.A. Kemp
Music Neil McArthur
Sound Designer Neil Alexander
Company Voice Work Patsy Rodenburg
Dialect Coach Claudette Williams
Musicians Steve Russell, Juldeh Camaram, Atongo Zimba
Original Songs Kwame Kwei-Armah, Neil McArthur,
    George Harris, Oscar James

Characters

Digger
Deli
Anastasia
Ashley, *Deli's son*
Baygee
Clifton

Act One

Prologue

The stage is in darkness. A single spotlight slowly reveals a costumed man, standing absolutely still with a gurkel (a one-string African guitar famed for possessing the power to draw out spirits) in his hands. His head moves sharply as if smelling something distasteful. The music starts. It is a slow lament-sounding concoction of American blues and traditional African music.

The man then covers the length and breadth of the stage flicking handfuls of powder on to the playing area. The music ends.

Blackout.

Scene One

It's Tuesday, mid-afternoon. It's raining. We are in Elmina's Kitchen, a one-notch-above-tacky West Indian takeaway restaurant in 'Murder Mile' Hackney. The walls are littered with 'Dance Hall' advertisements and Whey and Nephew-type posters. Amid the Budweiser series of posters celebrating African-American heroes there is a big sign saying 'NO DRUGS ARE PERMITTED ON THESE PREMISES. RESPECT.' *The TV that is attached to the left wall closest to the counter is blaring out the ragga tune 'Sufferer' by Bounty Killer. To the right is a rack of spirits. There is a telephone on the counter. Behind the counter are two wooden swing doors that lead to the kitchen. Above that is a huge picture of a middle-aged West Indian woman, Elmina,* **Deli**'s *mother. Next to that is a framed laminated poster that reads, 'Life is beauty, admire it. Life is costly, care for it. Life is wealth, keep it. Life is love, enjoy it. Life is a dream, realise it. Life is a challenge, meet it. Life is a duty, serve it. Life is a game, play it. Life is a mystery, know it. Life is an opportunity, benefit from it. Life is a promise, fulfil it.'*

Standing behind the counter is **Deli** *(thirty-four), a happy spirit. He is a born struggler and optimist, but today he is a little restless. Although* *slightly overweight, we can see that he once possessed a fit, athletic body. His personality is slightly soft at the core. He has his head buried deep in a letter while mouthing the words to the song being played on the TV. 'Born as a sufferer, grow up as a sufferer, struggle as a sufferer, fe mek it as a sufferer, fight as a sufferer, survive as a sufferer, move amongst the ghetto ah most ah dem ah sufferer ah!', etc., etc.*

When he raises his head we see that he has a big bruise above his eye and a few cuts on his forehead.

Sitting on a stool close to the counter is **Digger** *(mid-thirties). He is very powerfully built and looks every bit the 'bad man' that he is. His hair is plaited in two neat sets of cane rows which meet each other at the top of his head. At the ends of the cane rows are multicoloured ribbons, the kind traditionally seen in young girls' hair.* **Digger** *is from Grenada but came to England aged fourteen. His clothes are not flash but are brand-name street clothes. The Chopper bicycle that we see chained outside the restaurant is his.* **Digger***'s accent swings from his native Grenadian to hard-core Jamaican to authentic black London. He has his hands-free adapter permanently plugged into his ear. He is busy reading the* Daily Mirror.

Digger *(to himself but loud)*   You mudder arse!

Deli *glances up at* **Digger** *and then to the picture of his mother.*

Deli *(as if on autopilot)*   How many times I got to tell you about language like that in here, Digger?

He returns to the letter. **Digger** *raises his head from his paper momentarily and gently kisses his teeth in* **Deli***'s direction. He's got to get back to the article.* **Deli** *finishes reading the letter, screws it up and throws it in the bin. Suddenly* **Digger** *shouts out.*

Digger *(in disbelief)*   Blood CLATT.

Deli *(irritated)*   Digger!

Digger   What?

Deli   Ah you me ah talk too yuh na!

Digger *(vexed)*   You can't see dat I reading som'ting?

He ignores **Deli** *and carries on reading.*

Deli   Man, you're ignorant!

Digger *doesn't like being called ignorant.*

Digger (*half playful*)   Char! You only lucky I don't want eat wid dem drug-selling niggas down Yum Yums, why I don't boo you down and tek my business dere. Gimme fritter an a Ginness punch.

Deli   Please!

Digger   What's wrong wid you today?

Deli   Cos I ask you to say please something must be wrong with me? See my point? You're ignorant.

He brings the fritter and the punch he has poured out over to **Digger**.

Deli   Two pound twenty-five. Please.

Digger (*checking his pockets*)   Give me a squeeze na?

Deli (*almost laughing*)   Squeeze? You *own* more money than anyone I know.

Digger   But dat's my business, Deli.

Deli   Just gimme me fucking money.

Digger   See you. You coming jus' like your cousin Sofie, a rhated Englishman.

Deli *pauses for a moment, confused.*

Deli   Please explain to me how my female cousin, can be a white male?

Digger   You know what I mean, she love too much blasted Englishman. (*Shaking his head.*) You British blacks, boy.

He shows him a picture of her in the paper.

Every time she dey in the paper, she have a rhated white man on she hand. Wha' appen! Ghetto willy too big fe her or what?

Deli   What the hell that has to do with putting your mean hand in your pocket to pay for your fritters? It's low-life dregs like you that probably send her dere.

Digger *(taking umbrage)*   Low what? See me and you, we go fall out one day, you know! I not no low nothin'. I's a legitimate businessman!

Deli   You forget I know where the butcher knife is!

Digger *pulls out his gun and points it at* **Deli**.

Digger   Yeah, but what's that gonna do against my tech nine, motherfucker?

Deli *(vexed)*   Don't fuck about, Digger, how you gonna be pulling that ting out in here? . . .

Digger   Sorry! Sorry! . . .

The phone rings.

Deli   What happen if a customer walk in now? I done told you about that x amount a times. Damn. Hello! Elmina's Kitchen, takeaway and delivery, how can I help you? . . . Chicken? We have jerk chicken, curried chicken, fried chicken, brown chicken, stew chicken and our new vibe is sweet and sour chicken. Yeah, West Indian style . . . Yeah, yeah . . . Where'd you live, bra? Berringham Road, seen, gonna be forty-five minutes, you alright wid dat? . . . What's your name? Badder youth? Seen, Badder, that'll be five pounds fifty cash handed over to my delivery boy before he takes the food out of the heated rear box, yeah? Nice.

Digger *who has returned to the paper, looks up at* **Deli** *and shakes his head.*

Digger   Da'is why you nigger people go fail every time. How you go tell a hungry man he have to wait forty-five minutes for he food?

Deli (*shouting from the kitchen*) You can't run a business on lies.

Digger You think a Indian man would do that? That's why the black man will always be down. He don't know how to analyse his environment.

Deli What graffiti wall did you get that from, Digger?

Digger Your mudder's. Sorry!

He bites into his fritter. He grimaces.

Bombo! Deli, your cooking is shit! How can a man fuck up a fritter?

Deli (*smiling*) Don't watch that, Dougie reach and you know his cooking is baddd!

Digger What! He's gonna sit down in the kitchen and cook? Ha ha!

The phone rings.

Deli Elmina's Kitchen, takeaway and delivery, how can I help you? . . . Sweet and sour chicken? . . . Where'd you live, bra? . . .

He looks up at **Digger** *and hesitates for a moment.*

Deli Well, that'll be . . . that'll be the next one out. Yeah, yeah, respect.

Digger *laughs at him.*

Digger See, I told yu you was coming like dem English man. Fork-tongued motherfucker.

Deli (*feigning ignorance*) What? Man, since I've put that sweet and sour shit on the menu the phone's been off the hook.

Digger I don't mean to be disrespectful but your shop is never, has never and I doubt will ever be, off the hook.

Deli Some things shouldn't be measured in financial terms.

Digger   A business is one of those thing that should!

Deli (*kisses his teeth*)   Digger, fuck off.

Digger   Oh, it's alright for you to use all manner of
Viking exple, exples, swear word, but as soon as a
motherfucker uses language of our heritage you start to cuss.
Dat is what I talking about when I cuss you British blacks.

Deli *kisses his teeth and ignores* **Digger**. **Digger**'s *phone rings. He
takes out three. He finds the right one. He switches his accent to hard-
core Jamaican.*

Digger   Yeah, yeah? Tricky wha you say, rude bwoy? . . .
Seen . . . Seen . . . Na!!! Wha you ah say? . . . Alright . . .
usual tings ah go run . . . seen . . . tie him up wait for me . . .
Tricky, don't be a pussy and get trigger happy, wait for me,
you hear? Alright, what is it, three now? I'll see you 'bout
four thirty. Later . . .

He ends the call.

I gotta get myself some new blood. Tricky stewpid!

Deli   Thought you was a lone operator?

Digger   I subcontract on a job-by-job basis. Eh, you know
who I had business with de odder day? Spikey!

Deli (*not really interested*)   Spikey who?

Digger   Spikey, who own the hair shop down by
Stamford Hill lights.

Deli (*suddenly interested*)   What Roy's from across the road
big mouth friend with the hair? You lie?

Digger   Oh ho! You interested now?

Deli   Who Spikey did owe money?

Digger   Me!

Deli   Before you, fool?

Digger   Matic posse.

Deli   I knew that motherfucker had to be dealing. How else could he move from one fucking blow-dryer and Sat'day girl to employing twelve fit woman in under nine months?

Digger   I thought you doesn't watch odder people tings?

Deli   Shut up. How much was he down for?

Digger   Nothin' real big. Twenty.

Deli   Twenty?

Digger   Well, he owe Matic dem fifteen and once I put my fee pon top . . .

Deli   . . . Twenty? Damn.

Digger   When I put de gun by he head, you know what he do?

Deli   What?

Digger   He offer me him fifteen-year-old daughter?

Deli   To do what wid?

Digger   To fuck of course.

Deli (*outraged*)   You lie?

Digger   I buck him with me pistol. Who the hell you take me for, Rodent?

Deli   Rodent?

Digger   The Yardie bwoy that rape all them people dem pickney when he was collecting. Motherfucker gave the trade a bad name.

Deli   Ras! He pay yuh you money yet?

Digger   I told him I'd kill his family across the whole world. He had my money to me in five days.

Deli   So that's why the shop's closed!

Digger   I give him an extra lick cos me did hear he was an informer.

Deli   Yeah? Fucking bitch. Should'a give him two.

The men sing together.

Deli/Digger   Man fe dead lick a shot inna informer man hend.

Enter **Ashley**, **Deli**'s *son (nineteen), hooded street clothes, headphones. He has his hair in two bunches. Trousers falling off the arse. Has no respect for anyone older than himself except for* **Digger**. *He walks in slowly talking on the phone.*

Deli   Yo! Ashley, what took you so long? How you let the man cut up your head so? Look like Zorro.

The men laugh together. **Ashley** *kisses his teeth, grabs the TV remote off the counter, changes the channel to MTV base and attempts to sit down.*

Deli   What you sitting down for? Can't you see there's ting waiting here to get delivered?

Ashley *looks at his dad's cut head.*

Ashley (*nonchalantly*)   It's raining out there, you know! Give me a second to catch my breath.

Deli   You wanna catch you arse out street and deliver the people dem food.

Ashley   Nigger needs to chill, boy!

Deli   Hey, I ain't no nigger with you.

Ashley (*to himself almost*)   No you're not, what they calling you on street now? Deli the sissy punk.

Deli   What?

Ashley   How am I supposed to walk the street an look my bredrens in the eye when mans all grip up my dad by his throat and you didn't deal wid it?

Digger (*still confused*)   What?

Deli *doesn't answer.* **Ashley** *does.*

Ashley   Roy from over dere coarse up my dad . . .

Deli   Coarse up who? . . .

Ashley   . . . and he didn't even lift a finger to defence. Can you believe that?

Digger   You let Roy da coolie coarse you up?

Ashley (*under breath but loud enough to be heard*)   It's a good thing uncle Dougie's coming home that's my word . . .

Deli   He never coarse me nothin'. We had a little someting . . . and I decided not to deal wid it THERE and THEN.

The guys stare at him in amazement.

Digger   Rasclaat!

Deli (*to* **Ashley**)   Me will deal wid him right! What?! I can't see me fucking brodder! Is pass me must pass him in the jail van? (*Beat.*) Did you buy the banner ting for your uncle?

Deli'*s explanation has meant nothing to him.* **Ashley** *slams a big roll of banner tape on counter and pushes it towards his father.*

Deli   Thank you.

Ashley *looks at the address he has to deliver to.*

Ashley   Berrington Road? I ain't delivering no cold food there. Trust me. You better heat it up dread or no can do!

Deli (*sharp and fast*)   Who you talking to like that? Don't mek me have to lick you down you know! Your mouth too quick these days.

Ashley *pushes out his chest.* **Deli** *catches himself, pulls back and takes the container back into the kitchen, kissing his teeth.* **Ashley** *nods* *his head to* **Digger** *who just about acknowledges him.* **Ashley** *pauses for a moment then approaches* **Digger**.

Ashley   So, yes my don, what a gwan?

Digger (*back to reading his paper*)   Just cool ya.

Ashley   You still busting the TT?

Digger (*short*)   Yep.

Ashley   Sweet but when I get my dollars, mine's a BM boy. You done know!

Digger *does not reply*.

Ashley (*checking to see that his dad can't hear*)   Listen, I kinda wanna talk some tings through wid you, you na mean?

Digger   No, I don't know what you mean.

Ashley (*taken aback but bounces back*)   Seen, seen. You're hooked up and dat, and mans needs to get hold of proper tings, not no air pistols runnings, you get me? So I wondered if . . .

Digger (*firmly*)   No.

Ashley   No what?

Digger   No.

Ashley (*with attitude*)   What what? Mans ain't looking a free tings, you know!

Digger   Yes you is. Don't ever be forward enough to ask me about tings like that again, seen?

Ashley   Seen.

Enter **Deli**. *Hands food to* **Ashley**.

Deli   Take it na! And hurry come back. You gotta to help me sort the room for your uncle.

Ashley *does but he's staring at* **Digger** *as he exits.* **Digger** *takes the remote and puts it back on to the old school music channel.*

Digger   Dem blasted young children duh' have no respect. You know, some parts ah de country fucking big man like you and me 'fraid to come out dey yard because young punks like him wanna shot dem down to get stripes? Not me a rass!

Deli *stares at the door that* **Ashley** *just exited with great concern in his eyes.*

Deli   What! . . .

Enter **Baygee***, a hyper lively old Bajan man in his sixties who often speaks at a hundred miles an hour. He's the last of West Indian door-to-door salesmen. Defying logic he is carrying about twenty different designer bags. He is wearing a three-piece suit with trilby hat to match that have all seen better days. We can see his long grey hair sticking out of the sides. He rushes into the restaurant.*

Baygee   Hey, Delroy, give me a quick shot of Clark's and have one you yourself, I win ten pounds on the lottery today. What James Brown say? (*Sings.*) I feel good, dadadada, I knew that I would now.

Deli   You still playing that stupidness?

Baygee   Be happy for a fella na! You know how many years I giving them people me money and never get fart back?

Deli   Congratulations, Baygee.

Baygee   Thank you. I have some niceeeeeeee new clothes for the children this week, you know, Deli. (*He searches to find the right bag.*) Tracksuits, jeans, baggy trouser that show dey underpants, nice tings, boy. I even have a Donna Karen Los Angeles dress for the wife . . .

Deli   New York.

Baygee   She on holiday?

Deli   Donna Karen New Y . . . Forget it. And it's the ex-wife, Baygee.

Baygee (*smiles*)   Even more reason why you should buy it.
Anyway take a look through, I coming back. Just popping to
see Ms Mary on Abbots Road.

He decks the shot of rum in one.

Deli (*knowing full well*)   She have something for you?

Baygee (*trying to front*)   She owe me twenty pound.

Digger (*teasing him*)   I'll buy that debt off you for fifteen
pound.

Baygee   White boy, I wouldn't sell you my stepmodder
piss, and she been dead twenty years, God bless her soul.
Give me one more, Deli.

*He selects the bags he's going to walk with and makes for the door. He
looks at the picture of Elmina and turns back to* **Deli**.

Baygee   Oh God, how many times I have to tell you?
I love that you have you modder up there but you need to
have one of yourself too. You could have been one of the
greatest, boy. Clifton took me to see him fight once and
I said, Cliff, he could be one of the greats, you know. He
smiled and said, I know. Put up the picture, boy.

Deli   Soon, Baygee. Soon. Your usual curry goat and rice?

Baygee   Who cook?

Deli   Me!

Baygee   Na, just line me up a patty and a Guinness
punch. In fact, make that two Guinness punch. I go need a
little energy when I leave Ms Mary's. I gone.

He's gone.

Digger   You British blacks, boy.

Deli   And I don't know why you gots to be dissing us all
the time, you been here since you was blasted fourteen,
you're as 'British' as the rest of us.

Digger (*shoots out*) Never! I was born in Grenada and I've lived in jailhouse all over the world. I know who the fuck I am, don't you ever include me in all you stupidness.

Deli Five years in a New York jail don't make you a citizen of the world, motherfucker.

Deli *starts to tidy up.* **Digger** *takes the remote control for the TV and points it towards the screen attempting to change the channel. It doesn't work.*

Digger How you get this thing on the news again?

Deli You got to watch the news every time it's on? Square then tick.

Digger What happens up there today, happens on the streets tomorrow.

The news channel is on. **Digger** *is really concentrating.*

We hear the chime that accompanies the opening of the shop's door. The boys look up. Enter **Anastasia** (*forty-two*). *Although dressed soberly, we can see that she has the kind of body that most men of colour fantasise about. Big hips and butt, slim waist and full, full breasts. There is something incredibly sexual about her presence. Beneath the very well applied 'make-up' we can see that she must once have been a real beauty. There is an insecurity, a soft sadness about her even though she attempts to hide this with a veneer of coarse West Indian confidence. Although black British, she too swings into authentic, full-attitude Jamaican at the drop of a hat. She speaks with confidence if not a little attitude.*

Anastasia *scans the shop quickly then pauses for a second. Then, as if she is somehow rooted to the spot, looks around again but this time slower, more deliberate, as if trying to see something that is not visible, something that is hiding. Subtly, she inhales slowly and then exhales. She snaps out of it and smiles genuinely at* **Deli**. *She has a bag in her hands.*

Anastasia (*firm and confident*) Hi! I come to apply for the job in the window.

Deli/Digger Really!

Anastasia   No, I just like opening me mouth and talking stupidness!

The boys clock each other.

Deli   Right, um, you have any experience?

Anastasia, *full of natural sexiness, walks and puts her bag on the counter. She takes out a Pyrex dish of macaroni pie and steps back.*

Anastasia   Macaroni pie. I cooked it yesterday, but next morning food is always the sweetest.

Digger (*half under his breath*)   Mind she obea you, boy!

Deli   Shut up, Digger! (*To* **Anastasia**.) So you've worked in an West Indian restaurant before?

Anastasia (*almost winking*)   No. But I figure it's not beyond me!

Deli (*a little surprised*)   What makes you would want to work here?

Anastasia   The truth? You're in serious trouble my bredren! Anyone that names his restaurant Elmina's Kitchen is in need of help. The good news! It's the help that I can give . . .

Deli   Elmina's my mother's name!

Digger   Ras!

Deli   And your name is?

Anastasia   Anastasia, it's the name of a princess. Brudder, you can't have a picture of a woman on the wall and the place look so! But what really makes me wanna work here! You is the best-looking man I have seen in a very long time.

Digger *looks up.*

Deli (*taken aback*)   Really?

Anastasia   No, but I knew that would sweet you. So how about you taste my macaroni pie na?

Deli   Are you smoking rock?

Anastasia (*shakes her head*)   No, I don't do drugs and I don't drink.

Deli   . . . Cos, girl, you got brass balls coming in here and tell me about my mudder! People have dead for less.

Digger   True!

Beat.

Anastasia (*seriously*)   Forgive me, I have a warped sense of humour.

Pause.

Deli *takes off the top of the Pyrex dish.* **Anastasia** *takes a pre-package plastic spoon from her bag and hands it to* **Deli**. *She also takes her book out and clenches it like a Bible. It is* The Celestine Prophecy.

Anastasia   Don't you want to heat it up?

Deli *shakes his head. He tastes the pie.* **Digger** *shakes his head.*

Deli   Ummmm, that's good . . . wicked in fact. Wow. You got anything else in there?

Anastasia   I have a goat ready for stewing.

Deli (*gets serious*)   Well, it's a full-time post we have here. It may not look busy now but it can get real rushed at lunchtimes.

Digger *coughs.*

Deli   And we have a reputation in the area for excellence.

Anastasia   So, you offering me the job?

Deli   Why, don't you want it?

Anastasia   You know what I mailed my son last night? I tell him that me walk into a restaurant named after a slave castle but couldn't see the castle.

Deli *doesn't quite know how to respond.*

Digger (*exclaims*)   Rasclaat!

Deli (*ignoring*)   So, when can you start?

Anastasia   Whenever.

Deli   Thursday? . . .

Anastasia (*before it's come out of his mouth*)   . . . Thursday? Fine.

She gathers her things and gets up to leave.

Do you read?

Deli   What do you mean?

Anastasia   How you does feed your mind if you don't read? Typical man.

Deli   I haven't mentioned pay?

Anastasia   It's gonna be more than I'm earning now, right!

He nods. She exits.

Digger (*getting out of his seat*)   That's a rasclatt madwoman! How you could employ dat?

Deli (*ignoring*)   Digger, shut up, man.

Digger (*sitting back down*)   Rhated madwoman.

Lights down.

During the blackout we hear the voice of the **Newsreader**.

Newsreader   The headlines. As the case of John and Peter Goodyear enters its fifth day at the Old Bailey the brothers go on record saying they murdered their parents 'for the hell of it'. We talk to Denton Philips, the Jamaican gangster, or 'Yardie', brought into Britain by the Metropolitan Police to supposedly help in the fight against crime. And thirty-five million pounds of personal assets were seized from celebrated Ranter frontman, William Forsheve, in the biggest pension scandal to hit the private sector in a decade. (*Music.*) Scenes of astonishment at the Old Bailey today as a spokesman for the two brothers . . .

The lights slowly come up to reveal:

Scene Two

Baygee, **Digger** *watching the TV. The fourth screw is in. They have glasses of rum in their hand.* **Anastasia** *and* **Deli** *are putting the finishing touches to the 'Welcome Home' decorations for Dougie while watching the TV when they can. The freshly painted banner reads 'Yes, dread, you reach! Respect due!'* **Anastasia** *steps down from a chair and heads towards the kitchen. The restaurant looks a little cleaner. Nothing serious but it looks better.*

Digger   Thirty-five million, you know!

Baygee (*conversationally*)   My father use to say when a black man tief one man cry, when the European dem tief, whole continents bawl. (*Holding up the rum glass to* **Deli**.) Give me one last quick one.

Deli *heads behind the counter to do it.*

Deli   No problem. (*Referring to banners.*) What you think, Baygee?

Baygee   Look good.

Digger   How's a man suppose to enjoy his food when all he can smell is paint to bloodclaat?

Anastasia (*referring to decorations*)   Yes, dread, you reach, now there's a fitting welcome for a black man. 'Bout welcome home.

Deli (*smiling at her*)   OK, you were right.

Anastasia   My God, these tablecloth, Renk! . . . You worse than my son. If I don't change the bedclothes he'll sleep on the same ting for a year!

Digger *and* **Baygee** *clock each other.* **Digger** *puts out his hand.*

Digger   One week before he sex that! Twenty pound.

Deli *hears and looks up at* **Digger** *disapprovingly.* **Baygee** *ignores him.*

Baygee   What time you brodder reaching?

Deli (*kisses his teeth*)   Ahh you know Dougie, he said today *sometime* but I'll believe it when I see him.

He smiles, excited at the prospect.

Baygee   You shouldn't make the boy find he own way home, you should'da pick him up from the gates?

Deli (*flash of anger*)   Alone, is how he wants to come out.

Digger   Yo! Gal, gimme me a next dumpling.

Anastasia (*flash of temper*)   Is who you talking to so? Cos believe, it better not be me.

Digger *is slightly taken aback.* **Deli** *jumps straight in.*

Deli   I bet a hundred pound it's informer business that catch that thirty-five million man.

Digger   Your money would be better spent teaching you staff how to talk to people. (*Changing back to subject at hand.*) Informer, yes!!

Deli   Better you shot me before you ask me fe do that.

Anastasia *stares at* **Deli**, *disappointed. He recoils slightly.*

Digger   Dem man dere, you don't even waste bullet pon dem. (*Imitating stabbing.*) Just jook jook jook him till he dead.

Anastasia   Take it that's why they call you Digger?

Digger   Yep. It tells people who the fuck *I* am and what I do! Ask any nigger in the street and they'll tell you! Digger's like one of them African names. It's got meaning. Remember that!

Anastasia gets the dumpling from the heated cabinet. She brushes past **Deli** *– their bodies touch momentarily –* **Deli** *steps back, and looks away.*

Baygee (*annoyed at* **Digger***'s boasting*)   What you do, young white bwoy, is buy and sell black souls!

Digger   I buy and sell debts. Not no cheap-arse fake designer clothes, like some motherfuckers I know.

Baygee   Don't test me, young man. I lash a man last week and he is still falling down!

Deli   Baygee, cool na!

Baygee   Once upon a time, businessmen like me were the only street salesmen our community had. Now look what they got! You may frighten all them others round here, I don't 'fraid you young bad-johns. I hate you, but God blimey, I don't 'fraid you.

Digger (*about to get vexed*)   Wha?!!!

Anastasia *jumps in.*

Anastasia   Digger! Your dumpling! And here (*slams down a glass of rum*), cool your spirits na!

Beat while the men cool down. **Deli** *clocks that* **Anastasia** *saved the moment. He smiles at her.*

The phone rings. **Deli** *picks it up.*

Deli   Hello, Elmina's Kitchen, takeaway and delivery, how can I help you? . . . Ashley, what you phoning me on the business line for? Call me on the mobile.

He puts down the phone. **Anastasia** *looks to* **Deli***.* **Deli** *smiles, half apologising for his ignorance. His mobile rings.*

Deli   Yes, who's calling? . . . (*Gets serious.*) Yeah, mate, your uncle's been here an hour already . . . Upstairs . . . (*Vexed.*) Tell him what? . . . I'm not telling him nothing . . . No! I don't know if we'll be here when you finally decide to arrive!

He puts down the phone. **Anastasia** *exhales, shaking her head.*

Deli   Ani, I ain't seen the boy in three days, his uncle is due out and he ain't got the manners to be here first thing in the morning to greet him! Let the bitch stew.

Anastasia *doesn't comment but you can see that she disagrees.*

Anastasia   But he's a bwoy, Deli, dem do tings so.

Deli   Thanks. Think we're all done here? I'm gonna go and get ready.

Anastasia   What's wrong with what you've got on?

Deli   Need to put on something that hides the weight, mate.

Anastasia   You look good to me.

Anastasia *smiles.* **Deli** *stops for the briefest of moments and then carries on. As he steps through the swing doors* **Digger** *picks up the TV remote and switches the TV on to the horseracing channel.* **Anastasia** *(who has just picked up her book) automatically turns to the TV screen.* **Deli***, however, knew* **Digger** *would do this and pops his head back round the swing doors. He clocks that* **Anastasia** *is paying a lot of attention to the horses.*

Anastasia   Gwan!

She turns away from the TV screen when she hears **Deli***'s voice.*

Deli (*ignorant*)   Take the horse gambling off, Digger. Ladbroke's is up the bloody road. How many times do I have to tell you?

Digger *turns it back on to MTV base, looks at* **Anastasia** *and indicates to* **Deli***.*

Digger   Him luck salt.

Baygee   Turn that ting down, boy.

Digger *takes out a packet of cigarettes and offers one to* **Anastasia**. *She picks up her book and reluctantly accepts. She steps from behind the counter. He lights it for her.*

Digger   Your face is very familiar to me. We meet in a bashment or something?

Anastasia   Bashment? (*Touch of bitterness.*) All the nice dance close up or full up wid pickney. I don't rave.

Digger   You don't drink, you don't rave. Wait, wait, I get it, I get it. I see you wid Bobbler and dem, don't it?

Anastasia   I don't move wid no crack crew!

Digger   Then how you know it's crack dey does run?

Anastasia (*stutters a little*)   Everybody know dat! (*Recovering, goes on the front foot.*) Wait, what you trying to say? Me look like one straygay street gal to you?

Digger   You's a feisty thing, innit? That's the way me like them. Ride better when them have a little spirit. What you say, Baygee?

Baygee   Why you don't leave the woman alone?

Digger   Wha?! I just getting to know Deli gal.

Anastasia (*aggressively*)   Who tell you that I was Deli's gal?

Digger   No one.

Anastasia   Young bwoy, I doubt if you could ah handle it. Excuse!

Anastasia *stubs the cigarette out semi-hiding the ashtray and exits through the swing door into the kitchen, picking up a pen in the process.*

Baygee (*prodding* **Digger**)   Eh, I see a couple of wild Yard boys driving up a one-way street yesterday. When a man show them the sign, the youth don't just take out he gun and threaten to kill him!

Digger *doesn't reply.*

Baygee   Figure it must be one of the new set of Yardies that eating up Hackney. They giving children BMWs, who could compete with that, eh? Hmm! People should always read street signs, don't you think, Digger? I gone. Tell Deli I'll pass back and pay on my way back from Mrs Alexander's house.

He exits with his bags. **Deli** *enters the restaurant dressed in black shirt and pants. He even has a black tie on but not done up. He rolls his head like a boxer preparing for a fight.* **Digger** *looks at him.* **Anastasia** *comes out after* **Deli**, *she looks approvingly at him.*

Digger   Bloodclatt, who dead? Where you going dress up so?

Deli   I ain't dress up, just wanna look good for my bra, innit? I spouse up the place, so wah! I can't spouse up meself?

Anastasia   Yes, man, you looks goooooods. Hold up.

She straightens **Deli**'s *tie so that it is hanging around his chest.* **Deli** *is not comfortable with her doing this.*

Anastasia (*straight, almost motherly*)   Now you look 'ready'.

Digger   Na na, you right, man should meet his brodder the right way and dat and it's nice that you clean up the place for him, but if you'd have come to me, I'd have give you the money to do it up proper, you know big picture of Haile Selassie, next to yuh modder, proper bamboo furniture, dim lighting and such!

Deli   Thanks but if I ever want to do that, I'll go to the bank.

Digger *bursts out laughing.*

Deli   What you laughing at?

Digger   What bank is going to give you money, nigger?

Deli   One that could recognise I've been a businessman from morning . . .

Digger   . . . And one that ignores your black skin?

Deli   Ahhhhh fuck that old school shit, Digger. That was some old eighties shit you talking.

Anastasia *goes to the kitchen. Enter* **Ashley**. *His hair has been done. Neat cane rows. He's aware he looks good. He's vexed.*

Deli   So you decide to show up?

Ashley   I can't believe it. See, Dad, I told you you shoulda deal wid that Roy.

Deli   That subject's dead, Ashley.

Ashley   They've not only gone and bought the Chini restaurant shop next to theirs.

Digger *looks away.* **Anastasia** *clocks this.*

Deli   What's the matter wid that?

Ashley *(surprised)*   You ain't read the note, have you?

He produces it out of his back pocket.

'Sorry for the temporary closure, reopening soon as Roy's West Indian restaurant.' They're taking the piss out of you.

Ashley *stares at* **Deli** *with hate in his eyes,* **Digger** *looks away.* **Deli** *rolls his head, clicks his neck. We can see the rage in his eyes. He clocks* **Anastasia** *and tries to cover it.*

Deli   Hey, it's a free world, man, people can do what they want.

Ashley   He takes away your pride, then your livelihood, and all you can do is stand dere like a fish? You've lost it, blood.

Deli *(flash of temper)*   I'm not no blood wid you.

Ashley   Regrettably, that's exactly what you are.

Anastasia *exits to the kitchen.*

Ashley   Char! Where's Uncle D?

Deli   He ain't here yet.

Ashley   I thought you said . . .

Deli (*quickly*)   . . . Don't worry about what I said. You ain't seen your uncle in seven years and the day he's due out you can't be bothered to get your arse here to greet him . . .

Ashley   I had runnings . . .

Deli   Runnings is more important than being here for your uncle?

Ashley *does not reply.*

Deli   So, it's not just me that lets the family down is it?

Beat. **Ashley**'s *face drops.* **Anastasia** *walks into the kitchen.* **Deli** *feels a little guilty so tries to change the subject a bit.*

Deli   You see your child today?

Ashley   Yep!

Deli (*gives him a twenty-pound note*)   Good. Give it to the mother this evening. Tell her thanks?

Ashley   I don't need it actually, Dad.

Deli   Oh yeah?

Ashley   Yeah.

Deli *snatches it back.*

Deli   Seen.

Anastasia *comes out with a tray of food. While speaking, she fills up the cabinet.*

Deli   Anastasia, you've met my son Ashley, right?

She pauses for a second. It is as if all of a sudden her breath has become very heavy for a beat.

Anastasia   What a good-looking boy you have, Deli. No we haven't met, nice to meet you, Ashley.

Ashley (*looking her up and down*)   Wha appen?

Turns to his dad. Sotto voce.

So what, you sex it yet?

Deli (*angered*)   Don't be stupid and have some respect.

Anastasia   Deli, I put on the pan ready to fry the plantain but I can't find any.

Deli   Oh shit!

Ashley   What?

Deli   I don't done forget to re-order the blasted plantain!

Ashley   How you gonna forget that? That's Uncle D's favourite.

Deli   I know that! Shit! Gotta run to the supermarket.

He runs to get his black jacket.

Ashley   Don't be long, you know!

Deli, *with jacket on, moves past* **Ashley**.

Deli   Ani, I'll be back in ten? Later, Digger.

Digger   Later.

As **Deli** *exits the phone rings. As* **Anastasia** *is closer* **Ashley** *indicates that she should answer it.*

Anastasia   I don't know what to say!

Ashley   You're taking an order not speeching da queen! Answer it then!

While **Anastasia** *is on the phone* **Ashley** *pours himself a brandy and begins to build up a spliff.*

Anastasia   Hello, Elmina's West Indian food shop –

Ashley   – Kitchen, takeaway and delivery!

Anastasia   Takeaway and delivery, how can I help you? No, he's out at present, you can probably catch him on his mobile, OK.

Ashley   Who was that?

Anastasia   The prison service.

Ashley (*smiles*)   Uncle Dougie's the original warrior boy. He's probably been put back in solitary.

Anastasia *suddenly remembers.*

Anastasia   Lard Jesus, the pan.

She dashes back through the swing doors.

Ashley *looks at* **Digger***'s glass.*

Ashley   You want a top-up?

Digger   Yeah. Mek it a brandy though. In fact, while you dere give me one of dem Chana ting that girl just done bring out.

Ashley *takes a Chana out of the cabinet and pours out the drink, then hands it to him.* **Digger** *already has a ten-pound note in his hand ready to pay.*

Ashley   Na, man. Dis one's on da house.

Digger   Did your father authorise you to give anyone anyting on da house?

Ashley (*pure admiration*)   No, but you ain't any old anyone.

Digger   Did your father authorise you to give anyone anyting on da house?

Ashley   No.

Digger *stares at him.*

Ashley   OK. That'll be four fifty.

He puts the money in the till but spends just a little bit too long looking at its contents. **Digger** *looks up at him. He quickly closes the till and* *gives* **Digger** *his change.* **Ashley** *then picks up the remote control for the TV.*

Ashley   You watching this?

Digger *shakes his head.* **Ashley** *changes it to VH1 music channel. There's a kicking garage video playing.* **Ashley** *starts 'chatting' with the tune. He's looking at the reflection of himself while he dances and chats.*

Ashley   Hold the mic while I flex, I'm a lyrical architect with the number-one set. Player haters get bang so what if dey get a back han' or else man will get jiggy, hear what! Man a pack him nine milli.

Digger *finishes his food and gets up to leave.*

Ashley   Digger!

Digger   Yow!

Ashley   Could I speak to you about som'um?

Digger   I'm busy.

Ashley   You don't look busy!

Digger   Looks can be deceiving.

Ashley   I know you don't like me . . .

Digger *doesn't answer.*

Ashley   But that's all good, cos you don't have to like people to do business wid dem, right?

Digger   I don't buy stolen phones.

Ashley   Very funny, but I ain't no pussy street punk.

Digger   Ah so?

Ashley   Ah so. No disrespect, this shit (*the restaurant*) is all good for my dad, but me, I wanna do big tings with my life, bredren. But mans needs a little leg-up.

Digger   Really?

Ashley *looks around to check that* **Anastasia** *is not about to enter.*
She is not.

Ashley   I was kinda wondering if mans could run wid
you? Give you little back-up and dat?

Digger   Wha appen you ears dem beat up? I don't deal
wid boys.

Ashley (*flash of temper*)   I ain't no fucking boy.

Digger *moves like the wind towards* **Ashley** *and punches him full in*
the face. **Ashley** *hits the deck, blood flowing from his mouth.*

Digger   What did you say to me?

Beat.

Ashley (*whispers*)   I ain't no boy.

Digger   No! Did you use a Viking expletive when talking
to me?

Ashley *is confused.*

Ashley (*staying on the ground*)   No . . . Yes . . . What's dat?

Digger (*cool*)   And you wanna be a bad man? Go back to
school, youth, and learn. You can't just walk into dis bad
man t'ing, you gotta learn the whole science of it. You step
into that arena and you better be able to dance wid death
till it mek you dizzy. You need to have thought about, have
played wid and have learnt all of the possible terrible and
torturous ways that death could arrive. And then ask
yourself are you ready to do that and more to someone that
you know. Have you done that, youth?

Ashley (*wiping the blood away from his mouth and finding his balls*)
I stepped to you, haven't I?

Digger   Seen.

He sees **Anastasia** *enter. She stares at* **Digger** *with hate. His*
phone rings.

Digger (*overjoyed*)   Bloodclatttttttttt. Is when you reach? Haaaaaaa. Where you dere? Dem let you in the country? Bloodclattttttt.

He exits. When **Ashley** *turns and sees* **Anastasia** *he is momentarily taken aback.*

Ashley   How long have you been there?

She doesn't answer.

(*Trying to flex his manhood.*) Don't you understand English?

Anastasia (*motherly*)   I just reach.

She moves towards **Ashley** *to help him up. As if to hold him. As she kneels down, he jumps up.*

Ashley   What you doing? Get off.

She steps back.

You talk anything of this and you're dead!

Anastasia   How old are you?

Ashley   Nineteen. Why? You looking for a fit young tings to wok?

Anastasia (*pointed*)   When my son was nineteen you think he would talk to a big woman like dat?

She moves away. Enter **Deli**, *with plantain box under one arm and his mobile in his hand. His face is drained of all life. He stands unable to move for a moment.*

Anastasia   Wha' wrong wid you?

Deli (*quietly to himself*)   They've killed Dougie. The man was practically home and they done kil . . . kill him. (*Holding his head.*) Ahhhhh.

Ashley *jumps up to comfort his father.* **Deli** *pushes him off.*

Deli (*screams*)   Oh God, dem catch me again. I could kill a bloodclaat man tonight.

Lights down.

As the lights go down we hear a haunting eight-bar refrain played on the gurkel.

Scene Three

Day. We are in the restaurant. **Anastasia** *is stacking the heated cabinets with food with one hand and reading a book.* **Ashley** *is on the phone taking an order. Seated with* **Digger** *and* **Baygee** *is* **Clifton** *(sixty-three, but looks mid-fifties). He is a large man with a mouth full of gold teeth. Dressed in a very flash three-piece suit, his cashmere coat is over the back of a chair. His suitcase is visible. He is a boastful man who defines himself very much by how much attention he gets from those in his immediate surroundings. There is a slight shake in his left hand from time to time. With his catchphrase 'you see',* **Clifton** *uses his eastern Caribbean accent to full effect when storytelling. He is mid-story when we join the scene.*

Ashley   It'll be with you in twenty minutes. (*To* **Clifton**.) Carry on.

He hands order to **Anastasia**. *She enters the kitchen.*

Clifton   . . . Well, you see, this man was at least six foot . . .

Ashley   Six foot . . .

Clifton   . . . five. And in dem days dere that was a giant . . .

Ashley   In any day, boy . . .

Baygee   Clifton, every time you tell that story, the man has to grow two inches? . . .

Clifton   Shut up and let me tell the youth the story.

Ashley   Yeah, Baygee, let the man tell the story na.

Clifton   So, like I saying, he say to me, 'Who tell you you could speak to my woman? You want a cut arse?' Well, it so happen that them days was when the Teddy boys weren't making joke, and man had to have some defence . . .

Baygee   That's right!

Clifton   . . . So I gently brush back me coat and show him my blade. One big arse heng man ting, and I said in a low Robert Mitcham drawl, 'If you is me fadder. Do it na! Let we see who is the man and who is child.' And I just leave that in the air hanging. Well, I see a flash in he eye as if he was going to rush me, *you see*, cos the eye betrays an untrained man. I go to grab me ting but something deep inside me, and I swear to this day it was the voice of my old mudder, say, 'Wait till he mek he move.' Well, let me tell you it was that voice save me old mudder having heart attack when she hear Clifton come to England to get hang. Cos he look at me but the monkey must have realised that this would have been his last night on earth cos he just let out a little 'Ha' and walk off. Not another word.

Ashley   Gwan.

Clifton   But you know what the real funny thing was about that evening? When it all done, tell me where the woman was?

Ashley   All over you!

Clifton   Gone. Nowhere to be seen. The two stewpid black men would have finish their lives over a woman that didn't give a coconut leaf about either of dem.

Baygee   Huh, dem was the days when they use to feel you bottom to see if you had a tail. Clifton, you remember what Mary Lou do you?

Clifton   Yes, but that's another story for another time.

Anastasia *with her usual look of concern in her eyes comes out with the order and places it in front of* **Ashley**. *He ignores it.*

Ashley   Raaaaaaaaa, you got stories, man, you're smooth.

Clifton   Me, na. I coarse like saltfish skin. But I believe in living life to the full, and it is only possible to live as long as life intoxicates us. As soon as we sober again, we see it all as a delusion, a stupid delusion, and death provides the only alternative.

He decks his rum in one.

You at college, right?

Ashley *nods.*

Clifton   Who said that?

Ashley   I don't know.

Clifton   Baygee? Come on, you had the benefits of West Indian education, which European writer said that?

Baygee   Is me you asking?

Clifton (*sizing up* **Digger**)   Young fellow? Or should I say 'bad man'. You know the answer?

Digger (*cool and mellow*)   No I don't know who said that, do you?

Clifton   Now, you see, there's a clever man. Flip the script, turn the tables. The truth is I don't know either, but it sound pretty good, don't it?

Digger's *phone goes off. He answers.*

Digger   Yow! . . .

Anastasia (*annoyed at being the only one not asked*)   Tolstoy!

Clifton (*shocked*)   What?

Anastasia   Tolstoy. The minor Russian aristocrat . . .

Clifton, *who knew all along, doesn't like being upstaged. He automatically goes into verbal slap-down mode. The speeches overlap.*

Clifton   . . . who is reputed to be Gandhi's direct inspiration. And without Gandhi, you have no Martin Luther, and without MLK you have no civil rights, and without civil rights you have no equal rights which means women, blacks, none of us would be standing on the soil we do today.

Digger   Seen . . . Seen . . . Don't fuck about, yu hear, star! Me will kill a man dead fe dat . . . Stone dead . . . Me soon come . . . Hold it right ya dere so . . . Move an inch and coffin lid have fe close.

Digger *leaves some money on the counter and begins to leave hurriedly.* **Anastasia***'s eyes follow him.*

Digger (*kisses his teeth*)   People just can't do what they suppose to do in this world, can they?

Ashley   I can!

Digger *stops and stares at* **Ashley** *for a moment. Almost instinctively, he's about to tell* **Ashley** *to come with him, but he doesn't.* **Anastasia** *stares at* **Ashley***.*

Anastasia   Ashley!

He turns to her momentarily.

Ashley   What?

Digger   Mr C. Later.

Clifton *clocks this interaction.* **Ashley** *runs to the door and watches* **Digger***. After a beat he turns to* **Clifton***.*

Ashley   Sorry, carry on. I like to hear you, you're proper clever.

Clifton (*takes in* **Digger** *leaving*)   What's the point in being clever and none of you children take you foot? One end up a bloody thieve, the next a brok-hand boxer. Tell me what I did to deserve that, eh? Where me brains go, Baygee?

Baygee   Life don't go the way we want it.

Clifton (*decking his glass of rum*)   You don't lie, partner, you don't lie. Maybe you'll be the one that'll take me mind, eh, junior?

Deli *walked in near the end of the conversation with a box under his arm, but was not seen.*

Deli   Maybe he will, but that'll be because his father was around to nurture and support him.

Clifton *turns to* **Baygee** *embarrassed.*

Clifton   Oh God.

His hand begins to shake slightly. He calms it.

Hello son.

Deli *checks* **Ashley** *who is watching him closely.*

Deli   Hello, Clifton.

Clifton *and* **Baygee** *clock each other.*

Clifton   I come to pay me respects to you and help bury me first-born.

Deli   Is that so?

Clifton   I didn't mean nothin' by –

Deli   – Ashley, did you give your grandfather something to eat?

Ashley (*he's never seen his father treat anyone like this*)   Yeah.

Deli   Good. Then, Clifton, your respects are accepted and thank you for your visit.

He opens the door for **Clifton** *to leave.*

Clifton (*calm and cool*)   Oh, I haven't quite finished my food. You wouldn't put a man out on an empty belly, would you?

Deli *closes the door.*

Clifton   So I hear I'm a great-grandfather? (*Jesting*.) Bonjey! How you let the child age me so? (*Beat*.) The place don't look all dat but I hear you're doing OK? That's good!

Deli (*pointed*)   Bad luck is always just around the corner.

Clifton   Must be doing well to have bought two acres of land home!

Silence. **Clifton** *clocks that this is not public information.*

Deli   Like I said, man never knows what's around the corner.

Clifton (*changing the subject. To all*)   Eh! You know the first man I see when I reach Hackney?

Baygee   Who?

Clifton   Macknee the old Scottish man.

Baygee   Oh ho!

Clifton   I laugh till I couldn't laugh again. You see, I knew this was going to be a good trip when I saw that mean-nose bastard in a wheelchair, drunk, raggedy, throwing himself in front of people car shouting abuse.

Ashley (*shocked*)   You know the old drunken Scottish man, Grandad?

Clifton   Me use to rent a room from him. If I think hard, you fadder may have been conceived dere.

Ashley   Boyeeee, he's off his head, dread. Bare swearing and ramming people's vechs with his wheelchair. Man's due to get spark!

Anastasia   The man in a wheelchair, have some pity on him na.

Baygee   The bitch can walk. Sorry. (*To* **Anastasia**.) I mean, there's nuttin wrong with his leg.

Clifton   Is all the wickedness he do people that haunting him.

Baygee   If he was West Indian I'd say somebody wok obea him.

Clifton   Is only black people that know witchcraft?

Baygee *shrugs.*

Clifton   The most witchcraft is practise by the white man. How do the arse you think he managed to take Africa from we. That white man –

Deli *explodes, 0–60.*

Deli   . . . Don't bring none of your white this and dat in here, Clifton. I don't want to hear that.

Baygee   That's no way to speak to your father, Deli.

Deli (*trying to hold it down*)   Baygee, please!

He clocks **Anastasia***'s response.*

Clifton   No, the boy's right. In his place, his word is *the* word.

Beat.

Baygee   Clifton, come let we go over to the betting shop na? The old boys in there they go shit when they see you.

Beat.

Clifton   I coming, I coming. Baygee, you mind if my son and I have a few minutes?

Baygee   Of course.

He steps to the back of the restaurant.

Clifton   I know your brother meant a lot to you. I'm sorry. But this is the way of the world.

Deli *stares at him blankly.*

Clifton   You see, death is around us everywhere.

Deli   Ah ha.

Beat.

Clifton   I need somewhere to stay just until the funeral finish.

Beat.

I was wondering if . . . Until I see the doctor for me hand, and attend the funeral . . .

Deli *still doesn't reply.*

Clifton   I wouldn't burden you. A sofa will do. Two weeks max.

He stares right into **Deli***'s eyes.* **Deli** *thinks. He sees* **Clifton***'s hand shake. Silence.*

Deli   I can't have you stay here. This is Elmina's place. I'll call Ashley's mother and see if she'll put you up in the spare room. But once Dougie's buried I want you to leave, Clifton.

Clifton *looks at Elmina's picture and picks up his suitcase.*

Clifton   I'll be in the Black Dog across the road. When you ready, send for me. (*Taking in* **Deli**.) Baygee, come na! The boys go say, 'Big time Clifton, what you doing back in England, boy?' And I go tell them the Queen send for me. You mind if I leave my suitcase here?

Baygee   How you could ask the child that? Of course he don't. Come, boy.

Clifton   I coming. I coming.

Baygee   Stop coming and come.

They leave. **Ashley** *takes the food to deliver off the counter and looks at his father before leaving. As if paralysed,* **Deli** *stands rooted on the spot.* **Deli** *looks up to the picture of his mother. He is disappointed in himself for not outrightly refusing* **Clifton***.*

Deli (*whispers to Elmina*)   I tried.

Anastasia   Your pops is a character eee!

Deli   Before I knew myself, I knew I was Clifton's child.

Anastasia   They fuck you up, your mum and dad.

Deli   That's what Digger says about women.

Anastasia   You think that too?

He shrugs.

(*Innocently.*) Do you get on with Ashley's mother?

Deli   I'd rather not talk about her actually.

Anastasia   OK.

Silence.

How did the meeting go?

Deli   'To find the information needed to start the case would be' – how did they put it? – 'cost prohibitive' was the common phrase. Everybody knows your last day in prison you keep you fucking head down. But Dougie, no! He was a troublemaker, Anastasia, that's why no one wants to take the case, no one that I could afford right now anyway.

Anastasia   He left you money, right?

Deli   Sorry?

Anastasia   Dougie left you a whole heap ah money, right, everybody knows dat.

Deli *doesn't answer.*

Anastasia   Even if you have to spend you last cent, find someone. You can't mek people kill you family and left it so! There must be somewhere else you could go?

Deli *flashes a steely glance.*

Deli (*flash of anger*)   No, there is not somewhere else I can go, I have been everywhere, alright?

Beat.

Anastasia   You know that tone you just employed, you're sure that's the choice you wanna stick with?

Deli   Pardon?

Anastasia   Cos I don't know what kind of women you are use to but, baby, I don't let men speak to me like that.

Awkward silence.

Deli   Sorry.

Anastasia   Apology accepted.

Beat.

She runs over to her bag and gets out her Acts of Faith. *She rips out a page.*

Deli   What you doing?

She sticks it to the counter.

You don't find there's enough posters on the wall? What's that, Anastasia?

Anastasia   It's a page I don't need any more.

She enters into the kitchen through the swing doors, whistling. **Deli**, *intrigued, gets up and reads the page. Shaking his head, he laughs while reading it.*

Deli (*kissing his teeth*)   What rubbish . . . rubbish.

Anastasia *pops her head over the swing doors. The speeches tumble over each other.*

Anastasia (*surprised*)   Why's it rubbish?

Deli *walks away.*

Deli (*taking the piss*)   'In every disaster lies a lesson' . . .

Anastasia   It's true . . .

Deli   . . . 'If you can truly learn that lesson' . . .

Anastasia (*increasingly frustrated*)   . . . I know it in my own life . . .

Deli   . . . blah blah blah . . .

Anastasia (*vexed now*)   . . . It ain't no blah blah blah, this is, this is, life-healing stuff . . .

Deli   . . . Healing? What you healing for? . . .

Anastasia (*firm and straight*)   . . . So when the good tings come along you're ready?

Deli (*vexed*)   Good tings don't happen to me, Anastasia . . .

Anastasia   What stupidness . . .

Deli   . . . Ah my life me ah talk 'bout you na! And you know what me discover? Man is not suppose to want. I wanted, I could have been da don, and what happen? Bam, it get mash. I wanted to, I fucking worked hard to be there with Ashley and his mum! Bam, it get mash. I wanted my brother home, here with me and what happen? One step from the fucking gate, bam, he get mash. Don't tell me about my life.

Anastasia (*bitter*)   Oh you's one feeling sorrow for yourself, motherfucker?

Deli   What? . . .

Anastasia   You have things others dream of. This place . . .

Deli   . . . This place! Tell me what's so great about this place? I have a handful of customers who spend five pound a shot and talk nonsense all day! What did you say I have again?

Anastasia   You have you child. 'Anyting better than having you child –' How could anyting good happen to you when you don't look after the shit you have.

Beat.

Deli (*angry*)   And how am I suppose to do that?

Anastasia (*growls with passion, close up to his face*)   You supposed to clean up your environment, Deli. This restaurant stinks. People walk in here, they smell Digger and walk straight back out. I've seen it. But you, my friend, you're comfortable with the stench of death around you?

Deli   There's nothing wrong with Digger that a couple of years' intense hard labour wouldn't put right.

Anastasia   If you're gonna joke forget it. You mek me tired.

Deli   You know that tone you just used with me? Do you always talk to your bosses like that? Cos I ain't use to my employees taking to me like that!

Anastasia   You know what? You're right.

Anastasia *walks to get her coat.*

Deli   Where you going?

Anastasia (*screams, visibly upset*)   Why are my men too weak to raise their head above the fucking water. I don't want to be around another loser, Deli! I lose too much in my life already.

She's putting on her coat.

Deli   It's cos Digger's in here that them other punks don't come looking for money.

Anastasia (*stops*)   What money?

Deli   Ah, so there's something's you don't know, Oprah? Protection money.

Anastasia   You pay protection money?

Deli   No, that's the point. So Digger helps me, OK!

Anastasia (*tired*)   Whatever, Deli, whatever!

Coat in hand she makes to leave. **Deli** *thinks for a moment.*

Deli   Hold up na!

She carries on walking.

Do you like plantain?

Anastasia (*stops, unsure where he is heading*)   Ummm! Sure!

Deli   Well, wait na!

He enters the kitchen leaving her outside now. He laughs.

Huh! Look up there, what do you see?

Anastasia   Ummmmm, picture of your mother?

Deli   That was the last person to talk to me like that and still have dem head.

Beat.

'We have entered a stranger's dream, and for trespassing he has rewarded us with his worse nightmare' is what my father use to say about living in England.

Anastasia   He come back here though, innit?

Deli *enters with two 'plantain burgers' and hands one to* **Anastasia**.

Deli   Da da! You ever had a plantain burger before?

Anastasia   No!

Deli   Here, try this. Breast of chicken, sitting on crisp lettuce with three slices of succulent plantain, all in a sesame toasted bun.

Anastasia   I hope you're not trying to obea me!

They laugh. She takes a bite.

Anastasia   Ummmmmmmmmmmm!

Deli   Good, huh?

Anastasia   Yeah, almost as good as my macaroni pie!

Beat.

Deli   About a week before Clifton left, right, I was about ten and it was around midnight, I had the munchies bad. So I went downstairs and looked in the pot. There was one piece of juicy-looking chicken. But I didn't fancy that by itself so I opened the fridge door and there it was, a plantain. So I took it out and commenced to fry. (*Laughing at*

the remembrance.) And it came out alright. I jammed that
chicken in a bun and threw the burnt-up plantain on top ah
it and boyyyyy that ting taste gooooood. I was so digging on
that bun, I had forgotten to switch off the frying pan. And
yeah, it went up. Blacked up the whole kitchen. Mum and
Dad heard me scream and ran down. Eventually, Dad put
out the pan. My mum was just pleased that I had survived
but first thing my dad did when the smoke had cleared was
open the chicken pot. When he saw it had gone he ran
upstairs and got his belt boy and beat my claat. He said it
was because I nearly burnt down the kitchen, but I know it
was because of the chicken breast.

Anastasia *laughs.*

Deli   I haven't made it since then.

Anastasia *(excited)*   Deli, you's a fool. You know you have
the answer right here, you know?

Deli   What?

Anastasia *(excited)*   Blouse and skirts, West Indian fast
food! That's wicked. You sell dis and do up a place likkle bit
and different mans would come into your restaurant. I take
back all I said, damn, I knew I liked you for a reason.

She throws her arms around him. He's unsure how to react.

Deli   You can't take back! . . .

Anastasia   . . . Yes I can! . . .

Deli   . . . No you can't . . .

Anastasia *(close to his face)*   . . . Yes I can . . .

*She kisses him. He kisses her back. After a few beats, though, he violently
stops and pulls away.*

Deli   Na, na. Sorry.

Anastasia *(searching for his eyes, trying to convince)*   It's OK . . .
I liked it.

He walks to the other side of the counter. **Anastasia** *steps back, a little rejected.*

Anastasia   What's wrong?

Deli *doesn't respond.* **Anastasia** *walks to him, gently puts her hand on his face again.*

Anastasia (*without emotion*)   I'll do the wanting.

Deli (*vexed, moves away*)   No, I can't do this. You're not a bore-through gal, Ani.

Anastasia   Well then, don't just bore through.

Deli   I ain't got nothing else to offer you right now.

She doesn't reply.

(*Angry.*) The boys are betting on when I'm gonna fuck you, Anastasia! Ashley's betting.

Anastasia   I don't watch what other people think.

She slowly pulls **Deli**'s *head to face her and kisses him gently on the mouth. He kisses her back. Just as the shop bell rings he pulls back, holds her face in his hands and stares at her carefully.*

Enter **Digger***. He looks well vexed. Frustrated,* **Anastasia** *walks and stands near the swing doors to the kitchen.* **Deli** *is unsure what* **Digger** *has seen.*

Deli (*embarrassed, says the first thing that comes into his head*) Hey! You're back?

Digger (*snaps back*)   What kind of question is that? Of course I'm back. Give me a cocoa tea.

Anastasia *exits to the kitchen, shaking her head. Silence.*

Digger (*convincing himself*)   Me have fe talk it. Me just have fe talk it. I'm not vex, you nah, I'm vex na pussyclaat. I just had to deal with tricky. The fool na just switch pon me!

Deli *is not really that interested. He looks in the direction of the kitchen.*

Deli   Switch?

Digger   Switch, that's what I fucking said, innit? Switch! He na go collect money that is mine, and give it to Renton crew as a 'gift-offering'.

Deli   Wha?

Digger   Yes, gift, so that they would accept him inna dem crew! My fucking money! What the fuck is happening around here? I had to mark him str −

Deli (*holding his hand in the air to stop* **Digger**)   Yo! Digger −

Digger   − Don't cut me in mid-flow! You na hear what the advert say − it's good to talk. Me, I need to get this off my chest. Anyway, when me finally hunt down Tricky I tek out my blade − the long one with the bend on the top − and me slice −

Deli   − Digger, don't pollute up my vibes wid dem talk dey − !

Digger (*exclaims*)   . . . Pollute?! Deli, you went to prison for GBH, on three men and their dogs. How de fuck I gonna pollute you?

Deli (*losing it a little*)   A restaurant is not the place to discuss fucking murder.

Digger   Where else me suppose to talk about it? On the street?

Deli   Digs, right now I don't care, just not in here, not today.

Digger   I didn't murder him, I just cu −

Deli (*shouts*)   Digger! You can't hear me? I said I don't want to hear about it. If you can't hear me, man, come out!

Digger (*disbelief switches to cold*)   What? Of your restaurant?

Deli (*a little defensively*)   I ain't saying that, Digger, I'm just saying, what if someone walked into the place and overheard this kind of talk? They'd have heard all your bizness. You didn't even check, you just come in and start fe talk. Suppose 5.0 was in here?

Digger   But they ain't! Nobody comes inside here.

Deli (*losing it a bit*)   Well maybe that's the problem. Look, I don't want no dirty talk inside yere, take from that what you want.

Beat.

Digger   Well, I shocked, Deli. When you does call me ignorant I don't like it but I take it, but now my talk is not good enough for you and your restaurant? Me that sit down in here for a lifetime, is not good enough? . . .

Deli (*tired*)   . . . I didn't say that, Digger.

Digger   Seen, so you, like all them other niggers round here, switching on me?

Anastasia *comes to the swing door.* **Deli** *looks to her.* **Digger** *looks to her.*

Deli   Let me get some more cocoa from the back.

Deli *and* **Anastasia** *clock each other for a moment before exiting into the back, leaving* **Digger** *in the restaurant alone.*

Digger (*vexed, to himself*)   Keep your fucking tea. Ah wha de?!

Ashley *enters.*

Ashley   Yes! Digger!

Digger *turns to* **Ashley**. *He pauses for a moment. Looks to see if* **Deli**'s *about. He's not.*

Digger (*slow but over-friendly*)   Yes, Ashley, what gwan?

The lights slowly fade.

Act Two

The lights are down. We hear the voices of all the characters sing a slow blues called 'You Gotta Move'. While they are singing the lights slowly rise so that we can just about make out the figures. Facing upstage, the characters are at Dougie's funeral. Set to the side is a lone female figure in traditional African headgear playing the gurkel.

All

You may be rich
You may be poor
You may be young
You may be old
But when the Lord gets ready you ga'da move
You may be black
You may be white
You may be wrong
You may be right
But when the Lord gets ready you ga'da move
You ga'da move
You ga'da move
You ga'da move child
You ga'da move
And when the Lord gets ready you go'da move
And when the Lord gets ready you go'da move

The lights fade during the final chorus.

Scene One

Restaurant. Night, three weeks later.

Lights snap up on a refurbished restaurant. It looks good. The newly painted walls no longer have any posters. And the stools have been replaced by new Ikea-type modern ones. The only thing that remains is the picture of Elmina above the swing doors. And the TV, which is on. Above Elmina's picture, however, is a new sign that reads, 'ELMINA'S PLANTAIN HUT'. On the back wall is a picture of Dougie with the words 'Dougie Andrews, 1959–2003 RIP. They have just had the opening-night party. **Deli** *is closing the door behind the last customer/party attendee.* **Anastasia** *is clearing away the glasses and plates of food.* **Baygee** *and* **Clifton**, *who are very tipsy, are sitting at the counter.* **Baygee** *is playing his guitar and* **Clifton** *is singing loudly to the calypso rhythm being played. As he sings his eyes follow* **Anastasia**. **Deli** *is in buoyant mood.*

Clifton (*sings*)
Jooking, jooking, jooking
Gal her you bottom do so much stunt
Jooking, jooking, jooking
Let we try disting from de front
Jooking, jooking, jooking
I hope it's good seed you does lay
Jooking, jooking till de break of day.

Deli   Clifton, stop dat na, man.

He shouts to the customers who have just left. He is in new businessman mode.

Bye, thanks for coming. Don't forget for each ten burgers ordered you get the eleventh free . . . OK . . . Thanks again.

Clifton *mocks him to* **Baygee**.

Clifton (*sings*)   For each ten burgers ordered you get the eleventh free! (*Speaks.*) Black people buying ten ah anyting, eh, Baygee?

Ashley (*swigging from champagne bottle, looks at his watch nervously*)
Right, that's the family ting done!

Deli (*friendly*)   So what, you can't help me clean up the place?

Ashley   What?!

Anastasia   Thank you for helping, Ashley, tonight, Ashley.

Ashley *doesn't quite know how to react, so quickly smiles.*

Deli *turns to* **Clifton**.

Deli   And I hope you're proud of yourself?

Clifton   What happen to you?

Deli   The need for you to get on the table, start singing blasted rude calypsos and running the blasted customers was what. It was supposed to be an upmarket launch.

Beside herself, **Anastasia** *laughs under her breath.*

Clifton (*taking the piss*)   Upmarket launch? It was a party! And when man have party people suppose to dance, not stand up and chat. What de arse this generation coming to?

Deli   It's the opening of a new West Indian restaurant, Clifton, not a blasted shebeen!

Clifton   There was nothing West Indian about it. You have a master calypsonian sitting right here, you know, and would you let him play? NO! We had to mek coup in the name of culture and take matters into we own hand.

Deli (*matter-of-fact*)   No disrespect, Baygee, but that was not the image we (*looking at* **Anastasia**), I, want people to connect with this restaurant. It's a new vibes we ah deal in right now.

Anastasia   Listen, the man from the council pre-ordered a month's delivery of plantain burgers for black history month and paid upfront. We should be proud ah we ourselves. West Indian fast food reach.

Just as she is about to hug him, he steps back, takes the bottle of champagne away from **Ashley** *and returns to* **Anastasia** *with a glass.*

Clifton   If you ask me, fast and West Indian is a contradiction in terms.

Deli (*to* **Anastasia**)   Here.

Anastasia (*pointed*)   I've had too much already. Any more and you'll have to carry me home on your back.

Deli   Drink the drink na. Tonight is well special, it's also my bir . . .

Baygee *changes to an old-time kinky reggae rhythm.* **Clifton** *instantly recognises it, stands on the stool and starts to sing at the top of his voice.*

Clifton (*sings*)
   Soldering ah wha de young gal want, soldering.
   Welding ah what de young gal want, welding.

Deli   Jesus!

Ashley (*nervously checks his mobile*)   Gwan, Grandad.

Deli   Clifton, will you stop you noise?

Clifton *stops momentarily.*

Clifton   What de arse do this, boy?

Kisses his teeth.

Anastasia   Maybe you should call your dad and Baygee a taxi!

Clifton *is offended by* **Anastasia***'s comment.*

Clifton   What you trying to say, I is drunk?

Deli   Finish up you drinks, Clifton, home time.

Clifton   Answer me this! Can a drunk man extemporise?

Anastasia   I don't know, Clifton.

Clifton (*concentrating hard*)   Well, think about it. See! You can't answer because, the answer would be contri, contradictory to your current thesis.

Anastasia *laughs.*

Clifton   Baygee! Prepare me a rhythm.

Deli   Oh man!

Baygee *starts to play an old-time calypso rhythm.*

Clifton   You ready? You ready? Young boy, give me a subject quick while the rhythm hot! Quick!

Anastasia *pours herself a drink.*

Ashley   Um, um football! Football!

Clifton   Here we go. They use to call me culture master. Be prepared to get teach. (*Sings.*)

> History is a funny thing,
> History is a funny thing,
> Listen to me, people,
> Cos is about football me ah sing.
> Clive Best the greatest
> Baller West Ham ever had,
> But from the stands they'd shout each game,
> Go home you black bastard.

Deli   Oh here we go!

Clifton (*sings*)
> Oh England, what a wonderful land,
> In England what you must understand,
> Is whatever you do, wherever you rise,
> Please realise, you could never disguise
> You's a black man in a cold cold land.

Deli   That isn't about football! It's you on your high horse again.

Clifton (*vexed*)   Did you hear the word football?

Deli   Yeah . . .

Clifton (*turning to* **Ashley**)   . . . Did you hear the name of a footballer?

Ashley   Yes.

Clifton   Den it was about football, wasn't it?!

Ashley   Grandad, you give me jokes, boy!

Deli   I'm going to put the rubbish outside and I'm calling you a taxi, Clifton.

Anastasia   I'll help you!

Deli (*softly*)   You ain't paid for dem kinda work dere, girl.

Anastasia *exhales quietly.*

Clifton   Sweet gal, give me a subject na!

Anastasia   Um, love.

Clifton   That easy, man. Something hard.

Anastasia   OK. Trust!

Clifton   Alright, you ready now? Slow down the rhythm, Baygee.

Baygee   Oh God, man, you's a dictator!

He slows down the rhythm. **Clifton** *sings.*

Clifton
I look at you, you have eyes that I could trust,
The way you look me up and down on da number
    seven bus . . .

Baygee (*disgusted*)   Number seven bus?

Clifton (*quickly*)   Shut up. (*Continues to sing.*)

I think you is a lady,
But I don't know maybe,
Tonight if you'll give yourself to me.
(*Chorus:*) Give it to me.

Baygee (*sings back-up*)
Give it to me.

Clifton
Give it to me.

Baygee
Give it to me.

Clifton
Nice and soft, soft and hard, give it to me.

Baygee
Give it to me.

Clifton
Give it to me.

Baygee
Give it to me.

Clifton
Cos tonight you'll live you fantasies.

He ends kissing **Anastasia***'s hand.* **Ashley** *applauds.*

Anastasia   Clifton, that was rubbish, but you're brilliant!

Clifton *turns to* **Baygee**.

Clifton   Don't stop, boy, eh, eh, you losing you touch!

He grabs **Anastasia** *by the hand to dance with him.*

Anastasia   No, no!

Clifton   Get up, girl.

She gots up.

Baygee, sing one of them love song you use to play when we was young na!

Baygee *starts to sing.*

Baygee   Darling, I can feel you sweet aroma, *etc. etc.*

While **Baygee** *is singing* **Anastasia** *makes to leave, but* **Clifton** *pulls her close to him. They slow-rub.*

Anastasia   You're very strong for a, a, a older man.

Clifton *smiles.*

Clifton   Iccceeettch! It's been a long time.

Anastasia   Since you danced with a woman?

Clifton   Since *you* danced with a man. I can tell a woman's history by simply touching her. See, when I *grabbed* you, you flexed vex but now that I hold you softly, you don't know what to do with yourself, do you?

Anastasia   You are very sure of yourself!

Clifton   Am I wrong? Or am I wrong?

Beat.

Anastasia (*matter-of-fact*)   Actually, you're not. I haven't had . . . let a man touch me with tenderness for a lifetime.

Clifton   Why?

Anastasia   Cos men kill things.

Clifton (*ignoring*)   What about my son, hasn't he touched you with, how you say, tenderness?

Anastasia   I don't think your son is interested in me that way. I'm a bit old for him, Clifton.

She loses her balance. **Clifton** *holds her.*

Anastasia   Oh!

Clifton   Whereas I, on the other hand, *like* a sprightly young thing?

Anastasia *stands and then steps away from him.*

Enter **Digger***. He pops his head round the door. As soon as* **Ashley** *sees him he drops the champagne glass he has in his hand. Everyone clocks this, except* **Clifton** *who is still deadly focused on* **Anastasia***.*

Digger   So all you have big-time party and nobody doe invite me?

Clifton   Eh, eh, Digger, where you been, I thought you was dead!

Digger (*cold*)   Wha! You miss me?

Ashley *moves out.*

Ashley   Laters, people.

He touches **Digger** *with his fist very casually.* **Digger** *nods back again very casually.* **Ashley**'s *gone.*

Anastasia   Ashley, where you go(*ing?* . . .)

Enter **Deli** *from the back.*

Deli   Ashley!

He sees **Digger**. *He is slightly taken aback.*

Deli   Yo! Digger. Good to see you, man. What gwan?

Digger (*very cool*)   Just cool, yu nah! Hmmmm, all you fix up the place good.

Deli   Thanks. Want a burger or something?

Digger   Nah. Dem fast ting dere just give a man wind. Innit, Clifton? . . .

Clifton   . . . You doe lie, you doe lie.

Deli   I could probably cut up some chicken, stew it up and put it in a bun or something?

Digger   Nah, man, I wouldn't want you to mess up you new kitchen and dat. Anyway, just passing, yuh na! Later.

Clifton   Digger, where you going!? You don't hear me sing yet?

Digger   When business calls, Clifton!

Digger's *gone.*

Deli   Where's Ashley?

Anastasia   He just popped out.

Deli (*contained anger*)   Jesus.

Deli *picks up his mobile and speed-dials.*

Anastasia   Deli, come and dance man, deal wid de rubbish later.

It's engaged. **Deli** *kisses his teeth.*

Deli (*still elsewhere, cold*)   . . . I don't have time for that! I don't, Clifton, your taxi's gonna be about five minutes. Gonna have to share one with Baygee, they're running low!

He exits.

Anastasia   Clifton, something look wrong wid me? Excuse.

She leaves for the toilet. **Clifton** *sits next to* **Baygee**. **Baygee** *is looking at the swing doors, thinking of* **Deli**.

Clifton   You see she, dirty gal that!

Baygee   What you talking about, man?

Clifton   You don't see how she push up she hot tings pon me!

Baygee (*with a drunk man's directness, still strumming*)   You too nasty! I know you, you know! Take you eyes off the man woman.

Clifton (*all innocence*)   Is not the boy woman yet. Anyway, there's only two woman in the world I wouldn't trouble, me modder and me sister. And both ah dem dead.

Baygee *cuts his eyes at him.*

Baygee   I find since you come back that boy turn cold, you know.

Clifton (*kissing his teeth*)   Man should be glad not mad to see him fadder. In my day . . .

His hand is shaking.

Baygee   . . . Eighteen years is a whole heap ah time . . .

Clifton   . . . Too fucking soft. What happen between his mother and me is between his mother and me. He's a fucking divorced man, he should know that.

Baygee (*goes into performance*)   That's why I never marry, you know. I like a cat, I hunt alone, eat alone and the only time I want to be stroked is when I giving 'thunder'.

Clifton   Alas, a good philosophy, but too late for me.

Baygee   What is really wrong wid you, Clifton?

Clifton   Ah, a little sugar, little pain in me foot dem. Nothing I can't lick.

Baygee   Yeah?

Clifton   Personally, I blame the white man.

Baygee   Oh gosh, how you reach there, boy?

Clifton   Is true. People who feel discriminated against, you see, have higher blood pressure, die earlier, have more heart disease and die of cancer in higher numbers. Dem prove it. There's a test case in America right now that women bringing against men.

Baygee (*not really interested*)   So you sick bad?

Clifton   Baygee, a batman's can be called out several ways. Caught in the slips, clean bowl like a fool swinging for a huge six . . .

Baygee   . . . That's the way I want to go . . .

Clifton   . . . or he can get LBW'd. But it's not until the umpire raise he finger so, that you leave the crease. An he don't even look in my direction yet. Heaven go have to wait, boy.

He raises his glass. The men finish off their drinks. **Baygee** *plays the guitar. We hear the toilet flush.*

Baygee (*sings*)   Here's to life, joy and prosperity, may I be in mid-stroke when death call on me.

(*Speaks.*) Woooooooooooow! How that ting does just spring up on you so. The other day man was in full action when all of ah sudden me feel like me have to piss.

Clifton   You should'a let it out! She wouldn't ah know.

Baygee   Shut up, man. You too damn nasty.

Baygee *runs to the toilet.* **Anastasia** *enters. She has a rejuvenated sensual air about her.* **Clifton** *puts his head in his hands and lets out a slight groan. She stops when she hears this.*

Anastasia   I know that sound.

Clifton *looks up, surprised.*

Clifton   You do?

Anastasia   You don't fool me, Clifton. I can hear the pain.

Clifton   . . . Pain? . . .

Anastasia   . . . Of losing your first-born . . .

Clifton   It's the cramp in me foot actually. The diabetes does bring it on terrible.

Anastasia   Oh!

Clifton   But I'm glad you're concerned. Listen, I'm a direct man. You look good and I look great. What you say we keep each other company tonight? It's a long time since I really talk to a woman, maybe you show me how to grieve?

She understands loud and clear what he is trying to say.

We hear the loud tooting of the minicab.

Baygee *enters the room doing up his flies.*

Baygee   Ah, lovely! The only thing that can compare to sex! A good leggo water.

Enter **Deli**, *with a very dirty heavy carrier bag. He puts it under the counter.*

Deli   That will be your cab, gentlemen. Ani, you have to jump in with the guys, they're out of cabs.

Anastasia   It's OK! Do you want me to wait till you finish what you doing and you can drop me?

Deli   No, I can't do that. Get in the cab.

Anastasia *stares at him hard.*

Anastasia   Fine, I will. Clifton, you ready?

Clifton *jumps up.*

Clifton   Right, let's not keep the driver waiting. Your carriage awaits you, madam.

She quickly puts on her coat. She doesn't look at **Deli**. *She exits.*
Baygee *has finished packing away his guitar and has his coat on.*

Baygee   Deli, sometimes when tings staring you in the face you must take it you know. I gone!

Clifton *and* **Baygee** *exit.*

Deli *spots* **Anastasia**'s Acts of Faith *book. He runs to the door.*
We hear the car door slam and the cab drive off. **Deli** *walks back in.*
Book in hand, he switches off the TV, gets the keys out of his pocket and
is about to lock the door when **Ashley** *barges in.*

Deli   What the arse!

Ashley   Sorry, Dad, I didn't see you there.

Ashley *is making his way through to the kitchen. He is slightly hyped.*
Deli *searches for something to speak to him about. Before* **Ashley**
disappears behind the swing doors it comes.

Deli   Hey, Ash, what date is it today?

Ashley   Oh shit, it's your birthday!

Deli   Yeah.

Ashley   Oh shit, sorry, Dad.

Deli   It's all good. The event tonight was my party. That's why I was glad that even though you've not been around much lately, you were around tonight.

Ashley   Yeah, well, um . . .

Deli   Come, let we break some bread together na, just you and me!

Ashley   Well, I kinda wanted to go up . . .

Deli   Stay there, I'll get us a piece of chicken each.

Ashley   Let me get it. (*Wanting to go and wash his hands.*)

Deli   Na, man, you'll only make a mess.

Ashley (*shrugging shoulders*)   Alright.

Ashley *sits by the counter. He picks up some napkins and wipes his bloody hands.* **Deli** *exits with the chicken. He puts it in the microwave.*

Deli (*entering, genuine question*)   Hey, Ashley, do you read? You know, like for fun?

Ashley   Why am I going to that?

Deli   Feed your mind maybe?

Ashley   They make all the good books into films, innit?!

Deli   Seen!

Ashley (*laughing*)   I ain't never seen you pick up a book. Oh, except *now*, yeah, you reading all bred of self-help manuals like you's a blasted white man!

Deli   Reading's for whites? I'm trying to open up my mind to different tings, what's wrong with that?

Ashley   If that's your ting, nothing, man.

The bell on the microwave indicates the chicken is heated. **Ashley** *makes to get up, but* **Deli** *moves off first.*

Deli (*exiting*)   I'll get it.

Ashley *doesn't quite get why he's being served in this way.*

Deli (*entering*)   So where was I? Oh yeah, you said there was nothing wrong with education.

He gives **Ashley** *the food.*

Ashley   Happy birthday, old man.

Deli   Thank you.

He pulls out the dirty carrier bag from beneath the counter.

Then why did I find all of your college books in the rubbish?

Deli *puts the bag next to* **Ashley**. **Ashley** *stops eating.*

Beat.

Deli *won't say another word.*

Ashley   Char! I ain't got it for this.

He gets up to leave. **Deli** *instinctively pushes him back into the chair. He backs off, but only a little.*

Deli   Why are your college books in the bin, Ashley?

Ashley   You know what? They're there, cos I put them em there!

Deli *(calm)*   Don't be rude.

Ashley *(shouts)*   I ain't got time for college!

Deli   You don't have time? What do you have time for? Fucking Machino and garage raves?

Ashley   Don't come doing this whole good caring dad number right now! . . .

Deli   . . . I've never asked you about college before now? . . .

Ashley   . . . I stand corrected, you did ask me about college, when you wanted me to take a day off to run fucking food errands . . .

Deli *(vexed)*   . . . Who you swearing at, boy . . . ?

Ashley   . . . Forget this. College does not fit into the plan I have for my life. You want to keep selling your little plantain burgers, good luck to you, may you always be happy. Me, I'm a man.

Deli *loses it. He raises his hand to hit him but pulls back at the last moment.*

Ashley   Go on na!

Deli   You'd like that, wouldn't you? Yes, you'd like me to punch your lights out, so you could walk street and say, 'See, see, I told you man dad weren't no punk.'

Ashley   Why would I say that? You are a punk.

Deli   Don't you push me!

Ashley   And what? . . .

Deli   . . . And *what*? . . .

Ashley   . . . Yeah, what you gonna do, with your old self?

Deli   . . . Take you the hell out . . . (*He pulls back.*)

Ashley (*laughs*)   . . . You're joking bredren. You can't touch me! . . . I'll deck you before you can raise your hand star.

Beat.

Deli (*trying to defuse*)   And how you gonna put your hand on your father and think that you gonna live good?

Ashley   Man lives how he can.

Deli   Ah so?

Suddenly he springs forward and grabs **Ashley***'s arm before he can move. He twists it behind* **Ashley***'s back.*

Do it then! If your name is man, put your hand on me! . . .

Ashley   . . . Ahhhhhhh . . .

Deli   . . . No, not ahhhhhh, put your hand on me!

Ashley   . . . Get off . . .

Deli (*firm*)   You know what I read in one of those 'white' books the other day? The true sign of intelligence is how man deals with the problems of his environment . . . (*Shouts.*) I don't want to live like this, Ashley, it ain't fun . . .

Ashley   . . . Get offffffffffff, you're hurting me . . .

Deli (*from his heart*)   . . . I'm trying, I'm trying to change shit around here, but you ain't on line, bra! Where you are trying to head, it's a dead ting, a dark place, it don't go nowhere.

He releases the grip. Emotionally exhausted, he throws his hands in the air in near surrender. **Ashley** *is silent for a moment while he adjusts to the new freedom from pain.*

Ashley (*screams*)   Don't you ever touch me again! Do you hear me? Put your hand on me ever again, father or no father, you're a dead man. Do you hear me?

Deli   Calm down, Ashley. Calm . . .

He notices blood on his own hands. He scans **Ashley** *and sees that it has come from cuts on his hands. One cut is still bleeding.*

Deli   What happened to your hands?

Ashley *pulls his hands away.*

Ashley (*slightly taken aback*)   Ummmmm, cut them, innit.

Deli   Don't take the piss.

We hear the sounds of approaching sirens. **Ashley** *becomes alert.* **Deli** *notices his nervousness even though he is shielding it well. We hear them pull up.*

Deli   Are you – you're charlied to rass! (*Beat.*) What the fuck is going on, Ashley?

Ashley (*losing it*)   Then don't ask me nuttin. What the hell you think this is?

Deli   I don't know, son. That is why I'm asking you?

He goes to the door and looks outside.

Bloodclaat, ah Rose's place dat ah burn so?

Surprised, he turns to **Ashley**. *After a beat* **Deli** *runs to get his coat to go out and help. We hear more fire engines pulling up.*

Deli   We'll come back to this!

Ashley (*shouts*)   You know what I don't like about you?
You don't do nothin but sit back and let the world fuck you
over. Not me, dread!

Ashley *exits.*

Deli   You coming or what?

But **Ashley** *has gone. He looks around for a beat and then rushes out.*

Lights down.

Scene Two

Restaurant. Day.

Deli *is sitting by the counter, he looks a little dazed, unsettled. After a
beat or so* **Anastasia** *runs in a little flustered.*

Anastasia   Sooooo sorry I'm late . . .

Deli (*snaps back*)   No problem . . . I heard traffic was bad.

Anastasia (*ignoring him*)   . . . I overslept like a fool. It must
have been the champagne! Eh, what gwaning across the
street? When dat burn, last night?

Deli   Look so. Man, Roy's in Homerton, x amount of
burns. Rose's life work gone. That's why you got to live life
while you can, boy!

There's silence for a bit.

Hey, Ani, you're quiet today?

Anastasia   Am I? Just a little tired.

Deli *shakes his head in understanding. He wants to say something but
can't quite find the right words. Eventually it comes out.*

Deli   I cleared out Dougie's room in the flat today, you yuh!

Anastasia   Positive move, well done.

Silence.

Deli   Ani, how old did you say your son was again?

Anastasia   Nineteen.

Deli   Look at that, huh, we must have been doing it at the same time.

Enter **Clifton**, *with an extra spring in his walk.* **Anastasia** *moves swiftly back into the kitchen.*

Clifton   Bonjour, good morning good morning good morning. And how is everybody this bright fine morning? Well, noontime?

Deli   Someone woke up on the right side of bed!

Clifton   Oh yes, I had a very good night's sleep.

Deli   Lucky you.

Clifton   Yes, lucky me indeed. Anybody dead across de road?

Deli   No!

Clifton   Dem is Indian, innit? Insurance man.

Deli   Clifton . . .

Clifton   . . . Anyone in the labast? I wanna bust a piss!

Deli   No.

Clifton *exits to the toilet.* **Anastasia** *enters with a new batch of burgers and fries.* **Deli** *steals a few of the chips. She starts to put the burgers and fries in their takeaway bags.*

Deli (*struggles through this*)   Ani, I was thinking, as the business expands we gonna be kinda busy. If you wanna, you could stay in the flat upstairs you know! Save you getting bus in to work every day and dat?

Anastasia *looks up at* **Deli**, *surprised and pleased.*

While **Deli** *is speaking,* **Clifton** *re-enters but is unseen by the other two. His face drops when* **Deli** *mentions the flat.*

Anastasia (*genuine sadness*)   Oh Deli . . .

Deli (*jumps in*)   . . . You don't have to worry, I ain't using this as an excuse to jump you bones or nothing . . .

Anastasia (*straight and fast*)   . . . Why not? I'm a woman, Deli.

Deli (*struggling*)   . . . Of course you're a woman, Ani, a beautiful one, but . . .

Anastasia   But what? You know what, I got to think this through!

Deli (*covering defeat*)   OK! . . . But the offer's there if you want it.

Anastasia (*looks lovingly at* **Deli**)   Thanks, I'll think about it!

Deli   Cool.

Clifton *makes a bold entrance.*

Clifton   Baygee don't reach yet?

Deli (*pissed*)   He won't be here for at least another hour, you want something to eat?

They clock each other momentarily.

Clifton   What! That stupidness you have there?

Deli (*not surprised*)   Alright, I got some rice and peas upstairs from Sunday.

Clifton   How all you English people does eat three-day-old food I will never know. You could never be strong like my generation.

Deli   Yeah yeah yeah.

Anastasia   I'll go and get it for you!

Deli   No, it's alright.

He exits. **Clifton** *comes and stands close to* **Anastasia**. *She moves away.*

Anastasia (*firm, fast, whispered and very violent*)   What de arse you doing? I told you not to follow me in so quickly, what the hell you think it look like?

Clifton (*not whispered*)   It look like we had something nice last night!

Anastasia   Let me tell you, what happened last night was . . .

Clifton   . . . Beautiful? . . .

Anastasia   . . . Horrendous would be closer. It was a mistake that's not going to happen again.

Clifton   Um-hum!

Anastasia   Now, can we, no, I want us to keep this between me and you.

Clifton   Um-hum.

Anastasia (*struggles*)   This, it could . . . really mash up . . . Deli and . . .

Clifton   . . . And what is it that you and my son have today that you didn't have when you whining on top of me last night?

Anastasia (*angry, looks over her shoulder*)   We never had sex!

Clifton   Damn well near as. I wonder if it could be the offer of a ready-made family that is making this conversation have an air of desperation.

Anastasia (*stutters a bit*)   What you mean by dat? I don't need no family.

Clifton   . . . Oh I think you do.

Anastasia   I have my family an believe I'm not desperate for nothin', I'd just prefer if we keep it . . . to weselves.

Clifton   And from this arrangement I get what?

Anastasia   What could I possibly give you?

Beat while he thinks.

Clifton   What you didn't last night?! But in fact you know what? I've changed my mind about that. You, young lady, have a disproportionate amount of influence over my son, and I don't like it. So I tell you what I want, I want you to leave. Leave this place before I tell Deli what you taste like, and believe, he'll put you out on your arse before I've finished.

Anastasia   I beg your pardon?

Clifton *grips her tightly.*

Clifton   My son don't need his heart broken by a dirty gal who'll lay down with any man that hold her the right way.

Anastasia (*outraged*)   Who you calling dirty gal, you bomberclaat rude.

She's about to slap him. He squeezes her arm tighter.

Clifton   . . . You think you found yourself a little sucker in Deli, eh? You stick around long enough you'll share the big money he get from he brodder? Ah ah! Too many in line for that, my friend.

Anastasia *forces herself away from* **Clifton**.

Anastasia   You're a, a, *wicked* man.

Clifton   Oh, you ain't seen nothing yet! Trust me!

We hear **Deli** *enter from the kitchen. He comes through the swing doors into the shop. He is carrying* **Clifton**'s *plate of food.*

Deli   Here. I'm not doing this again, you know. You eat what's in the restaurant from now on, or nothing at all.

Clifton *shifts the plate away.*

Clifton   If it's so you going to talk to me over a little piece of food, best you keep it.

Deli   OK! Don't eat it then.

Clifton   Gimme the food.

Anastasia   Deli, I got to run over to the internet shop for five minutes. I really need to –

Deli   . . . It's not there any more . . .

Deli *can see that she is upset.*

Is the council order ready?

Anastasia (*dashing out*)   Yeah, it's on the counter.

She leaves, bumping into **Ashley** *at the door. He is really dressed like a street hoodlum. She doesn't say sorry but carries on running.* **Ashley** *has a stronger stand about him, a more fixed hardness.*

Ashley   What's this world coming to, your woman bumps into me and can't even say excuse!

Deli   Don't . . . (*He catches himself.*) Listen, Ashley, about last night . . .

Ashley   Don't watch dat, I've come to get my clothes.

Deli   Why?

Ashley   How you gonna ask big man his business?

Ashley *accidentally on purpose drops his car keys on the floor. And walks on. He picks up his keys and waves them in the air singing.*

Ashley   Who am I, the gal dem love, zim zimmer, who's got the keys to a bimmer.

Deli   Whose car you thieve boy?

Ashley   I ain't thieve nothing, I bought it bra!

Deli   You bought a car?

Ashley   Yep. Cash money!

Deli (*laughing*)   What car is that?

Ashley   A bimmer . . .

Deli   A BMW!? . . .

Ashley   Yep.

Beat.

Deli   Huh! You insurance it?

Ashley   I would have, but I ran out of money!

Deli   Ohhh! So that's why you're here flashing keys!

Ashley   I ain't here asking you for nothing star. You ain't got nothing that I can't get!

Deli   You always gots to be rude innit? Drag us back!

Ashley   No old man, it's bear forward motion *I* deal in.

Deli *stares at him hard.*

Ashley   Actually you know what? You're right I was rude. Hear what! Let me tek you for ride, old man, let me show you *my* world. You na mean?

Deli   Your world?

Ashley   Yeah!

Deli   You're joking aren't you?

Ashley   Sorry?

Deli   Look at you, you little monkey. Dressed up like a fucking circus clown! You want me to partake in that?

Ashley (*aside to* **Deli**)   What boy! That is poetry!

Deli   Where you get the money Ashley?

Ashley*'s phone rings. He checks the number but doesn't answer.*

Ashley   That's long talk.

Deli   Dere's nothing long about it. It's an easy question, where'd you get the money?

Ashley   Some things, when you do em right, life rewards you.

Deli   . . . life rewards you? Where the fuck (*you get that shit from*)?

Ashley   I'm living proof of it.

Clifton *is about to intervene but* **Deli** *stares him down, at the same time continuing with* **Ashley**.

Deli   Do you honestly expect me to come in your car and sanction your nastiness?

Ashley (*angry*)   No, I expect you to be happy for me, happy at my progress. What I don't expect, want or need, is you fronting your jealousy with petty excuses!

Deli (*even angrier*)   Jealousy? I'm a hard-working man who's survived because I don't watch other people's tings. What makes you think I'd be envious of your stupid car, I haven't even seen it?

Ashley (*overjoyed*)   Wait till you do, it's crisp!

Deli   It can be as crisp as it wants. I want nothing to do with you and your nastiness. Come out that world, Ashley.

Beat.

Ashley (*laughs*)   You're a punk, Dad. I was giving you a chance. A chance to let the whole area know that ooooh you're Ashley's father and so we roll! But no, you want to stay small, insignificant, weak. You, you disgust me. I'll be back for my clothes.

He turns to leave. His phone rings. He answers this time with his bluetooth headset.

(*Deliberately.*) Yo! Yes, Digs . . . ? Soon come, yeah, soon come.

Deli*'s face drops at the mention of* **Digger***'s name.* **Ashley** *exits the shop.* **Clifton** *looks at* **Deli**.

Clifton   You should have at least looked at the car.

Deli *stares back at him with contempt.*

Lights down.

Scene Three

Restaurant.

The news item is playing as the lights come up.

Deli *walks into the restaurant from the kitchen. He has a huge knife in his hand. He places it under the counter. He then walks back into the kitchen and comes on with a metal baseball bat. He places that behind the front door out of sight.*

Newsreader   This is not just one isolated incident. Last month Catherine Henderson, an accident and emergency consultant at Homerton Hospital, called for staff with experience from cities such as New York and Johannesburg to join her team because NHS workers were simply not equipped to deal with the flood of gunshot wounds pouring into the department.

Deli *switches the channel back to MTV or whatever music channel he can find. As he is flicking through he passes the God channel. An American preacher is screaming out.*

Preacher   It shouldn't be no surprise our inner cities are burning up. It is the sinnnnnnns of the *fathers* bearing down on our youth.

Deli *kisses his teeth and finds the music channel. Playing is the ragga video to 'Satan Strong'. As if stiff, he moves his fists, almost warming-up style, and punches the air.*

Enter **Anastasia**. *She has a bag over her shoulder.* **Deli** *sees her and stops. He clocks the bag. He smiles.*

Deli (*surprised*)   Hey!

Anastasia   Hey!

She doesn't move from the door. Pain is etched all over her face.

Deli (*pointing to bag*)   I didn't think you were coming back. You want some help with that?

He makes to the door to pick up the bag. **Anastasia** *puts up her hand to stop him.*

Anastasia   No!

He stops.

Deli   Ani, I've been thinking that maybe I should just talk straight. What I meant this afternoon was . . .

She moves to a table and opens the bag. She begins to take out some clothes. The first thing is an Averix leather jacket.

Anastasia (*ignoring him*)   . . . This belonged to Marvin, my son. I know kids don't like wearing other people's clothes but I figured Ashley might like this . . .

Deli *is unsure why she is doing this.*

Deli   That's a wicked jacket, doesn't Marvin still (*wanna wear that*) . . .

Anastasia   . . . Unless you think it's bad luck to give him dead clothes?

Deli *stops in his tracks. He stares at her at first not understanding, then understanding. There's a long pause while they speak to each other without words.* **Anastasia** *finally answers the question* **Deli** *has been trying to articulate.*

Anastasia   Long.

Deli   Why . . . ?

Anastasia   I'm sorry. Tell Ashley that I hope it fits and, um . . .

Deli   You're leaving?

Anastasia *nods her reply. Their speeches overlap till they reach an emotional climax.*

Deli   Don't!

Anastasia   If you hit the canvas one more time brother, you ain't getting back up. I will hurt you, Deli . . .

Deli   Is this because I asked you to move in with me? . . .

Anastasia (*flash of anger*)   No. It's because the stink around this place is getting stronger and I got to run (*before it takes me down*).

Deli   But I cleaned up the place, Anastasia!

The horn is honked.

Anastasia (*looking out*)   I better go. That's my cab.

Deli (*frustrated, it stumbles out*)   I could, shoulda, woulda coulda right now but you know what? You got to give a brother time to turn shit around, to talk what's in his heart. You can't just walk so!

Anastasia (*tender but hard*)   Sometimes you should listen to people when they say they're no good for you. It might be the truth.

The car horn honks again. She doesn't move.

Deli (*pulling himself together*)   Right.

Anastasia   Hope Ashley likes the jacket.

She leaves. **Deli** *stands still for a moment. He doesn't quite know what to do with himself. He starts to pace up and down the restaurant, fretting, frustration building. To hold back the tears he starts swing-punching the air. We hear the car drive off. He doesn't notice that* **Clifton** *has entered the shop and is watching him. Eventually he falls on to one of the stools, head in hands.*

Clifton   It's all right, son.

Deli *springs up.*

Deli   Clifton! What you doing?

Clifton   It's all right. Do you want me to give you a little time to yourself?

Pause.

Deli   No.

Pause. **Clifton** *smiles to himself.*

Clifton   No woman no cry.

Deli   . . . I liked her . . . She could have taught me . . . things.

Clifton   Yes she could have, but listen to your father when I say she wasn't for you. She was using you for lifeboat, child.

Deli (*with a little attitude*)   And how do you know that?

Clifton   I'm a man of the world . . .

Deli   Oh and I'm not? You know what? Go away! I don't need you to stand above me gloating.

Clifton   Now wait a minute, I'm trying to be sympathetic and you're insulting me? . . .

Deli   I don't want your sympathy, Clifton . . .

Clifton   . . . I'm not giving you my sympathy, Deli, I'm giving you some fatherly advice . . .

Deli   . . . Well, I don't want it! Not from the man that ran left my mother for some Irish woman.

Clifton   Oh! Well, it had to come out sometime.

Deli   Yeah, I hear that after you spend out all your money on her, she run leave you for a younger model! You think we didn't hear? We heard and we laughed.

Clifton   Well, it's good to know that the gossip express is still going strong . . .

Deli   Don't mamaguy me, Clifton. Your money ran dry. You mug me mother and now you're trying to mug me.

Clifton   I didn't thieve nothing from your mother!

Deli   Yes you did. You build big house with swimming pool off my mother's savings.

Clifton   Your mother and I split the proceeds of the house . . .

Deli   . . . that my mother put the deposit down on, that she paid the mortgage on when you spend out the money down the pub and the bookies or running next woman?

Clifton   I put down my wage packet every week on your mother's table . . .

Deli   And then thief it right back.

Clifton (*snaps*)   . . . You're a grown man, for Christ's sake, stop acting like a child and use you mind. Your mother going to tell you both sides of the story?

Deli   There is no other side to the story.

Clifton   Yes, I did leave, but why, Delroy? . . .

Deli   Irish pussy!

Clifton   I didn't have to leave my home for pussy.

Deli   Really?

Clifton (*calmly*)   If I hadn't left, Delroy, I would have died. Your mother suffocated me, child. She suffocated me . . .

Deli   . . . My mother was a brilliant woman . . .

Clifton   Yes she was. Too brilliant for me. And boy, she never let me forget it. Way I talked was too rough, way I spoke was too loud. The way I walked, the way I ate. Jesus, living with that woman was like being in an airless room. It drew all of the life from me.

Deli   . . . That's fucking rubbish, she loved you like –

Clifton   No she didn't. She was stuck with me.

This stops **Deli** *momentarily.*

Your mother was not interested in me, or any other man. You ever see her with anyone new after I left?

Deli   Raising two children on one income doesn't leave much time to fraternise with the opposite sex.

Clifton   Sex! Don't let me start, your mother hated sex . . .

Deli (*puts his fingers in his ears*)   . . . Don't wanna hear this!

Clifton   She never loved me. Not the way a wife should. And let me tell you, you and Anastasia would have walked down the same street.

Deli   Rubbish, Anastasia was the only decent thing around me.

Clifton   Decent!? That gal asked me to fuck her last night because I threatened to expose her dirty nasty ways to you. How decent was that?

Beat.

Deli (*stunned*)   What did you do?

Clifton   I fucked her to prove I was right. She was a thieving little whore who was only after you and Dougie money.

Deli   No she wasn't!

Clifton   I smelt her the moment I walked in here.

Deli *runs at his father.*

Deli   How could you do that?

Clifton   Was she your woman?

Deli   No. But you must have known?

Clifton   Which is exactly why I had to prove her to be the woman I knew she was. She was here to thieve your money. Like all of them. You don't need people like that around you, Delroy, you need people around that love you.

Deli *looks at him. Enter* **Digger**. *He's in a bad mood. He brings his Chopper bike into the restaurant.*

Digger   Boyyyyy, I just done nearly kick up this fucking ambulance man. I'm driving in my car and I hear the siren so I wait for the right spot to pull over. Instead of the man wait, he swings in front of me and then cuts across my front. The fucking man doh just clip me wing! So I jump out and instead the man say sorry, he come open up his big mouth and come call me an ignorant idiot. You know I don't like that people call me that already. I had to threaten him. You been watching too much fucking 'Casualty', mate. I'll punch down your claat. When he saw that, he calmed himself and just freed up his insurance details. Fucking chip my new TT, you know, shouldda shoot him clatt.

Clifton   Wasn't there someone in the back waiting to reach the hospital?

Digger   I don't give a bombo! Deli, give me a roti.

Deli   We don't do roti no more, Digger.

Digger   Oh yeah, me forget.

Deli *throws a glance at the baseball bat behind the door.*

Deli   Eh! The police came round about the Roy ting today.

Digger   Oh yeah? What you tell them?

Deli   What Rose told me.

Digger   Which was?

Deli   That some Yardie men in mask asking for protection money burnt down the place, after beating the hell out of Roy.

Digger   Really? She told the police that?

Deli   I told her she should. How else we gonna rid this place of such vermin.

Digger   I wouldn't have thought that would do her much good. Nobody likes an informer. Not even you.

Beat.

From what I hear she refused a reasonable deal.

Deli   Did you get my son help you in your nastiness, Digger?

Digger   What you talking about? Don't be stupid.

Deli   I don't believe you. How much odder dirty youth out there you gonna recruit, you gonna take my son? I don't want you anywhere near anything of mine again, Digger. My son, myself, my shop.

Digger   You don't? . . . You should think about that. Particularly after the recent events.

Deli   You threatening me?

Digger   No. Just reminding you of who protects who! Shit's gonna change, Deli, dey run tings now. They was going to send a next man to talk to you but I said, true say that you and me go back, that I would do it and negotiate the best price for all involved.

Deli   The best price?

Digger   Best price.

Deli   After I already pay rates, tax and employees' insurance, Renton crew want me to pay protection money?

Digger   Yep. I might could a get you less but ah, pay you do.

Deli   What appen, Digger? How you gonna go and join them lowlives?

Digger   Watch you mouth, Deli.

Deli   Ha, well, run tell your new employees that no. Not me.

Digger   Don't be stupid. You don't want dem kinda friction dere.

Deli   I been here ten years, Digger, what makes you think I'm gonna start paying some 'off the boat' bloody Yard boy money that I don't have?

Digger   Because they said so. It's not like you can't afford it. Everybody knows that Dougie left you a whole heap ah money.

Deli   Dougie never left me shit. You know what? Tell them they can come burn down my place, before they get a red cent from me, that they can fuck off.

Digger   I ain't gonna tell them that, Deli.

Deli   That's your business.

Digger   No, this is. Once I say you have to pay, you pay, Deli, or else I look bad.

Deli   So it's money you want, well, here, Digger, have some money.

He empties out his pockets and throws the coins at **Digger**.

Digger   Ah wha de bloodclaat!

Clifton   Delroy . . .

Digger   Deli, calm and settle youself before I have to.

Deli   Take the money, Digger.

He throws more money that he has found by the till.

Clifton   Deli, calm the hell down.

Deli   Take the money na!

He grabs hold of the till and rips it out of the counter and throws it at **Digger**.

Take the blood money.

Digger   Deli!

Digger *goes to pull his gun out but before he can get it out* **Deli** *is at his throat with the big knife.*

Deli   Do it na! See if you could shoot me before I cut your bloody throat!

Digger   Deli, you're behaving like an arse. Calm down and move the knife from my throat unless you plan to use it this very minute.

Deli   Digger, you used my son, you used my blood, to do my neighbour. You knew the first place the police were gonna come to was here.

Digger   He wanted to defend your manhood. Is not me!

Deli   My son doesn't have to defend me, Digger.

Digger   Take the knife from my throat, Deli.

He doesn't.

Clifton   Delroy, use your mind. Take the knife from the man throat.

Digger   I told him no. But all you got on the street is your rep, bro, and my youth wants rep.

Deli   I see you close to Ashley again, Digger, and I will kill you.

He takes the knife away.

And take back your stinking BMW!

Digger *stands up.*

Digger   That's a very silly ting you jus' do. (*Beat.*) I hope you can defend that.

Digger *exits, staring* **Deli** *out.*

Clifton   Was that wise?

Deli *stares at* **Clifton** *and then backs out towards* **Digger**.

Lights down.

An intense gurkel melody plays until:

Scene Four

Restaurant. Day.

Baygee *is sitting with a half-eaten plantain burger in front of him. He is mid-story to* **Clifton** *who is in the kitchen area.*

Baygee   Now you know Charlie! Twenty years he dere in this country and doe miss a day work. But that afternoon, out of the blue, he head start to hurt him bad. He beg the manager not to send him home but they order him, so he go. Well, is just by chance I meet him on the street, vex he vex. I say, Charlie boy, go home and enjoy the missus. Huh, well, is den he start to tell me ting. Apparently, before Thelma would give him anyting he had to agree to put out the bins and wash de wares and all breed ah stupidness!

Clifton   What?

Enter an aproned **Clifton** *with a tray of plantain burgers. He starts restacking the shelves.*

Baygee   Yes, blackmailing de man before she get him he tings, and even then he say, no matter what he tell her, all she doing is laying stiff so dreaming ah Trinidad. Not even a little (*he imitates a female groan of pleasure*) ahhhhh to sweet him.

Clifton   Is he that wrong, he should a grip woman long! Me I would a . . .

Baygee   Wait hear de story na! So I give him a few sweet boy tips and I send he on he way. De next time I see the man, is not in burial ground!

Clifton   You lie?

Baygee   Well, the story go that when he reach home flowers in hand and ting, he hear one set a noise from upstairs. Well, he say somebody break in and must be beating he wife. So he run into the kitchen grab one big knife and creep up de stairs so as to catch the criminal in the act . . .

Clifton   Surprise him yes . . .

Baygee   When he bust into the room, tell me what he see?

Clifton   The wife beating the man?

Baygee   Thelma head stick out the window leg cock up so, and a man half he age woking it hard from behind.

Clifton   You lie?

Baygee   I look like I lie? . . .

Clifton   What he kill de man?

Baygee   Well, he sister tell me that the wife tell she, that he just look at her, and then he look at this young stallion dat making Thelma shout ting he doe hear in he life and he heart just give up so, bang, he drop and dead.

Clifton   Just so? . . .

Baygee   Just so.

Clifton   Bonjay! Ha! Well is so he had to dead. Me old man use to say, if you have to drown you can't burn.

Baygee *downs the rum in front of him in one and salutes* **Clifton**.

Baygee   He don't lie, Clifton, he don't lie.

Enter **Deli**. *He doesn't greet either of the men. He is in a world of his own.*

Clifton   Where the France you been, boy?

Deli *looks at* **Clifton** *but doesn't reply.* **Clifton** *addresses* **Baygee** *at first.*

Clifton (*to* **Baygee**)   But look me crosses na! Delroy, you going deaf? I had to set up the shop by myself, you know. Where you been?

Deli   In a meeting.

Clifton   Meeting, what kind of meeting?

Deli   I said a meeting, OK!

Clifton   You don't know we have a business to run here. None of the things going to be ready for lunchtime, you know?

Deli   Clifton, Clifton please. We miss lunch, we miss lunch.

Baygee *looks up at the two men, checks his watch and decides it's time to leave. He takes one last shot of Clark's and slams the glass on the table and stands to go.*

Baygee (*laughs*)   Gentlemen, I promised I'd drop something before twelve o'clock.

Clifton   I go have you food ready. What time you passing back?

Baygee   No, it's OK, dey just reach back from Trinidad. She go have a little home food for me.

Clifton   Who is that?

Baygee   Ms Thelma. I gone.

He exits and leaves the shop. There's silence for a bit.

Clifton   You's still a suspect?

Deli   You see Ashley this morning?

Clifton   No! (*Beat.*) I feel rather proud, you know. We seem to be running this ting well. Don't you think?

Deli   We?

Clifton   Yes, it wouldn't be unfair to say we. In fact, you know what I was thinking? You should let me move into the flat with you, son, that way we'd always be ready!

Deli   Clifton, I'm selling this place.

Clifton   Because them Yardies want a little money from you? It's better you pay them than you run away. Men don't run, son.

Deli (*fed up with everyone questioning his manhood*)   So what do they do, Clifton?

Clifton   They stay at the crease till the umpire's hand go so. (*Pointing up and out.*) Running is never the answer.

Deli   I'm not running.

Clifton   I thought you had more brains than that, man!

Beat.

Where you going if you sell this place?

Deli   I don't know. Somewhere far.

Clifton   You going to take Ashley?

Deli   I want to.

Clifton   What about me?

Deli   What about you, Clifton?

Clifton   Aren't you going to need someone to help you run the business?

Deli   Who said anything about a business?

Clifton   What else you go do? Who's going to employ someone that has no qualifications, spent a year in jail and ran away from the one positive thing he has achieved in his life. Where's your respect?

Deli   Respect for what?

Clifton   Ashley, me.

Deli   You?

Clifton   Yes actually, me. As your father you owe me respect. The respect that says, 'Daddy I know you're not well, as your son I'll take care of you till you're strong again.'

Deli   Clifton, this is the wrong time for us to be having this debate.

Clifton (*losing it*)   No, this is exactly the right time to be having it. As a child, did I ever let you walk the street raggedy?

Deli   No, but . . .

Clifton   Exactly!

Deli   That was about you, you and your children always had to be the smartest in the street!

Clifton   Exactly, I looked after you . . .

Deli   To a point.

Clifton (*to himself*)   Once and man, twice a child. Jesus. Your generation curse. You British blacks pick up worse and leave best. Instead ah you pick up the Englishman thirst for knowledge and learning you pick up his nasty habit of dumping their old people in some stinking hole for them to rot when they are at the prime of their wisdom.

Deli   Clifton, is you that said when the doctors give you the all-clear that you going home . . .

Clifton   . . . I lied. I don't have nowhere to go, Delroy.

Deli   What do you want me to do? I can't help you, Clifton, believe me, I don't have nothing!

Clifton   You and your brother bought some land home! You got money hidden away, I know. Let's go home together na? Open a little something in town. Show them bitches that Clifton can bounce back. Clifton have something. He children amount to something. You know they does laugh at me home? Yes. Your own uncle laughs at me. 'Look,' he does say, every time he sees his daughter in the paper hug up with a next white man, 'she doing well, innit? By the way, Dougie come out of jail yet.' Laughing at my seed. Let we go home show them that my seed is something. We are somebody.

Deli   Clifton, listen to me, you are not going to want to be where I am, believe me.

Clifton (*loses it*)   Don't say that!

He begins to throw over the chairs and tables.

What have I got to show for my life, Delroy? Parkinson's! What do I have to do, beg you? Fight you for it?

Deli   Calm down.

Clifton   No, you fucking calm down. Calm down? Calm down? Come and make me na, think the old man can't knock you down.

He starts swinging his fists in the air. **Deli** *stares at him, bewildered. He loses steam eventually, falling to the floor.*

Ashley *enters. He stares at* **Clifton** *on the floor and the messed-up restaurant. He doesn't say a word. Eventually, he goes to help* **Clifton** *stand up.* **Clifton** *shrugs him off and picks himself up.*

Clifton   Get off me. All you generation curse. You go rot, mark my words.

He leaves the restaurant. **Ashley** *stares at his grandfather leaving.*

Beat.

Ashley   Where's he going?

Deli   I don't know.

Ashley *(cool and deadly)*   I hear you was down the police station this morning?

Deli   Yeah, how you know that?

Ashley   What did they want?

Deli   More details of your whereabouts when Rose's place was burn.

Ashley   What did you tell them?

Deli   What I have before, that you were here with me. Why?

Ashley   You sure?

Deli   Yeah!

Ashley *walks up and hugs his dad.*

Ashley   Thanks, Dad.

Deli (*slightly taken aback*)   It's alright.

Ashley   You know I was only looking out for you?

Deli *pushes him off.*

Deli   No, you were looking out for yourself. But it's my fault. Should have got you out of here years ago. But I didn't have the resource, the wherewithal . . .

Ashley   . . . What you talking about?

Deli   They know it was you. They know it was Digger. It's only a matter of time. If Roy dies they coming to get you, son, no matter what.

Ashley *is about to say something but* **Deli** *stops him.*

Deli   Ah . . . Now I know you's a big man and dat but it's up to me to protect you the best way I know how. If I was to say that I've arranged a place away from here for us, what would you say?

Ashley   I'd say why?

Deli *struggles to find the words. Eventually.*

Deli   OK. I did go to the police station today but it wasn't about you entirely.

Ashley   No?

Deli   No. I went because I've struck a deal. You . . . for Digger.

Ashley (*shocked to his core*)   Noooo! You can't have done dat? You're many things but you're not an informer, Dad.

Deli   I knew Digger was bad but, son, he's terrible.

Ashley   He does what he has to do to survive.

Deli   Don't talk shit to me. What do you want me to do, son, protect Digger and throw you to the wolves? This is about your survival, you better know.

Ashley (*sickened*) You didn't have to inform, Dad. Where you ever going to go in the world and not have to look over your shoulder?

Deli That's not better than being in prison?

Ashley Is still prison, just bigger cells.

Deli Well, I've been in a cell, son, and it is not very nice. Each generation is suppose to top the previous one. If I have to die on the street to get you out of that dere runnings, wouldn't I be doing my job?

Ashley I don't believe you did this?

Deli I did, now listen to me. The police are going to arrest Digger today, but they're only gonna be able to hold him for forty-eight hours. After he's released, he's gonna know that I shopped him, then he's going to come right here and deal with me.

Ashley You're damn right he will!

Deli But if you speak to the police and say that you'll testify that Digger told you to do all that happened that night, we will get fifty grand and a safe house out of the country. Coupled with the money I already have, when we ready we could fly back home and live the lives of kings.

Ashley Hackney's home.

Deli It won't be when Digger gets out. What? He's gonna have an informer's son in his crew?

Ashley (*realisation*) You did that on purpose?

Deli Yes I did.

Ashley (*screams*) I don't believe you.

Enter **Digger**.

Digger You better do! Didn't I tell you your father would do this. Didn't I?

Deli *stands. A little afraid but ready whatever comes next.*

Digger   How did you think you were going to get away wid dis? Wha, you think you could just pull knife on me, inform pon me and me would let you get 'way?

Deli   Man has to tek his chances in life, you get me, don't you, Digger?

Digger   I get you, but what about your son? What have you done to your child, Deli? Branded him for life. Ashley, the informer's boy.

Deli *stares him out.*

Digger   What did you think was going to happen, Delroy?

Deli   Stop all the long chat, Digger, if you come to deal wid me let's get it on like men.

Digger *pulls out a packet of crack rocks and throws them on the floor. He then removes another bag from his pocket. It is pure cocaine. He opens it and, as if releasing magic dust from his hand, throws a handful at* **Deli***.*

Digger   Um-um. It's not me that's gonna deal with you. You don't know what we do to informers these days, do you? Well . . .

He turns to **Ashley***.*

My youth. Deal wid this properly and you go straight to the big league. Rep is everything, and yours is gonna be huge after this.

Ashley *slowly takes out his gun.* **Deli** *just stares at him.*

Ashley   You let me down, Dad.

Digger   OK, let's do the solicitor's work for him. Put one in the roof, shows we had a struggle.

Ashley *shoots the gun off in the air.*

Deli   You ready for this life, Ashley?

Digger   Alright, now point the gun at your punk-arsed dad. The one that gets beat up and does nothing, has his business near taken away and does nothing, but then informs on a brother man to the other man for what? A piddling fifty grand! I could ah give you that! Is this the type of people we need in our midst? Weak-hearted, unfocused informers? No, I don't think so. Do you, Ashley?

Ashley's *hands are shaking a little. After a beat.*

Ashley   Digger, I don't think . . .

Digger (*screams at him*)   Is this the type of people we need in our midst?

Ashley   No.

Digger   OK then, raise the gun, point it.

Ashley *does.*

Digger   Good. Is your finger on the trigger?

Ashley   Yes.

Digger   Good.

Digger *pulls out his gun and shoots* **Ashley** *dead.*

Deli   Noooooooooooooooooooooooooooooooo.

Digger *looks to* **Deli**.

Digger   Yes. Ah so dis war run!

He exits.

Deli *kneels, still, by his dead son. After a few beats he rises, takes the jacket that* **Anastasia** *left for* **Ashley** *and covers his body and head. With one final glance around, he stares at the picture of his mother, then walks out of the restaurant. The violent ragga tune plays as we fade to black.*

Anthony Neilson

Realism

Anthony Neilson was born in Edinburgh and lives in London. His plays include *Welfare My Lovely* (Traverse Theatre, 1990); *Normal* (Edinburgh Festival, Finborough Arms, 1991); *Penetrator* (Royal Court Theatre Upstairs/Traverse Theatre/ Finborough Theatre, 1993); *Year of the Family* (Finborough Theatre, 1994); *Heredity* (Royal Court Theatre, 1995); *The Censor* (The Red Room at The Finborough Theatre/Royal Court Theatre, 1997), which won the Writers' Guild Award 1997 and Best Fringe Play and the *Time Out* Live Award 1997; *Edward Gant's Amazing Feat of Loneliness!* (Theatre Royal, Plymouth, 2002); *Stitching* (Traverse Theatre/Bush Theatre, 2002), which won the *Time Out* Off West End Award 2002; *The Lying Kind* (Royal Court Theatre, 2002); *The Wonderful World of Dissocia* (Tron Theatre, Glasgow, 2004); *Realism* (Royal Lyceum Theatre, Edinburgh, 2006); *God in Ruins* (Soho Theatre, 2007); *Relocated* (Royal Court Theatre, 2008); and *The Séance* (National Theatre Connections, 2009). He has also written for TV, radio and film. Credits include: *The Debt Collector* (Dragon Pictures/Film 4, 1999), which won the Fipresci International Critics Award; *Spilsbury*, a 90-minute single film for TV (Stone City/BBC, 2009); and *Spooks* (Kudos/BBC, 2009). He is currently RSC Literary Associate.

For Amy

Realism was first performed on 14 August 2006 by the National Theatre of Scotland at the Royal Lyceum Theatre, Edinburgh, as part of the Edinburgh International Festival. The cast was as follows:

Paul; Galloway,
  Independent Politician;
  Minstrel, Bystander   Paul Blair
Angie, Presenter, Bystander   Louise Ludgate
Laura, Right-Wing Politician   Shauna Macdonald
Stuart McQuarrie   Stuart McQuarrie
Father, Pundit, Simon, Minstrel   Sandy Neilson
Mother; Left-Wing Politician   Jan Pearson
Mullet, Minstrel   Matthew Pidgeon

Director Anthony Neilson
Designer Miriam Buether
Lighting Designer Chahine Yavroyan
Sound Designer/Composer Nick Powell

Notes

While the dialogue in this play is largely my own, the material herein was hugely influenced by the suggestions, criticisms and improvisations of the actors and creative team, whose names are listed in the text.

As ever, what follows is a record of a show that was presented in 2006. Elements of the sound or production design may be described, but should only be taken into account; they represent no stipulation on my part (except where indicated).

The play contains references to topical events, localised matters and personal issues that may limit its relevance in other territories or times. Where possible, I have attempted to explain the dramatic relevance of these moments so that the imaginative translator may find a way to adapt them.

Though *Realism* is divided into acts, it should be presented without an interval.

Please note that though there are several phone conversations during the play, at no point should a phone ever be present (or represented) onstage.

THE SET

In the original production, the stage was raked from front to back with a slight imbalance upstage left.

All the elements of a normal home were present. From front of stage to back: a sofa, a fridge with work surface, a washing machine, a toilet, a bed, a dining table and chairs, an armchair, etc. Various practical lights (both standing and hanging) were also arranged around the set.

However, the stage itself was covered with several tons of off-white sand. All of the aforementioned furniture was cut off to varying degrees (and at varying angles) so as to appear 'sunk' into this sand. The television was placed at the very front of the stage, seeming almost completely submerged, allowing only enough space to use it as a lighting source for the sofa.

The walls on all three sides consisted of large pillars, grey and textured, which hinted at concrete. Actors entered and exited between them.

PRE-SHOW

As the audience arrived, we played a medley of UK traditional tunes which was famously (until 2006) used as the opening music for BBC Radio 4. It not only set the play's beginning firmly in the morning; it also inspired a spirit of joviality, which I would recommend – as *Realism* is, to all intents and purposes, a comedy. If you have any kind of equivalent – a light tune that your audience finds synonymous with morning – I would respectfully suggest that you consider its use.

'Breakdowns' are presented in square brackets at the scene beginnings. These describe what is actually occurring in the play's 'real' time-line. I wrote them for my own benefit and present them for your interest only. You may prefer not to read them, and experience the show in the same vague sense of confusion that the audience did.

Characters

Stuart
Paul
Mother
Father
Mullet
Angie
Presenter
Pundit
Right-Wing Politician
Left-Wing Politician
Independent Politician
Audience Member
Laura
Minstrel 1
Minstrel 2
Minstrel 3
Simon
Cat
Bystanders

Act One: Morning

One

[*In which . . .* **Stuart** *gets a phone call from his friend* **Paul.** **Paul** *wants him to come and play football.* **Stuart** *declines the offer. He puts out some food for the cat. He remembers a dream he had the previous night. He goes back to bed.*]

Stuart *sits on the couch, in his bedclothes. He has one hand down his pants, absent-mindedly squeezing himself – it is not a sexual gesture. He looks very tired.*

Paul, *wearing a suit, is looking in the fridge.* (*Note: at no point in the following scene do the actors make eye contact.*)

Paul   Did I wake you?

Stuart   No, not really.

Paul   Not really?

Stuart   I was awake.

Paul   Were you still in bed?

Stuart *smells his fingers.*

Stuart   Yeah, well, it's Saturday morning so . . .

Paul   So I woke you up. I'm sorry.

Pause.

Stuart   What's going on?

Paul   Were you out last night?

Stuart   For a while.

He tries to look at a birthmark on his shoulder. It's itching.

Paul   D'you get pissed?

Stuart   A bit.

Paul   A bit?

Stuart   Paul – I've not even had a cup of tea –

Paul   I was just wondering what you're up to. You playing fives later?

He starts dribbling a football back and forward.

Stuart   I don't know. I don't think so.

Paul   You've got to.

Stuart   Why have I got to?

Paul   We're already a man down.

Stuart   I don't think I can.

Paul   Why not?

Stuart   I just – I don't really feel like it.

Pause.

Paul   What do you feel like, then?

Stuart   What?

Paul   What do you feel like doing?

Stuart   Not much.

Paul   Aw, come on – come and play footie. We'll have a few pints.

*For the first time we see **Paul** from the front. His shirt is half open and his suit jacket has vomit down it.*

Stuart   I really don't feel like it.

Paul   So what are you going to do? Just mope about your flat all day?

Stuart   I've got stuff to do.

Paul   Like what?

Stuart   Just boring things.

Paul   Like what?

Stuart   For fuck's sake . . .

Paul   I'm just asking.

Stuart   Like washing, cleaning up – domestic shit.

Paul   You can do that tomorrow.

Stuart   I can't.

Paul   Why not?

Stuart   Cos I just – I haven't got any clean clothes . . . I just need to get myself together.

Paul *crosses to the couch and sits beside* **Stuart**.

Paul   I could come over after. Get a few cans in. Get a DVD out.

He instantly falls asleep. During the next exchange, he nods in and out of consciousness.

Stuart   Paul, I really – I just want to do nothing.

Paul   You want to do nothing?

Stuart   Yeah, I just –

Paul   We don't have to do anything. We can just kiss and cuddle a bit; there's no pressure.

Stuart   That's tempting.

Pause.

No, really, I just – I said to myself I was just going to do nothing today. It's been a fucking hellish week at work and I'm just knackered; just want to chill out.

Paul   What good – do you?

Stuart   Eh?

Paul   That going to – ?

Pause. Annoyed, **Stuart** *stands. Damned reception.*

Stuart   Fucking things.

Paul   I said what good's it going to do you, moping about your flat all day?

Stuart   I'm not going to be moping.

Paul   You are – you're going to mope.

Stuart   I'm not going to mope.

Paul   Mope, mope, mope; that'll be you.

Stuart   Right, well, so if I want to mope I can fucking mope, can't I? I mean, I'm not planning on moping but I reserve the right to mope in my own fucking house.

Paul   All right, all right; calm down, calm down. I just don't want you getting all depressed.

Stuart   I'm not, I'm fine.

Paul   All right.

Stuart   Just want to spend a bit of time on my own.

Paul   Fair enough.

He staggers to his feet.

Will I give you – tomorrow?

Stuart   Will you give me tomorrow?

Paul (*louder*)   Will I give you a *shout* tomorrow?

Stuart   Yeah, give me a shout tomorrow.

Paul   If you change your mind –

Stuart   I'll give you a bell.

Paul   Give us a bell. We'll be in the Duck's Arse from about five.

Stuart   All right, cheers.

Paul *exits.*

Pause. **Stuart** *yawns.*

Stuart *goes to the fridge, opens it. He takes out a tin of cat food and prises back the lid. He fills a bowl with food. Some of it drops onto the floor. At the top of his voice he shouts:*

Here, kitty kitty kitty kitty!

He considers staying awake, but then walks back towards his bedroom.

On the way, his **Mother** *appears. He stops.*

Mother   Have you seen the sky?

Stuart   What do you mean?

Mother   It's full of bombers.

Stuart   Where from?

Mother   Israel? [*At the time of writing, in 2006, Israel had invaded Lebanon. Substitute a more topical/timeless reference if necessary.*]

Pause. **Stuart** *continues on his way.*

Mother *takes a seat at the dining table.*

Stuart *climbs back into bed.*

Lights fade. Music – during which **Father** *enters, carrying a morning paper. He takes a seat at the dining table, handing part of the paper to* **Mother**. *They read.*

Two

[**Stuart** *gets up again. He remembers another fragment of a dream. He makes himself a cup of tea, and gets a mild electric shock from the toaster. Feeling bad about himself, he attempts to exercise but ends up pretending to be a rabbit. He remembers a friend chasing him with a shit-covered stick. The same friend got him to taste a crayon, which was horrible. He watches a news report about the Middle East crisis.*]

Stuart *wakes up with cramp. He hits the side of his leg. The pain passes. Pause.*

Paul *enters behind* **Stuart***, carrying a huge carrot.* **Stuart** *doesn't see him.*

Paul   Stuart.

Stuart   What?

Paul   That fucking squirrel's back.

Stuart   What does he want?

Paul   He wants his guts back in.

Stuart   That'll cost a fortune.

Paul   Yeah, but Angie'll pay for it. She's on her way out.

Paul *sits in the armchair.*

Stuart *gets up and collects a cup from the cupboard.*

Father   Stuart, don't bother me.

On his way to the fridge, **Stuart** *looks inside the cup, checking that it's clean. He turns on the electric kettle.*

Mother   Can you see it? There – a castle, look. The tea leaves make a turret, and the tea's like a moat at the bottom.

Stuart   What's a moat?

Mother   It's the water round a castle, to keep the folk from getting in.

Simultaneously, **Mother** *and* **Stuart** *sing a fairly buoyant, very British wartime song – the sort of song a mother used to sing:*

I like a nice cup of tea in the morning,
I like a nice cup of tea with my tea . . .

But **Mother***'s voice fades away, leaving* **Stuart** *groping for the lyrics. A sound arrives, punching into him the realisation of her absence.*

Stuart *takes a moment to recover, then puts the cup down. He looks at the jars in front of him.*

Stuart   Coffee – tea? Tea – coffee?

Stuart *opens a box of tea bags. He drops a tea bag into the cup.*

He opens the fridge.

He takes out a packet of bread. He snaps off two pieces and pushes them into the toaster. He takes some milk out of the fridge. He smells the milk.

The sound of children playing

The sound of the water boiling in the kettle becomes the sound of horses galloping. It reaches a crescendo . . . then stops.

He pours the hot water into the mug.

Smoke is beginning to rise from the toaster. The bread is trapped in there.

Stuart *tries to get the toaster to eject the toast but it isn't working. He's beginning to panic.*

Mullet *appears behind the couch. He looks like a child from the seventies. He is hyperactive and extremely irritating.*

Mullet *(in an annoying sing-song voice)*   Stewpot! Stewpot! Stewpot! [*This is what many children called Stuart were nicknamed in the seventies.*]

Stuart   For fuck's sake, what?!

Mullet   The toast's burning!

Stuart   I know! I can't get it out.

Mullet   Use a knife!

Stuart   I'll get electrocuted.

Mullet   You won't.

Panicked, **Stuart** *runs to the cutlery drawer and runs back to the toaster.*

He plunges the knife into the toaster and is immediately thrown on to his back by the resulting shock. **Mullet** *finds this hilarious.*

Mullet (*gleeful*)   You fucking knob!

Angrily, **Stuart** *smacks the toaster off the surface.*

Mullet   That was a fucking beauty!

Stuart   My heart's going like the clappers!

Pause.

Fucking hell.

He picks up the toaster and the burnt toast. He takes a knife to the toast and starts to scrape off the burnt bits.

Angie *appears behind him, wearing a dressing gown. She stops, annoyed.*

Angie   Why do you do that?

Stuart   What?

Angie   Scrape the fucking toast into the sink?

Stuart   I don't like burnt toast.

Angie   So scrape it into the fucking bin! It just clogs the sink up. And then you smear it on the side of the Flora [*a type of margarine*]. You're a dirty bastard.

She continues across the stage.

Stuart   I thought you were going to call me?

She exits.

Pause. **Stuart** *throws the toast into the pedal bin.*

He walks over to the sofa, sits down.

Stuart   I've broke out in a sweat from that shock.

Mullet   That was a beauty. You went fucking flying!

Stuart *tries to look at his mole.*

Mullet   What's wrong?

Stuart   That birthmark's itching.

Mullet   Let's see.

He takes a look at it.

I'm not joking, man; that's cancer.

Stuart   It's not cancer. I'm too young to have cancer.

Mullet   You're joking, aren't you? Fucking Kylie's got cancer – look how young she is! If someone with all that money and an arse like that can get cancer, you think you can't? What else is wrong with you?

Stuart   My left eye's still funny.

Mullet   That's diabetes.

Stuart   It's not diabetes!

He goes to the mirror, distressed. Behind him, **Mullet** *makes faces and rude signs.*

Mullet   Why not? Your uncle had it.

Stuart   Doesn't mean I've got it.

Mullet   So why are you thirsty all the time?

Stuart   Am I thirsty all the time?

He thinks about it.

I'm thirsty a lot of the time. And I keep getting cramp. Is that diabetes?

Mullet (*mimics*)   'Is that diabetes?' You're such a fucking jessie.

Stuart   Fuck you.

Mullet   What's happened to you, man? You were going to be a choo-choo driver. You were going to be an astronaut. What's happened to that guy? What's happened to the guy who was going to build a rocket and fly to fucking Mars? I mean, look at yourself. What do you see?

Pause.

Stuart   A fat fucking shite.

Mullet   A fat fucking shite. And how do you feel?

Stuart   Like shite.

Mullet   Like shite. And what are you going to do about it?

Stuart   Fuck all.

Mullet   You're going to do fuck all. You could have gone out to play footie but you're going to sit around the house all day moping and why? Because of a girl! Because you're waiting for a girl to call you!

Stuart   I can't help it. I love her.

Mullet (*mimics*)   'I loooove her'! So why did you dump her then?

Stuart   I didn't.

Mullet   You did. You dumped her because she had horrible, wobbly thighs and a wonky fucking nose.

Stuart   Shut your stupid face.

Mullet   It's true.

Stuart   It's not!

Pause.

Mullet   Hey, Stu – do that thing with your pants!

Pause. **Stuart** *pulls his pants up over his belly. Cranking one arm, he lets his belly extend to its full size, as if pumping it up. Then he removes an imaginary cork from his belly and lets it deflate.*

Mullet   *That* – is fucking *genius*.

Stuart   I'm a fat sack of shit.

Mullet   So what? So's Tony Soprano and he gets shags. And you know why? Because only poofs care what they look like. And women know that.

Stuart *gets on to the floor.*

Mullet   What are you doing? Are you going to do press-ups? Only wanks do press-ups.

Stuart *starts doing press-ups.*

Stuart   I'm not listening to you.

Mullet *gets down beside him and moves and talks in rhythm with* **Stuart***'s increasingly laboured exercises.*

Mullet   Good. So you won't hear me say how *boring* they are, and what a *poof* you are, and how *boring* they are, and what a *wank* you are, and how boring they are, and how *fat* you are, and what a *weakling* you are –

Stuart *gives up, knackered and exasperated, and strangely amused.*

Mullet   How many was that?

Stuart   Four. (*Or however many he managed.*)

Mullet *derides him.*

Mullet   Four! You only managed four?!

Stuart   I'm going to build them up over time.

He stands up and starts to jump up and down, on the spot.

Mullet   Look at you now! You look like a fucking rabbit!

Stuart   Do I?

Mullet (*excited*)   Do this – Stu – do this.

Hopping alongside **Stuart**, **Mullet** *makes paws with his hands and sticks his teeth out.*

Mullet   Like a rabbit!

Stuart *does it.*

Mullet   Are you hungry, rabbit?

Stuart *nods.*

Mullet   You want some carrots?

Stuart *nods.*

Mullet   Say, 'I want some carrots, Mr Farmer.'

Stuart   'I want some carrots, Mr Farmer.'

Mullet *offers his crayons.*

Mullet   Right – Imagine these are carrots! Come and get
the carrots.

Stuart *follows after* **Mullet**.

Mullet   No, but you have to hop.

Stuart *hops after him.*

Mullet   That's it – come and get the carrots, Thumper!

Stuart *reaches him but* **Mullet** *suddenly produces a stick.*

Stuart   What's that?

Mullet   It's a stick!

Stuart   What's on the end of it?

Mullet   Keich! [*Scottish slang for shit.*]

Stuart   Fuck off – is it?

Mullet   Smell it.

Tentatively **Stuart** *does – he gags.*

Stuart   Aw, fuck off!

Grinning, **Mullet** *chases after him.*

Stuart   Fuck off! Fuck off, ya dirty bastard!

They run around laughing, and occasionally gagging.

Mullet *whoops like a Red Indian and suddenly lots of others appear,
as if in a playground. He chases them all around and for a moment the
stage is full of noise and activity. One by one they claim sanctuary by
the walls. Finally, out of breath,* **Stuart** *is cornered.*

Stuart   Put that down.

Mullet   Why?

Stuart   (*gags*) Just put it down. I'm telling you.

Mullet   Telling me what?

Stuart   Telling you to put it down.

Mullet *thrusts the shitty stick at him.*

Stuart   You better fucking not – I'm telling you.

Mullet   You want the carrots? Are you going to hop to the carrots?

Stuart   I'll hop to the carrots if you put it down.

Pause. **Mullet** *puts the stick down.*

Stuart *advances a little.* **Mullet** *quickly picks the stick up and thrusts it at him again.*

Stuart   Put the fucking thing down!

Mullet   All right, all right – I'm putting it down.

He puts it down, then throws the orange crayons.

Hop to the carrots, rabbit.

Stuart *hops over to the carrots.*

Mullet   Eat one.

Pause. **Stuart** *eats the end of one. He spits it out in disgust.*

Stuart   That's fucking awful!

The game's over – **Stuart** *sits on the couch.*

Mullet   Stewpot! Stuart! Stuart.

Stuart *ignores him.*

He picks up his tea and sips it. He turns the TV on – its light plays on his face.

Dejected, **Mullet** *gathers up his things and leaves, dragging his stick behind him.*

The sounds of war.

Behind him, people run screaming as if under heavy fire, taking shelter behind the appliances.

Oblivious to them, **Stuart** *crosses to the fridge and fixes himself a bowl of cereal.*

He arrives back at the couch as the same time as the others, who assemble themselves around him.

Three

[**Stuart** *gets annoyed by a radio discussion show in which the guests all seem to be in favour of the smoking ban (introduced in Scotland in 2006). A pirate radio station interferes with the reception. He imagines himself a member of the panel. He considers how to get* **Angie** *to call him.*]

Pundit   The simple fact is that this is a blight on our society and a drain on the already stretched resources of the Health Service; and if the pitiful souls that participate in it do not have either the ability or the moral fibre to control themselves, then it's actually our societal *duty* to make sure they can do as little harm to others as possible.

Applause.

Presenter   Remind me what your party's position on the ban is, Right-Wing Politician McDonald?

Right-Wing Politician   My party's position –

Left-Wing Politician   I don't think the Conservatives have a position.

A spattering of laughter and applause from the audience. **Stuart**, *sandwiched between them, continues to eat his breakfast.*

Right-Wing Politician   No, actually, our position is that we're broadly in favour of the ban –

Left-Wing Politician   Broadly.

Right-Wing Politician   But that we argued for certain exemptions, such as private clubs.

Left-Wing Politician   Conservative clubs by any chance?

Some laughter.

Presenter   And what's your personal view?

Right-Wing Politician   My personal view –

Presenter   Given that the question was whether the current smoking ban is an infringement of civil liberties.

Right-Wing Politician   Right, well – it obviously is an infringement on the civil liberties of smokers –

The sound of a pirate radio station cuts in – booming dance music.

Stuart   Oh fuck –

In unison, the panel members all get up and crab-walk across the stage, stopping here and there, until, finally, the reception returns.

Right-Wing Politician   But is their right to smoke more important than the rights of those who don't?

And then cautiously – so as not to lose reception – they back on to the couch, as one.

Independent Politician   So it's a question of whose rights are more important?

Right-Wing Politician   Exactly.

Independent Politician   Which is exactly the Labour Party's position.

Right-Wing Politician   I was asked what *my* opinion was.

Pundit   A more important question is why should the general public have to pay billions of pounds a year to help cure these wretched individuals of their self-inflicted ailments?

Applause.

Stuart   I'm sorry but the hypocrisy here is absolutely stunning. I mean, they've banned smoking at bus stops!

Pundit   I should think so.

Stuart   All right, well, tell me this: if cigarettes are *so toxic* that it's dangerous even to *stand near a smoker at a bus-stop* . . . why are we selling them at all? Why not ban them altogether?

Presenter   That's a good point, isn't it, Jan Pearson? Why not ban them altogether?

Left-Wing Politician   Well, that really *would* be an infringement on civil liberties –

Stuart   Oh, what bollocks! If you were concerned about civil liberties you wouldn't have banned the right to demonstrate outside Parliament!

A solitary cheer from the audience.

Thank you. I mean, let's say we suddenly found out that fucking – Pot Noodle – was so horrendously poisonous – that just being in the same *building* as someone eating it was potentially fatal: are you saying we'd keep it on the shelves?

Left-Wing Politician   A slightly different thing.

Stuart   Yes, it is, and we all know why; because the government isn't making £3.50 worth of taxes on every Pot Noodle sold!

Some applause. He gets up and crosses to the fridge to get more milk for his cereal.

All I'm saying is, make your minds up: if smoking's legal, then let people do it. Let the pubs and the restaurants and the workplaces decide whether they allow it or not. But if it's as dangerous as you say it is – and you're genuinely concerned about the health of the nation – then have the guts to ban it outright . . .

Applause. Warming to his theme (and still eating his cereal):

. . . but you won't, will you? Because you don't want everyone to suddenly stop smoking. Because if everyone stopped smoking, they'd have to raise income tax by about two pence in the pound; and the people that'd shout loudest about it are the same wankers that are shouting about having to pay smokers' health bills.

Hitting his stride now, he adopts the manner of a lawyer.

You see, what we have in the smoking ban is an unholy alliance between –

He stands in the spilled cat food. Disgusted, he scrapes it off his bare foot while continuing:

What we have in the smoking ban is an unholy alliance between the hypocritical and the sanctimonious. On the one hand, we've got a government who want the nation to get healthier, but not so suddenly that it jeopardises their chances of re-election. And on the other hand, we've got a society – a post-Thatcherite society – that is so fractured and dysfunctional that the only way a semblance of unity can be preserved is to feed it a constant stream of state-approved scapegoats for us to mutually fear or disdain.

Now to the audience:

In summing up, I can put it no better than the famous poem written by some Jewish guy or possibly a German:

When they came for the gays
I did not speak out
Because I was not . . . a gayboy. Or something.

When they came for the fox-hunters
I did not speak out,
Because I was not a toffee-nosed twat on a horse,
    with a little trumpet.

When they came for the smokers
I did not speak out –
Because I was not a yellow-fingered ashtray weasel.

But then they came for me.
And there was no one left to speak out.

And with this, **Stuart** *passes his empty cereal bowl to the* **Right-Wing Politician** *and makes his way to the bed.*

A stunned pause and then, one by one, the panellists begin to clap, and the audience begins to clap, and then the panellists stand, and so does the audience. The response is tumultuous.

Right-Wing Politician   Who was that man?

Pundit   I don't know, but he's turned my head around, I'll tell you that!

Independent Politician   He's turned everyone's head around!

The **Presenter** *attempts to get the audience to calm down.*

Presenter   All right, thank you, ladies and gentlemen, can we – ?

But now there is a thumping of chairs.

No please – please put down the furniture –

At this point, someone from the audience rushes up to the stage and throws a chair at the **Presenter**.

Audience Member   Fascist bastards!

The chair just misses her. The **Audience Member** *runs out of the doors.*

Presenter   Ladies and gentlemen, please stay calm! Please, no smoking, please – please don't light those – don't light that cigarette!

Smoke begins to curl onto the stage. The panellists begin to cough and splutter.

(*To panellists.*) I think we should go. (*To the audience.*) Ladies and gentlemen – listeners at home – I'm afraid we have no choice but to abandon this week's *Any Questions* due to a stunningly lucid intervention from a member of the public!

Left-Wing Politician (*into mobile*)   Get me the Prime Minister. (*Pause.*) I don't care about that – get him on the phone right now!

Pundit   Keep to the floor where there's air!

They drop to the floor and start to crawl away, a riot occurring in the audience.

Presenter   Next week we'll be in Stevenage – so if you want tickets for that visit our website or call us on 0800-777-444 –

*A fireman enters (the actor playing **Mullet**), his torchlight casting a beam through the smoke.*

Mullet   We've got to go now!

*He lifts the **Presenter** over his shoulder and carries her out.*

Presenter   And don't forget *Any Answers* after the break –

She is taken away.

*Through the smoke, **Stuart** is illuminated, sitting cross-legged on the end of his bed. His pot belly makes him look like Buddha.*

The sounds of the audience riot fade.

As the smoke clears, he stands and walks to the front of the stage.

He peers out at the audience, as if looking in a mirror.

***Stuart** says only a few of the following statements out loud. The rest are played on tape, creating a collage of sound. During this, **Angie** crosses the stage at the back in her dressing gown, towelling her hair; and the **Right-Wing Politician** takes her clothes off – she is wearing a nightdress underneath, and now becomes **Laura**.*

Stuart   It's me.
It's Stuart.
It's me again.
I know you're ignoring me.
I know you don't want to speak to me.
I need to speak to you.
I've got some things of yours.
You've got some things of mine.
You should come and get them.
I should come and collect them.
Please call me.

Will you call me?
As soon as you get this.
When you've got the time.
Today if possible.
I'll be in.
Or try my mobile.
But we need to talk.
I'd like to talk.
It'd be good to talk.
I miss you.
I love you.
I made a mistake.
It won't take long.
It's really urgent.
Please.
Please call me.

The smoke clears to reveal **Laura**, *sitting on the toilet.*

Four

[**Stuart** *lies in bed thinking. He tries to masturbate. He hears an ice-cream van outside and contemplates buying one; instead he opens some mail. It is a bill for the council tax. He makes up a little song. He takes a shit. He takes a shower.*]

Stuart   What are you doing?

Laura   What does it look like I'm doing?

Stuart   Number twos?

Laura   No.

Stuart   Number threes?

Laura   What's number threes?

Stuart   Both.

Laura   No, just number ones.

Pause.

Get out then.

Stuart   Why?

Laura   What do you mean, why? Cos I can't pee with you . . . standing there.

Stuart   Why not?

Laura   Cos I just can't. I can't pee with anyone in the room.

Stuart   Try.

Laura   No!

Stuart (*mimics*)   'No!'

Laura   Stuart . . .

Stuart   Do you not love me?

Laura   Yes. What's that got to do with it?

Stuart   'What's love got to do, got to do with it?'

Laura   'What's love but a second-hand emotion?'

Stuart   Do you not trust me?

Laura   Yes. Sort of.

Stuart   Sort of?

Laura   Look, it doesn't matter if I trust you or not, I still can't do the toilet with you sitting there! I can't even do it with my sister in the room.

Stuart   There's lots of stuff you do with me that you wouldn't do with your sister. Well – outside of my masturbatory fantasies.

Laura   You're disgusting. Do you really think about that?

Stuart   What?

Laura   About me doing things with my sister?

Stuart *shrugs.*

Laura   What sort of things?

Stuart   Just being tender and sisterly with each other. Sometimes using a double-ended dildo.

Laura   That's disgusting. You're a dirty old perv.

Pause. He's not leaving.

Please – I'm really desperate.

Stuart   Can't be that desperate.

Pause.

Two people that love each other – they should be able to pee in the same room.

Laura   See that's where we differ. I don't think peeing has anything to do with love.

Stuart   I don't want you to piss on my face. I just want you to pee with me here in the room.

Laura   But why, though?

Stuart   I don't know. Because it's something you've never done with anyone else.

Pause.

Laura   I don't think I can.

Stuart   Try.

Pause. He makes a peeing sound.

Laura   I don't think I can.

Stuart   Are you worried you'll fart?

Laura   No!

Stuart   It's all right. Sometimes you need to kick-start the bike. I understand.

Laura   I'm not worried I'm going to fart!

Pause.

Stuart   Just think of cool, clear water. Flowing. A rushing brook. Niagara Falls. Waves crashing against the pier.

She tries. Pause. A trickle.

Oh – something's happening . . .

Pause. He puts his hand between her legs.

Laura   No, it'll stop.

Stuart   I just want to feel it.

Pause.

I love everything that comes out of you.

He starts to touch her. She hugs him.

Enter **Angie**.

Angie   What's going on here then?

Music. Bad porn music.

They stop, startled. **Laura** *is still aroused.*

Angie   You don't have a fucking clue what you're doing. Get out of the way.

She pushes **Stuart** *aside and thrusts her hand between* **Laura**'*s legs.*

Angie   I'll show you how the little bitch likes it.

Laura *starts to breathe heavily. She clings on to* **Angie**.

Angie   That's it, you little slut. You like that?

Someone in the bed starts to masturbate.

This is how to do it.

Laura   Oh yes, oh yes, that's it – oh finger me, finger me.

Angie (*to* **Stuart**)   Do something useful with yourself and spank my fucking arse.

Stuart *starts to spank* **Angie**'*s arse.*

Angie   That's it – spank my big fucking arse!

Mother *appears.*

Mother   Does this dress look terrible on me?

Laura   Oh God, that's so good – oh finger me!

Mother   I've got a bum like a baby elephant.

Stuart (*to* **Mother**)   Go away!

Angie   Spank my big fucking arse!

Mother   It wobbles like a big bloody jelly.

Stuart (*and the bed-wanker simultaneously*)   Go away!

Laura   Oh that's it, that's it, just there –

Angie   Spank me harder, you fucking bastard!

Mother   What do you want for your Christmas?

Laura   Oh God, that's good – rub my little cunt!

Mother   I've got a bum like a baby elephant's.

Mother *slaps her bottom. The rhythm falls into time with* **Stuart**'s *spanking of* **Angie**.

Angie   Spank my big elephant bum!

Laura   What do you want for your Christmas?

Mother   What do you want for your Christmas?

Angie   What do you want for your Christmas, then?

Furious, **Stuart** *gives up. Simultaneously, the girls go limp like dolls and* **Stuart**'s *'double' swings up, out of the bed, to sit on its edge.*

Stuart (*to* **Mother**)   Will you stop going on about your arse?! I don't want to think about your arse! It makes me want to vomit! I don't go on to you about my fucking balls, do I?! How would you like that?!

Pause. He sits on the end of the bed, mirrored in posture by his double.

Pause.

I'm sorry.

Mother   It's all right.

Pause.

Stuart   You know that aftershave stuff you bought me?

Mother   The stuff you said was cheap shite?

Stuart   I know, I know, but listen: I've still got it. And you know, if there was a fire, I wouldn't save my CDs first or my iPod or anything; the first thing I'd save would be that aftershave.

Mother   Don't be silly. If there's a fire you just get on with saving yourself.

Stuart   Well, obviously, yes, but – I'm trying to tell you something. I'm trying to tell you what it means to me.

Pause.

It's funny that, isn't it? Of all the really nice things you gave me – it's the cheap shite that means the most.

Pause.

Will *you* tell her to call me?

Pause. The sound of an ice-cream van. **Laura** *leaves.* **Angie** *bends over the toilet and vomits.* **Stuart** *kneels beside her, rubbing her back.* **Mullet** *bursts in.*

Mullet   Ice cream, ice cream, we all scream for ice scream!

Stuart   Too old for ice cream.

Mullet   What then?

Stuart   Don't know. Sorbet?

Mullet   Fucking sorbet! You're such an old wank! I'll bet you're even starting to like ready-salted!

Stuart   I am, actually.

Mullet   Come on – let's get some ice cream! A 99. Or a push-up.

Stuart   They probably don't have any ice cream. It's probably just smack.

Mullet   Get some of that then.

Stuart   I'll become an addict.

Mullet   So?

Stuart   So then we'll have to live in rubble. You wouldn't like that, would you?

Mullet   You're so boring and fat and emotionally stunted! Go and see if the post's here.

Stuart *looks at his watch.*

Stuart   Fucking should be.

Mullet   Go on then!

Stuart   It'll just be bills.

Mullet   It might not be. It might be a birthday card.

Stuart   It's not my birthday.

Mullet   So?

Pause. They exit, in a kind of synchronicity.

A light breeze blows sand across the stage. The light bulbs sway.

Stuart *enters, opening a bill.*

He stops, and reads it.

Stuart   What the fuck . . . ?

Pause.

I fucking paid that!

He throws it in the bin and puts the kettle on again. Pause.

What a bunch of cunts.

As he waits for the kettle to boil, he repeats the phrase, singing it to himself.

What a bunch of cunts, what a bunch of cunts . . .
What a bunch of cunts, what a bunch of cunts . . .

Music begins. He sings along, the orchestration becoming more elaborate.

Behind him, female dancers appear.

He becomes involved in a song-and-dance number. The lyrics consist only of the words 'What a bunch of cunts' and sometimes 'What a bunch of fucking cunts' for variety's sake.

Male dancers join in − they are blacked-up, like Al Jolson.

[*Note: those of us who grew up in Britain in the seventies were treated, on Saturday nights, to a spectacularly incorrect show called* The Black and White Minstrel Show, *which featured white singers blacked up. The point of this and the following small section might be lost in more enlightened times and locations, and can easily be substituted or omitted. But it should not be omitted on the grounds of offensiveness alone.*]

The song reaches a finale, then ends. Only then does **Stuart** *see the blacked-up male dancers.*

Stuart   What the fuck is this?

Minstrel 1   What?

Stuart   The blacking-up?

Minstrel 1   What about it?

Stuart   What *about* it?

Minstrel 2   We're the Black and White Minstrels.

Stuart   I know who you are. It's a bit fucking racist, isn't it?

Minstrel 3   It was your idea.

Stuart   It wasn't *my* idea.

Minstrel 1   Whose idea was it then?

Minstrel 2   It wasn't fucking mine, that's for sure – I feel a right twat.

Minstrel 3   Me too.

Stuart   It was whoever thought up *The Black and White Minstrels.*

Minstrel 1   Yeah, but you liked it.

Stuart   I didn't like it – it was just on.

Pause.

Right, well, just – fuck off, the lot of you.

Minstrel 2   Don't fucking worry.

Minstrel 1   It *was* your idea.

They leave. **Stuart** *pulls his trousers down and sits on the toilet.*

Stuart   It was just on.

Pause.

Yes, it was a big surprise to me. I'd always thought that you split up with someone because you'd stopped loving them, or realised you never did. But actually none of my relationships – my serious relationships – have ended that way. I've always loved them. There's been some other issue: a different outlook, a different dream; sometimes just practicalities. Nothing you wouldn't love someone for. Just things you can't live with peacefully. But I've felt the loss of every one of them, like a little death. It gets quite tiring after a while, the accumulation of losses.

He wipes his backside and looks at the toilet paper.

The accumulated losses. The accumulated losses of life.

Pause.

My next record? My next record is that one that's got the bit that goes 'I think I love you' that Angie used to play. If you're listening, Angie, please call. You said you'd fucking call.

[Note: this is a reference to the radio programme Desert Island Discs, *in which famous people choose their favourite records. In the original production, this scene ended with a repetitive sample of that one line 'I think I love you', taken from the song 'Take the Box' by Amy Winehouse, but this can be substituted. The point being that we often fixate on one line from a song. The sample then segued into a musical composition which served as the bridge between acts.]*

Music.

Above **Stuart***, a shower unit comes on and he is sprayed with water as he sits there. He turns his face up to it, letting it clean him.*

Lights fade.

Act Two: Afternoon

[**Stuart** *washes his clothes. He is insulted by a telesales call.*]

Stuart, *now dressed, enters with a basket full of dirty washing.*

Stuart (*singing*)
   What a bunch of cunts, what a bunch of cunts . . .

He opens the door of the washing machine and starts bundling the clothes in; but, from inside the machine, he hears his **Mother**'*s voice:*

Mother (*muffled*)   Have you checked the pockets?

Stuart   What?

Mother (*muffled*)   Have you looked in the pockets?

He removes some of the washing.

Stuart   What are you saying?

Mother   I said, have you checked the pockets of your trousers?

Stuart   Yes . . .

Mother   Are you sure?

Stuart   There's nothing in the pockets.

Mother   Because you know what happened to those tickets.

Stuart *sighs.*

Mother   Why don't you check? Better safe than sorry.

Stuart (*exasperated*)   Right, I'll check the fucking trousers.

Mother   There's no need for language.

Stuart (*fondly*)   There's no need for language.

He drags out a pair of trousers and checks the pockets. He finds something.

Mother   What's that? Is that your bus pass?

Stuart   No.

Mother   So much for checking the pockets. Honestly, I think you'd –

Stuart *bundles the washing back in.*

Mother (*muffled*)   – forget your own head if you didn't –

Stuart   Yes, thank you, Mother.

He shuts the door. He empties powder into the tray, not sure how much to add. He sings a jingle from a washing-powder commercial:

'Washing machines live longer with Calgon.'

He crouches down to look at the settings.

What the fuck is a pre-wash? I never do a pre-wash. Maybe I should do a pre-wash?

Pause. He opens the door of the washing machine.

Mum – should I do a pre-wash?

A long pause. There is no answer. Of course not. He closes the door and turns the machine on. It trickles into life.

He looks in the basket. There's a sock in there.

Shit!

He tries to open the door but it's too late.

Exasperated, he takes the sock . . .

Right – you're going in the fucking bin!

. . . and throws it in the pedal bin.

He returns to the machine, watches it turn. The sound of the clothes sloshing.

Bored, he puts the basket on his head and clutches the slats as if they're the bars of a prison cell.

You've got to get me out of here!

This amuses him for a moment.

The sound of the machine gets louder and louder and more hypnotic. It reaches a crescendo and then stops.

The phone rings.

Stuart   Hello?!

Salesman   Is that Mr McWary?

Stuart   Mr McQuarrie.

Salesman   Oh, I beg your pardon – Mr McQuarrie: and can I just confirm with you that this is your home number?

Stuart   Yes, obviously.

Salesman   And is this a BT line, Mr McQuarrie?

Stuart   Yes.

Salesman   And if I was to tell you that you I could save you up to a hundred pounds a year on your phone bill, would that be of interest to you?

Stuart   Em – not really, no.

Salesman   I see. And what if I was to tell you that you could also enjoy over twenty extra channels of television at no extra cost – would that be of interest to you?

Stuart   No, it wouldn't, but thanks – (for asking).

Salesman   And you would also be able to enjoy free broadband at speeds of up to 8 MB depending on your area.

Stuart   I'm sorry, but I'm really not interested. And I'm actually not that keen on being – (phoned at home).

Salesman   Because all that can be yours with Teleport's Essentials package at an introductory price of just £13.99 a month for the first three months.

Stuart   Right, well, you don't seem to be listening to me, but I'm really not interested, I'm sorry.

Pause.

Salesman You're not interested?

Stuart Sorry, no.

A pause, and then the **Salesman** *hangs up.*

Stuart Hello?

Nothing.

Fucking cheeky bastard!

Mullet *appears from under the bedding.*

Mullet You are one totally pathetic fucking loser!

Stuart What?

Mullet That guy just made an absolute cunt of you.

Stuart I know he did!

Mullet He made a fucking tit of you in your own house.

Stuart I know!

Mullet And you just let it happen.

Stuart Well, what was I supposed to do? I said I wasn't interested – I was trying to be polite.

Mullet Exactly. He basically said, 'I'm going to fuck you up the arse,' and you said, 'Yes, sir,' and spread your fat arse-cheeks.

Stuart Cheeky fucking bastard!

Mullet So what are you going to do about it?

The phone rings.

Stuart Hello?

Salesman Hello, is that Mr McWary?

Mullet *urges him on.*

Stuart   If by Mr McWary you mean Mr McQuarrie, then yes.

Mullet *is disgusted with him.*

Salesman   Oh, I beg your pardon – Mr McQuarrie: and can I just confirm with you that this is your – (home number)?

Mullet   Is that it?

Stuart   Eh?

Mullet   'If by Mr McWary you mean Mr McQuarrie' – is that all you're worried about? That he got your name wrong?

Stuart   I was just starting.

Mullet   You still said yes though, didn't you?

Stuart   What am I supposed to say?

Mullet   Tell the cunt to fuck off!

The phone rings.

Stuart   Hello?

Salesman   Hello, is that Mr McWary?

Stuart   No, it fucking isn't!

Stuart *looks at* **Mullet**.

Salesman   Oh – I'm sorry –

Mullet   Tell him to fuck off!

Stuart   Fuck off!

Pause. They seem pleased with themselves.

Salesman   Hello?

Stuart   He's still there!

Mullet   Give it to the cunt!

Stuart   Give him what?

Mullet   It's a Saturday afternoon, for fuck's sake!

Stuart   It's a Saturday afternoon, for fuck's sake!

Mullet *nods.*

Stuart   Would you like me phoning you on a Saturday
afternoon?

Pause.

No, I didn't think so; and I don't want any more shit TV
channels so fuck off and don't call me again!

The phone hangs up.

That told him.

Mullet   Yeah, but he still hung up on *you*. He's still got the
power. He's phoned you up at your house, on your day off,
and he's made you feel angry and bad.

Stuart   What can I do about it?

Mullet   Make *him* regret calling *you*. Spoil *his* fucking day!

Pause.

Stuart   All right.

The phone rings.

Hello?

Salesman   Hello, is that Mr McWary?

Stuart   No, it's Mr McQuarrie.

Mullet *is annoyed with him. But* **Stuart** *indicates to wait.*

Salesman   Oh, I beg your pardon – Mr McQuarrie. And
could you just confirm that this is your home number?

Stuart   Yes it is. But listen – are you calling from
Teleport?

Pause.

Salesman Yes, I am.

Stuart Oh good, I was hoping you'd call.

Pause.

Salesman Were you?

Stuart Yes, and listen, I'm very interested in your product but would you mind calling back in about ten minutes? It's just that I'm wanking at the moment.

Salesman I'm sorry?

Stuart I said I'm wanking at the moment – but I should have come in about five minutes so if you could call back then, that'd be perfect.

Mullet *is delighted.*

Salesman Oh – right . . .

Stuart I mean, unless you'd like to stay on the line and talk me through it, you know – say something like, 'Ooh yes, ooh yes, wank it,' over and over again. Would that interest you at all, you little fucking maggot?

Pause.

I'm asking you a question, you subhuman piece of shit – would that interest you?

Salesman No, sir – it wouldn't.

Stuart Right – well, then, *you* can fuck off!

The phone goes dead. They are triumphant. They run around whooping in triumph.

Mullet That was fucking great!

Stuart He'll think twice about doing that again.

Mullet God, you were quite vicious there. 'Subhuman piece of shit'?

Stuart   Well, I'll take abuse up to a certain point –

Mullet   Yeah, but there's a line.

Stuart   But there's a line, and if you cross it – doesn't matter who you are –

Mother   Stuart!

They both jump out of their skins.

Mother   Stuart McQuarrie! What do you think you're playing at?!

Stuart   What?

Mother   Don't 'what' me! I heard the filth you were saying! What was the meaning of it?

Stuart   I didn't start it.

Mother   Who did then?

Stuart   The guy on the phone – he called me up, out of the blue –

Mother   I know what he did. I don't remember him saying any filth to you.

Stuart   No, well, he didn't; but when I said I wasn't interested, he just hung up on me. Which was pretty bloody rude.

She slaps him round the head.

Mother   There's no need for language!

Stuart   You shouldn't hit people on the head, it gives them brain damage.

Mother   I'll brain damage you.

Pause.

So he hung up on you. Which was rude . . .

Stuart   So I decided to be rude back.

Mother   Oh, the Big Man, is it? The Head Cheese.

Mullet *smirks.*

Mother   Making someone feel small over the phone.

Stuart   He hung up on me.

Mother   Did he? Are you sure that's what happened? Let's ask him, shall we?

Stuart   Ask him?

Mother   Yes – because he's here. Simon?!

She looks offstage.

Come and give him a hand.

Stuart *and* **Mullet** *look at* **Simon** *– who we cannot yet see – and then at each other.*

Mother   Come on then.

She nods them in an offstage direction. **Stuart** *makes* **Mullet** *acompany him. They exit.*

Muffled sounds of effort offstage.

They return with **Simon**. *He's in a wheelchair, attached to an IV drip.* **Mother** *helps bring him onstage. One of* **Simon***'s arms is tiny and malformed.*

Mother   Simon, this – I'm ashamed to say – is my son. Stuart – this is the man you called subhuman.

Simon   Hello.

He extends his small hand. **Stuart** *and* **Mullet** *shake it.*

Stuart   Hello.

Mullet   Hi.

Simultaneously:

Simon   Why don't you –

Mother   Listen, I just –

Simon   Sorry –

Mother   No, you go ahead.

Simon   I just wanted to say that it's really all right. I completely understand – we get enough adverts thrown at us without people calling you up at home and trying to sell things. Believe me, I feel embarrassed every time I call someone. It's just that, obviously, given my condition, you know – playing for England was never an option.

Stuart   Oh, I don't know . . .

Mother   Stuart!

Stuart   Oh well, look – I'm sorry that you're disabled and all that and obviously I feel a bit bad. But it doesn't change the fact that as soon as I said I wasn't interested, you just hung up on me; and that's just rude, whatever . . . condition you're in.

Mother   Oh, and you're such a big know-it-all, aren't you? The Big I-Am. Well, tell him, Simon.

Simon   Oh really, it's all right. He wasn't to know.

Pause.

Stuart   Wasn't to know what?

Mother   It just so happens, Mr Smarty-Pants, that Simon didn't hang up on you; he actually had a seizure.

Pause.

Simon   I felt it coming on during the conversation. I'd have said goodbye but my jaw sort of locks, so I can't speak.

Pause.

Mother   Thank you, Simon.

Pause.

I hope you're proud of yourself, Stuart McQuarrie. Maybe you'll not be so quick to judge in future.

She wheels him offstage.

Stuart *and* **Mullet** *are left there, in their shame.*

The sound of the washing machine turning.

Mullet *sits by it and puts the basket on his head, as* **Stuart** *had earlier.*

Stuart *makes his way back to the couch.*

Pause.

The **Cat** *ambles slowly in.*

Stuart   Ah, here he is. Where have you been all night? Chasing all the girl cats I bet.

Cat   Fuck you.

The **Cat** *walks straight to the bowl of cat food and smells it.*

Cat   Muck.

And with this, he turns and walks slowly out again.

Stuart *tries to stroke him as he passes, but the* **Cat** *shrugs him off.*

Angie *enters. She's trying on clothes for an evening out.*

Angie   What's wrong with Galloway?

Stuart   He's spoiled.

Angie   Well, if he's spoiled it's because you spoiled him.

Stuart   I don't spoil him. They must have been feeding him salmon or something.

Angie   At a rescue centre? I doubt it. Anyway, don't change the subject.

Stuart   What was the subject?

Angie   You being a homophobe.

Pause.

Pleading the Fifth, I see.

Stuart   I don't care if you think I'm a homophobe. I know I'm not.

Angie   But being gay revolts you?

Stuart   I didn't say being *gay* revolts me.

Angie   What did you say then?

Stuart   I don't care if people are gay. I'm actually in favour of it.

Angie   Why, because it narrows the competition?

Stuart   Exactly. And they're all the best-looking guys as well. Everybody wins.

Angie   You said it revolts you.

Stuart   No, I said that if you're a heterosexual man – regardless of how enlightened you are – you find the thought of, you know –

Angie   What?

Stuart   The thought of coming into direct contact with another man's . . .

Angie   Cock.

Stuart   Yes –

Angie   You can't even say it.

Stuart   Can't even say what?

Angie   Another man's cock.

Stuart   Another man's cock.

Angie   There, you see? Still heterosexual.

She kisses him.

Stuart   You are so fucking annoying, d'you know that?

Angie   And you're a homophobe.

Pause.

And a racist.

Stuart   How am I a fucking racist now?!

Angie   Cos every time you tell me what Mr Rajah's said you put on that stupid accent.

Stuart   That's not being racist.

Angie   It is so . . . 'All reduced – Mr Rajah's all reduced!'

Stuart   That's how he talks!

Angie   You don't have to do the wee shake of the head.

Stuart   So *The Simpsons* is racist, is it?

Angie   Yes.

Pause.

Stuart   I'm not a fucking racist. There's not a racist bone in my body. In fact I go out of my way to not be racist.

Angie   How?

Stuart   Well – if an Asian shopkeeper –

Angie   'An Asian shopkeeper – '

Stuart   Yes – if an Asian shopkeeper gives me change, I always make a point of just making slight contact with his hand.

Angie   What's that supposed to prove?

Stuart   Well, you know – just to make sure he knows I don't think I'll get the Paki touch or something. And – if I get on a bus, and there's an Asian person sitting there –

Angie   Don't tell me – you sit beside them.

Stuart   Yes! Even if there are other seats!

Angie   You are such a fucking wanker, Stuart McQuarrie.

Stuart   Ah, but who's more of a wanker? The wanker, or the wanker that loves the wanker?

Angie *pushes him away.*

Angie   I don't love you.

Pause.

You love me.

Stuart   Yes. I do.

He embraces her. Pause.

Angie   D'you want to shag?

Pause. He looks at his watch.

Stuart   Yeah, all right.

She pulls him down behind the couch. We hear their voices, as they struggle off with their clothes.

Stuart   Can you bum your girlfriend?

Angie   Can I bum my girlfriend?

Stuart   Can *one* bum one's girlfriend? I mean – you hear about men bumming each other but you never hear someone say, 'I bummed my girlfriend.'

Angie   I'll fucking bum you.

Stuart   You'll bum me?

Angie   Will you shut the fuck up?!

We hear the sound of them starting to make love.

Father *enters and stops as he sees them.*

Father   What's going on here?!

Suddenly, from behind the couch, up spring **Stuart** *and* **Laura**, *looking flustered.*

Mullet *suddenly springs into life.*

Mullet   Stewpot, look! Porno!

He waves a tatty old porno mag that he's found.

Stuart · Not now!

Laura *runs out, distressed, clutching her blouse to her chest.*

Stuart *half follows her.*

Stuart   Laura!

Mullet *finds more pornography in the sand.*

Mullet   There's more, look! It's like treasure!

Angie *appears from behind the couch.*

Angie   You dirty bastard!

She storms out.

Stuart   Angie – it's not mine!

Mullet   Look at this!

Stuart *runs to* **Mullet**.

Stuart   I can't just now.

Mullet   But look at the fanny on that!

Stuart   Christ.

Mother (*enters*)   Stuart!

Stuart   I've got to go

Mullet   Later, then.

Stuart   Yeah, later.

Mother   Stuart, get over here now!

Stuart *runs back and sits on the couch, shamefaced.*

Father   Well, I think we have to tell them.

Mother   Oh, shut your silly mouth. We don't have to tell anyone anything.

Father   If it was the other way round, we'd want to know.

Mother   Have you met Laura's parents?

Father   No, but – (that's not the point).

Mother   Then shut your silly mouth, you old jessie.

Father   Don't call me a jessie, Margaret. Not in front of Stuart.

Mother (*mimics*)   'Don't call me a jessie, don't call me a jessie.'

Father   Right, well, you sort it out then; because I give up, I just bloody give up!

He walks out.

Mother   'I just bloody give up.'

Stuart *and his* **Mother** *share a conspiratorial laugh.*

Pause.

Mother   So – what are we going to do with the two of you?

Pause. **Stuart** *shrugs.*

Mother   He may be an old jessie, but you know what they say, even a stopped clock's right twice a day. When we've got Laura under our roof, we've got a duty of care. We've got a responsibility, to make sure she doesn't get up to anything that her parents wouldn't want her getting up to. You know what Jesus said: 'Suffer the little children.'

Stuart *looks confused.*

Mother   What do you think of her?

She pokes at him.

Stuart. Stuart.

Stuart   Who?!

Mother   Don't act the daft laddie. What do you think of Laura?

Pause.

Do you love her?

Pause. He shrugs uncomfortably.

Just a shrug.

Stuart   Aw, Mum!

Mother   Don't 'Aw, Mum' me, it's important. You put your swizzle-stick inside a girl and babies are what's next.

Stuart *groans and puts a cushion over his head.*

Mother   Now don't be such a baby. It's a thing for a girl that age to have a child. She's just a little thing too. She's not got a big fat bum and hips like me. A baby'd rip her from front to back.

Stuart *groans. She prises the cushion away from him.*

Mother   Listen to me, Stuart. You know what Jesus said: 'Respect your mother.'

Stuart   He never said that!

Mother   You weren't there, you don't know. Now listen to me: do you get all excited when you think of her? And I don't mean your swizzle-stick –

Stuart   Stop saying that!

Mother   I mean, down your back, a little shiver. And do you want to say her name over and over? Do you find excuses to say it? Laura Laura Laura!

She teases him.

And do you hug the pillow and pretend it's her?

He throws the cushion aside.

Stuart   No!

Mother   Ah, you see – a picture tells a hundred tales.

Pause.

And is it like all the other girls just disappear? Like they don't exist? Like she's the only girl in the world?

(*Sings.*)
  'If you were the only girl in the world,
   And I was the only boy . . . '

She smiles. Pause.

Well, you listen to me –

He covers his ears. She wrenches the cushion away, so seriously it startles him.

I'm being serious, Stuart, this is important!

Pause.

Don't you pay any mind to what anyone says. There's nothing worse you can do in this world than marry for the sake of appearance. If you feel all those things about a girl, then maybe she's the one. But if you don't, or if you think you might not feel them ten years down the line, then you let her go, no matter how she cries; and do it sooner, not later. Let her be free to find someone who does feel that. You be alone rather than that; rather than fight like cat and dog all your life; rather than die a bit at a time. That's what a real man does for a woman. That's what he does for himself.

Pause.

Don't you settle for less than love, than true love, do you hear me? Don't you settle for less!

Pause.

Laura *enters.*

Mother   Here she is.

Laura *sits on the couch with* **Stuart***.*

Mother   You feeling better?

Laura *nods.*

Laura   I like your mirror.

Mother   Which?

Laura   The big one in the hall.

Mother   That was my mother's. Yes.

Pause.

My mother gave that to me.

Classical music plays, and **Stuart** *lies down to listen to it. With one hand, he half conducts.*

Mother, *bare-footed and parasol in hand, walks across the sand.*

[Note: in the original production, this next scene played out as if on a beach, but the location, in itself, is unimportant and you may wish to change it depending on your stage design.]

Mother *walks around a rock pool. She stares up at the sun.*

Suddenly she becomes unsteady on her feet, totters slightly, and then collapses, face down.

Bystander 1, *who has been talking on his mobile phone, runs to her. He crouches down beside her, unsure what to do.*

Bystander 2 *rushes in, having seen the collapse.*

Bystander 1 *calls for an ambulance.*

Seeing a coastguard, **Bystander 2** *rushes offstage towards him.*

Father *enters, in holiday clothes, carrying a bag of shopping. When he sees his wife collapsed, he drops his shopping and runs to her, but it is too late.*

He cradles her in his arms.

Bystander 2 *returns. Lights fade on this tableau. The music ends. The washing machine churns to a halt.*

Act Three: Night

[**Stuart** *has something to eat. He watches television. He goes to bed.*]

Stuart *looks at his watch.*

He gets up and goes to the fridge, opens it.

He takes out a ready meal.

Laura *enters.*

Laura   Oh Stuart!

Stuart   What?

Laura   What's that?

Stuart   It's a prawn curry thing.

Laura *is disapproving.*

Stuart   What?

Laura   I'll bet it's full of E-numbers.

Stuart   What's wrong with E-numbers?

Laura   They're bad for you.

Stuart   Everything's bad for you.

Stuart *pierces the film, puts the meal in the microwave and starts it cooking.*

Laura   You shouldn't use microwaves either. They make you infertile.

Stuart   Good. Won't have to bother with johnnies.

Laura   Don't say good. What if we want to have children?

Stuart   Laura, for fuck's sake – will you get off my back? If you want to go out with a leaf-eating, non-smoking, rice-eating wank then do it. But stop trying to turn me into one.

Pause.

Laura   I'm just saying it because I don't want you to die.

Stuart   Awww.

Laura   Who'll look after all the animals if you die?

Stuart   Oh I don't *know* . . .

Laura   Oh, oh – I've thought of another one! Koala bears! We've got to have some koala bears!

Stuart   Aren't they vicious?

Laura   Koala bears? They're lovely!

Stuart   I stand corrected.

Laura   But we'll have to grow eucalyptus trees because that's all they eat.

Stuart   Yeah, well – we're growing bamboo for the pandas anyway.

Laura   I think we'll have to build another biosphere, just for plants.

Stuart   This started out as a small farmhouse in France and now it's like Blofeld's fucking secret complex. Who's going to pay for all this?

Laura   I am!

Stuart   You are? Because it's going to cost about a billion pounds.

Laura   Yeah, well, it's a dream house. You can't put a price on a dream house!

She exits.

Stuart   You can't put a price on a dream house . . .

The microwave pings.

Stuart *takes out the meal. He peels back the film, stirs it, then places it back inside.*

He sits on the couch. Only the light from the TV on his face, which is fixed in an inane grin. A high-pitched noise sounds.

The doorbell rings. Lights up again. **Stuart** *looks puzzled.*

The doorbell rings again. He gets up to answer it, leaving the stage.

The light bulbs sway. A breeze shifts the sand. Pause.

Paul *enters, carrying a bag.* **Stuart** *is displeased.*

Paul I know, I know – you said you were doing nothing.

Stuart Yeah, and I sort of meant it.

Paul Yeah, well, there was nothing going on at the Duck. Fucking girlfriends, I'm telling you – they're ruining the world. D'you want to stick these in the fridge?

He hands him some cans of beer. **Stuart** *groans.*

Paul We don't have to drink them all. We'll just have a beer and see how it goes; if you still 'vant to be alone', I'll piss off – Scout's honour.

Stuart *puts them in the fridge.*

Paul *sits on the couch. He unwraps some food.*

Paul I got you some chips.

Stuart I just put something in the microwave.

Paul What?

Stuart A prawn curry.

Paul That'll go with chips. What's this? *Millionaire?*

He opens a can of beer and hands one to **Stuart***, then opens one for himself. They fill their glasses.*

Paul Look at this cunt. He's used a lifeline already and he's not even up to five hundred.

Stuart*, resigned to his fate, sits on the couch beside him.*

Paul D – Jon Pertwee.

Again only the TV light plays on their faces. They stare at the television, with those same inane grins. The same whining sound. It suddenly ends and they return to normality.

Paul   That was shite. It's about time they put that to bed. What's on the other side?

Stuart   Let's just see the headlines.

Again – the light, the grins, the sound. Lights up.

Paul   The Israelis are a deeply misunderstood people.

Stuart   Fuck . . .

Paul   What?

Stuart   I had a dream . . . something to do with Israel . . .

Paul   What's this?

*Once more – the lights, the sound. but only **Stuart** is grinning. **Paul** immediately falls asleep. Lights up. **Paul** wakes.*

Paul   Who did it?

Stuart   The guy with the haircut.

Paul   His mate?

Stuart   Yeah.

Paul   Told you. Shall we partake of another 'tinnie'?

Stuart   Yeah, go on.

Paul   On you go then.

Stuart   Me?

Paul   You're the host.

Stuart   Didn't get much choice in the matter, did I?

Pause. He sighs.

These are nice chips.

*He gets up to go to the fridge. **Paul** watches him intently.*

Stuart   Fuck . . .

Pause.

Paul   What is it?

Pause.

Stuart   I feel really funny.

Pause.

Fuck . . .

He drops to his knees. The chips spill out of his hand across the floor.

Paul, I'm not joking – something's really wrong . . .

He rolls on to his back. **Paul** *gets up to look at him.*

Stuart   Call – an ambulance –

Paul   Can you move?

Stuart   No –

Paul   Try and move your hand.

Pause. Nothing.

Stuart   Oh Jesus – what's happening to me?

Pause. **Paul** *looks around. He takes a cushion from the couch.*

He squats down beside **Stuart***.*

Stuart   Paul –

Paul   Have you got anything to say?

Stuart *can barely even make a sound.*

Paul   Stuart – look at me; have you got anything to say – you *cunt.*

Pause. With great effort:

Stuart   Tell Angie – that I love her. Tell her – I don't know – why I left her – like I did.

Pause. **Paul** *nods.*

He places the cushion over **Stuart**'s *face.*

We hear his muffled shouts for a while, then they fade.

After a while, **Paul** *removes the cushion.*

Breathing heavily, **Paul** *stares down at* **Stuart**'s *corpse.*

The doorbell rings, startling him.

For a moment he doesn't know what to do.

The doorbell rings again.

Paul   There in a minute!

With great effort, he drags **Stuart**'s *body out of sight.*

Mullet *appears, peering over the back of the couch, watching this.*

The doorbell rings again.

Paul *enters, out of breath.*

Paul   Just a moment!

And then he sees **Mullet***. Their eyes meet.* **Paul** *puts his finger to his mouth –* '*Shhhhh.*'

Paul *straightens himself up and goes to answer the door.*

The light bulbs sway.

Voices offstage.

Paul   Angie, hi.

Angie   Hi, Paul. Is Stuart here?

They enter.

Paul   Eh – he's not, actually.

Angie   Where is he?

Paul   I don't know. Is he not with you?

Angie   No, why? Did he say he was seeing me?

Paul   I think so . . .

Angie   No. I was meant to give him a call but I wasn't seeing him. Not as far as I know.

Paul   Oh right. I thought that was what he said.

She looks around the flat. **Paul***, nervous, positions himself in front of where he dragged* **Stuart***'s body.*

Angie   What are you doing here?

Paul   Do you want a beer or something?

Angie   No, I'm all right.

Pause.

What are you doing here?

Paul   We were down the Duck's Arse, you know – earlier. Had a couple of pints and then we were coming back here, but he had to do something – I thought he said he was seeing you, or calling you or something. So he said for me to wait here. I thought that was him.

She nods, obviously suspicious.

Angie   When was this?

Paul   Eight or so. I mean, I tried phoning him but . . .

Their talk fades, to be replaced by music. This is what we would hear them saying (or as much as you need for the moment).

Paul   . . . it always seems to be busy. I don't know, I just assumed maybe he was on the phone to you. To be honest I assumed you were maybe having a bit of a barney. Sorry, but you know how it is. Best not to interfere with these things. So, you know – I just made myself comfortable here, had a few beers, watched the TV, that sort of thing. But I am getting a wee bit worried. It's been a couple of hours now and if he wasn't seeing you, then I don't know who he could have been seeing. It isn't really like him whichever way you look at it.

Angie   No it's not.

Paul   I don't know – what do you think we should do?
Maybe we should go out looking for him. I'm sure there's
some explanation for it. Maybe he met someone. We could
always try the Duck, maybe he's gone back there. I did sort
of foist myself on him. Maybe he had some other plans that
he didn't want to tell me about.

But instead . . .

A spotlight – signifying **Angie***'s point of view – moves across the
floor, highlighting: the two glasses of beer, the two cans, the spilled
chips and then the tracks left in the sand by* **Stuart***'s dragged body.
The spotlight follows the tracks off into the wings.*

Mullet *still watches, silently, from behind the couch.*

The sound returns.

Paul   No, I'm sure there's an explanation for it.

Pause.

Angie (*scared*)   I'll try phoning him.

Paul   I've tried him a few times. There's no answer.

Pause.

Angie   Can't hurt to try again.

Pause.

Paul   Tell you what – let's try down the Duck. We can
give him a call on the way.

He puts his jacket on. Pause.

Angie   All right.

They exit. **Angie** *casts a look backwards as she leaves.*

Pause. The sand shifts again.

*A mobile phone rings: the ringtone is reminiscent of the ice-cream van
heard earlier.*

Mullet *slowly appears from behind the couch. He sits down cross-
legged and starts eating the chips from the floor.*

Music.

From everywhere come the mourners, all moving slowly.

Laura *looks like a grieving supermodel, her movements strangely jerky as she walks to position.*

Stuart's **Father** *enters slowly, in a black suit.*

Stuart's **Mother**, *all in white, descends from the ceiling to come to a stop only feet above the ground.*

The **Cat**, *Galloway, enters, dragging a dead bird.*

They take their positions around the room, forming a bizarre tableau.

The music ends.

Mother   I remember one winter, it had just snowed – this was back when it snowed in winter – I looked out of the window of our house, down into the square, and I saw him in his little school uniform –

Father   He could never keep his shirt-tails in, could he?

Mother   No, that's right. Or his laces done up. But anyway, I looked down and – before he came into the stair – I saw him deliberately rolling in the snow, you know; getting it all over himself. So I'd make a fuss of him when he came in. Give him a nice bowl of home-made soup. I think that was the only thing I cooked that he actually liked.

Pause.

Laura   Yeah, cos I remember when it was snowing; and I think we'd had a bit of an argument. No, I think we'd actually split up; yeah, that's right. And we both spent about a week in misery but not knowing if the other one was bothered. And then one morning I came out of my mum's house to go to school and all this snow had fallen and it was all untouched; except outside my door, and on all the cars, and everywhere, someone had written 'I love you Laura'. Everywhere you could see.

Mother   Stuart?

Laura   He must've got up really early and come over to my house and done it all before I got up.

Mother   He did love you, Laura. I know you had your ups and downs; but he really did. And you, Angie. But I think you've always got a soft spot for the first.

Angie *shrugs, absorbing the veiled insult.*

Father   Well, that must've been the only time he ever got up early. D'you remember – he got into terrible trouble for being late at school?

Mother   Oh dear, yes. What a palaver that was. They had us in, didn't they?

Father   They were going to expel him!

Mother   That's right, they were.

Father   They were going to expel him if he was late just once more. So he came up with this foolproof system – he put a bucket of cold water by his bed. The theory being, when his alarm clock went off, rather than just turning it off and going back to sleep as usual, he would immediately plunge his whole head into this bucket of water. Well – come the morning – off goes the alarm, Stuart bolts awake, rolls over – takes one look at the water, says, 'Not a chance,' and just goes back to sleep again!

Laughter.

Angie   If he had to leave before me in the morning, he'd always put one of my teddy bears in bed beside me, with its little arm over me.

Affectionate nodding. Pause.

Mother   Galloway – you must have a few stories about Stuart?

Pause. Galloway considers it.

Cat   He was a prick.

Pause. **Father** *raises his glass.*

Father   To Stuart.

They raise their glasses.

All   To Stuart.

Music.

Stuart *appears now. They all turn to see him.*

They begin to clap. They applaud him as he walks down to them, his arms open, almost messianic.

He kisses **Angie**.

He shakes his **Father***'s hand and tries, awkwardly, to hug him.*

He hugs his **Mother** *tight.*

He attempts to stroke Galloway, but the **Cat** *swipes him with his claws.*

He high-fives **Mullet**.

Finally, he embraces **Laura**.

Laura *and* **Angie** *remove his clothes until he is as he was at the beginning of the play.*

His **Father** *and* **Mother** *prepare his bed.*

The **Cat** *picks up the dead bird and leaves.*

Stuart *is led up to the bed. His* **Father** *tucks him under the covers. His* **Mother** *kisses his forehead. They exit.*

Mullet *takes one last look at his friend, peaceful in bed now, then leaves.*

The bed slowly lifts up to a vertical position. Over this:

Stuart (*on tape*)
   And now I lay me down to sleep
   I pray the Lord my soul to keep
   And if I die before I wake
   I pray my soul the Lord to take.

Stuart *sleeps, as if we are looking down on him.*

The phone rings. He wakes and answers it. **Angie** *is voice only.*

Stuart   Hello?

Angie   Stuart? It's Angie. Did I wake you?

Stuart   Eh – no, no.

Angie   Are you in bed?

Stuart   Yeah, but I'm awake. I thought you were going to call me.

Angie   I am calling you.

Stuart   I thought you were going to call me earlier.

Pause.

Angie   You wanted to speak to me.

Stuart   Yes, of course –

Pause.

Angie   I don't care about my things. Throw them away if you want.

Pause.

Stuart   That's not what I wanted to say . . .

Angie   What then?

Stuart   Is it a bad time?

Angie   A bad time?

Stuart   You seem in a hurry.

Angie   It's late.

Stuart   Whose fault is that?

Angie   Don't start or I'll hang up.

Stuart   Don't hang up.

Angie   Then say what you've got to say.

Pause.

Stuart   Jesus, Angie – does it have to be like this?

Angie   Like what?

Stuart   Look – I know you won't believe me, Angie. But I love you. I really do.

Pause.

Angie   Stuart . . .

Stuart   And I know, so why did I finish it? But you've got to believe me when I say – I don't know. I truly don't know. There was no reason for it; I'm not seeing anyone else, I wasn't unhappy. I didn't do it because of what's happening now. I did it because – of what would happen in the future.

Pause.

Angie   Why are you telling me this?

Stuart   Because I don't want to live without you.

Pause.

Angie   What does that mean?

Stuart   It means what it means. It means that I love you. That's a precious thing. Do you know how precious that is?

Pause.

I know you're hurt. But let's not throw everything away.

Angie   You're really confusing me.

Pause.

What are you saying? Are you saying you regret it – what?

Long pause.

Stuart   No. I'm not saying I regret it. I think it was the right thing to do, for both of our sakes. But I didn't do it because I don't love you.

Pause.

Why don't we meet up?

Angie   No.

Stuart   Why not?

Angie   You know why not.

Pause.

It's over, Stuart. It has to be.

Pause.

Stuart   We can't even be friends?

Angie   I don't know. Not now.

Stuart   But some day.

Angie   I don't know. Maybe – who knows? But for now – stop calling me. Please. Please, Stuart.

Pause.

I have to go now.

Stuart   Not like this.

Angie   What do you mean?

Stuart   I mean let's not make it a big goodbye. I can't handle it, not just now.

Pause.

Just talk to me for a while. Talk to me like we'll be seeing each other tomorrow.

Pause.

Angie   What do you want me to say?

Stuart   I don't know. Anything.

Pause.

Angie   How's Galloway?

Stuart   He's fine. Surly, as usual.

Pause.

Angie   What did you do today?

Stuart   Today?

Pause.

Fuck all.

The lights by now have faded to black.

Optional Epilogue

*[In the original production, the following happened. Obviously, it was
an expensive sequence and the play will work without it. If it can be
done, it should be, but it may be omitted if there is no reasonable way to
achieve it.]*

A box is flown in.

*When the lights come up, it is revealed as a kitchen. The furniture – the
washing machine, the cooker, the fridge, etc – is exactly the same as
that which was dotted around the set, but is now in its proper place. It
looks very real.*

A door opens and **Stuart** *enters. He then proceeds to make himself,
in real time and with little fuss, a cup of tea. This done, he sits at the
kitchen table.*

Angie *enters, wearing a dressing gown. She takes the washing out of
the washing machine (a stray red sock has caused the whites to come out
pink). Irritated, she leaves.*

Stuart *sits there.*

*The lights come up. The audience gradually realise they are expected to
leave.* **Stuart** *continues drinking his tea.*

Eventually, the theatre empties.

Bola Agbaje

Gone Too Far!

Bola Agbaje was a member of the Young Writers' Programme at the Royal Court Theatre and her first play, *Gone Too Far!*, premiered there in February 2007. The production won a 2008 Olivier Award for Outstanding Achievement in an Affiliate Theatre before transferring to the Royal Court Theatre Downstairs in July 2007. Her other plays for theatre include *Sorry Seems to be the Hardest Word* (Royal Court Tent at Latitude, 2007), *Reap What You Sow* (Young Vic, 2007), *Rivers Run Deep* (Hampstead Theatre, 2007), *Off the Endz* (Rough Cuts, Royal Court, 2008), *Legend of Moremi* (Theatre Royal, Stratford, 2008), *Good Neighbours* (Talawa Unzipped at the Young Vic, 2008) and *Detaining Justice* (Tricycle Theatre, 2009, part of their *Not Black and White* season). She is currently Pearson Playwright in Residence for Paines Plough and is adapting *Gone Too Far!* into a full-length screenplay for the UK Film Council and Poisson Rouge Pictures.

To my brother Ladi Agbaje who sometimes goes too far.
I hope you realise you can *turn back*

Gone Too Far! was first performed in the Royal Court Jerwood Theatre Upstairs, Sloane Square, London on 2 February 2007. The cast was as follows:

Armani	Zawe Ashton
Yemi	Tobi Bakare
Old Lady	Maria Charles
Razer	Ashley Chin
Policeman 2	Phillip Edgerley
Shopkeeper/Policeman 1	Munir Khairdin
Ikudayisi	Tunji Lucas
Flamer	Ricci McLeod
Mum/Paris	Bunmi Mojekwu
Blazer	Marcus Onilude

Director Bijan Sheibani
Designer James Cotterill
Lighting Designer Nicki Brown
Sound Designer Emma Laxton
Choreographer Aline David

Characters

Yemi, *sixteen, black, stubborn, short-tempered, does not understand or speak Yoruba, good-looking*

Ikudayisi, *eighteen, black, has an African accent which he changes to a fake American one when he is around other people, apart from Yemi; he speaks Yoruba*

Mum, *has an African accent and speaks Yoruba*

Shopkeeper, *Muslim Bangladeshi with an accent, wears a headscarf*

Armani, *fifteen, mixed race, speaks fast, with an attitude*

Paris, *sixteen, dark-skinned, pretty, very calm, with a soft-spoken voice*

Old Lady, *old and frail*

Razer, *seventeen, good-looking, dresses well*

Flamer, *seventeen, light-skinned, good-looking, wears the latest fashion, everything brand new*

Blazer, *eighteen, black, tall, well built; his presence shows he is not someone to mess with*

Police Officers 1 *and* **2**, *white, cockney accents*

Scene One

It is mid-afternoon and we are in **Yemi***'s bedroom. It is a small room which is suitable for one but is clearly occupied by two. A single bed with a duvet cover on it and a mattress on the floor with only the sheets take up most of the space. There are suitcases on the floor, opened with clothes hanging out from them, a mixture of traditional African and casual attire. There is a small TV on the floor with a PS2 attached to it.*

Ikudayisi *is squatting up and down, pulling his ears. He is performing some sort of punishment; he has been doing it for a while and looks tired, but does not stop. He is wearing jeans and a T-shirt, which represent a fashion trend a few months behind the current times.* **Yemi***, on the other hand, is kneeling down on the floor playing on his PlayStation; he is better dressed than* **Ikudayisi** *and is up to fashion in the clothing department. He has on the latest hoodie and a fresh pair of white trainers. He does not pay any attention to* **Ikudayisi** *behind him, who tries to glance over his shoulder every time he squats.* **Yemi** *is engrossed in his game.*

Ikudayisi   Can I play when you finish?

Yemi *does not respond.*

Ikudayisi   Oh, don't go that way-oh!

Yemi *looks round and cuts his eye at him.*

Ikudayisi   Is it games you are supposed to be doing or your punishment?

Yemi *remains silent.*

Ikudayisi   It's not fair-oh!

Yemi *still remains silent and continues to focus on his games.*

Ikudayisi   If you don't start doing your own I will tell Mum.

Yemi   LEAVE ME!

Mum *shouts from offstage.*

Mum *(off)*   Yemi. Is that your voice I'm hearing? Ahh ahh. Is that what I told you to be doing?

Yemi *jumps up from his game and begins his punishment.*

Yemi   It wasn't me, Mum!

Mum (*off*)   You better not be playing games up there. If I catch you . . . Ah! / You will not know yourself-oh!

Yemi   I'm not doing anything.

He starts to pack the games away quickly, and goes back to squatting like **Ikudayisi**. **Mum** *continues her rant from offstage; she is moving around so the volume goes up and down.*

Mum (*off*)   You these children, you these children, you are trying to kill me but I won't let you. Before I go from this earth I will show you pepper. People are always telling me I am lucky to have big boys like you. They don't know-oh, they don't know. You don't do nothing for me. You don't cook, you don't clean. All you do is give me problems. If I have to come up that stairs today . . .

The phone rings and she answers in a very English voice.

Hello. Oh yes, yes. Don't worry, I will be bringing it tomorrow . . .

Her voice trails off.

Yemi   You're such an idiot.

Ikudayisi   What level was you on?

Yemi   Don't talk to me, man.

Ikudayisi   Did you save it?

Yemi   Stop talking to me.

They continue their punishment in silent, **Yemi** *struggling more than* **Ikudayisi**.

Ikudayisi   Do you know the punishment you are doing, it is not the one she told you to do.

Yemi   Don't talk to me, man. Can't you just shut your mouth?

Mum (*off*)   Ah ah! Yemi, Oluyemi, is that you again. Do you want me to come up there today? If I have to walk up these stairs . . .

Yemi *moves to the floor to continue his punishment – left hand stretched out, with his right leg up in the air and his right hand behind his back.*

Mum (*off*)   . . . you will not like the side of me that you will see.

Yemi   It wasn't me, Mum, it was him that keeps on talking – he is tryna get me in trouble.

Ikudayisi   *Ma, mi o se nkon kon* – [Mum, I'm not doing anything –]

Mum (*off*)   IKUDAYISI!

Ikudayisi   Yes, Ma?

Mum (*off*)   *Wa bi baiyi.* [Come here.]

Ikudayisi   *Ma, mi o se nkon kon.* [Mum, I'm not doing anything.]

Mum (*off*)   *A bi ori ko pe ni?* [Is your head not correct?]

Ikudayisi   *Mon bo, Ma.* [I'm coming, Mum.]

Yemi   GOOD!

Ikudayisi *exits.*

Yemi *continues to do his punishment, but only for a little while. He looks at the door, waits for a sound and, when he does not hear anything, goes back to his computer game. As he is about to start playing,* **Mum** *calls him again.*

Mum (*off*)   YEMI OLUYEMI!

Yemi *jumps back to his punishment position.*

Yemi   Yes, Mum! Whatever he said he is lying. I'm still doing it. He is just tryna get me in trouble.

Mum (*off*)   Yemi, Yemi, I said come here.

Yemi   Mum, yeah, you told me do something, I'm doing it.

Mum (*off*)   Are you OK? Ah ah, nonsense. Is it me that you are talking to like dat? If I have to come up that stairs –

Yemi   AHHHH, MAN!

Yemi *leaves the room as* **Ikudayisi** *returns and barges into him on the way out.* **Mum** *is still ranting and raving.* **Ikudayisi** *picks up* **Yemi***'s computer game and starts playing.*

Mum (*off*)   – you have no respect. It not your fault, it not your fault. It's my own, I have spoilt you too much. When I should have taken you to Nigeria, to boarding school, I let you stay here and now look at you.

Yemi *and* **Mum** *continue their conversation offstage while* **Ikudayisi** *plays on the computer game, listening.*

Yemi   Yes, Mum.

Mum   You and your brother go to the shop for me.

Yemi   What? Why can't Dayisi go alone?

Mum   Don't start that nonsense with me. Don't start.

Yemi   But Mum, why don't he go?

Mum   He does not know de way.

Yemi   The shop is only round the corner.

Mum   You are going with your brother and that is final.

Yemi   But Mum, man!

Mum   Who are you calling man? Shut up, shut up your mouth. You listen up and you listen well. When I tell you to do something you do it. Don't ask me no silly questions. He is going to the shop with you and I don't want no trouble.

She shouts for **Ikudayisi***.*

Mum   Ikudayisi! Ikudayisi!

Ikudayisi   Ma?

Mum   *Mo fe ki ewo ati Yemi lo si shop fumi.* [I want you and Yemi to go to the shop for me.]

Ikudayisi   Yes, Ma.

He starts putting on his shoes, but then sees some Nike Air trainers in a box on **Yemi***'s side of the room and picks them up. He puts on the trainers and start profiling in front of a mirror.*

Ikudayisi (*to himself*)   Hey, fine boy. Cool guy!

He does a bit of breakdancing. **Yemi** *and* **Mum** *continue to talk offstage.*

Yemi   MUM! I don't want him to go with me. I will go by myself.

Mum   Yemi, don't start-oh, don't start. Do you think I'm stupid, do you think I'm stupid? When I send you by yourself, you will just go and galavant on the street. I said he is going with you. He is going! Always you, always you, giving me problems. I'm too young to die-oh. You better go and buy me milk now, and you better come back quick quick.

Yemi   OK!

Mum   It is always you. Always you giving me high blood pressure. I will kill you before you kill me. I will kill you!

Yemi   OK, OK! I'm going.

Blackout.

Scene Two

Yemi *and* **Ikudayisi** *walk out onto the estate. It is run-down, with graffiti all over the walls. It is the scene of a typical south London estate with rows of flats. The shop is at the far end of the stage and the* **Shopkeeper** *is outside putting up a newspaper stand. There is Islamic music playing loudly from inside the shop and he is singing along to it. He is wearing an England shirt and a headscarf. There are also England flags hanging all around the shop. He immediately notices the* *boys and hovers around the door watching them closely.* **Yemi** *has his hood over his head.*

Ikudayisi   How much did she give you?

Yemi   Don't talk to me.

Ikudayisi   If there is money left I want to buy chocolate.

Yemi *ignores him and bops ahead towards the shop. As soon as they get to the door, the* **Shopkeeper** *stands in the way.* **Yemi** *tries to walk past him, but he refuses to move away from the door.*

Yemi   Scuse, boss.

The **Shopkeeper** *clears his throat and points to the hood.*

Shopkeeper   No hoods.

Yemi   Uhhh.

He attempts to get past again but fails.

Can you move out of the way?

Shopkeeper   Sorry, no hoods.

Yemi   I wanna buy something dough.

Shopkeeper   I said no hoods allowed.

Yemi   And who are you?

Shopkeeper   My shop, my rule.

Yemi   Come out the way, I need to buy somink.

Shopkeeper   Take off hood and you can enter.

Yemi   This ain't Tesco, you nah.

Ikudayisi   Yo bro, why don't you just take off the hood, man, it will save a lotta trouble.

Shopkeeper   Yes, listen to friend.

Yemi, *stunned by the accent, turns and looks at* **Ikudayisi**, *puzzled.*

Yemi (*to* **Shopkeeper**)   Be quiet. (*To* **Ikudayisi**.) What's with the accent?

Ikudayisi   What accent, man?

Yemi   That one! You need to lauw dat, man, cos it don't sound good. We're not in America, we're in England!

He looks down and sees his trainers on **Ikudayisi**.

Yemi   What are you doing with my trainers on?

Ikudayisi   I'm borrowing them. Don't you think it looks nice on me?

Yemi   No, it don't suit you.

Ikudayisi   You know I look fine, fine.

Yemi   Look, yeah, what have I told you bout taking my stuff?

Ikudayisi   What's your problem? You can have it back when we get home.

Yemi   Just *don't* touch my stuff. Goss, man, do I need to start putting a padlock on my shit?

Bored by the conversation, the **Shopkeeper** *starts to go inside, and* **Yemi** *tries to follow. The* **Shopkeeper** *puts his hand in* **Yemi**'s *face to stop him.*

Shopkeeper   Still have hood.

Yemi   I ain't ere to teef nothing. I just need to buy somink. So *move*, man!

Shopkeeper   I don't want trouble.

Yemi   And no one ain't looking for trouble, boss. Just let me in.

Shopkeeper   Please, I don't want to call police.

Yemi   What! You're making me mad now. Why are you talking bout police for? We only here to buy something, you get me?

Ikudayisi   He doesn't get you, he not moving.

Yemi   Shut up! I'm not talking to you! Just stand over there, man.

Ikudayisi *moves to the side and watches* **Yemi**.

Yemi   Boss, stop the long ting and let me in.

Shopkeeper   Take off hood.

Yemi   Just move!

Shopkeeper   Please, no trouble.

Yemi   Don't you know nothing about human rights? You of all people should understand where I'm coming from – being a Muslim and dat.

Shopkeeper   Are you Muslim?

Ikudayisi   No, he is not-oh.

Yemi (*to* **Ikudayisi**)   You eediate, I said no one ain't talking to you. Just be quiet. (*To* **Shopkeeper**.) No I'm not a Muslim. But you're Muslim, innit?

Shopkeeper   Yes.

Yemi   See, that's what I'm saying, we're the same peoples.

Shopkeeper   I no black, I Bangladeshi.

Yemi   I know you're Indian –

Shopkeeper   Bangladeshi.

Yemi   Don't get it twisted, blud. Man, oh man, don't care where you're from. What I'm saying is I *know* you feel oppressed and dat when mans tell you, you can't wear your head ting in certain places. It the same like me! Bare people going around thinking you're gonna do dem something when all *we* wanna do is get on with our life. I understand you, blud!

Shopkeeper   Then no hood.

Yemi   You're not getting what – Hold up. (*To* **Ikudayisi**.)
Listen to the music this guy is tryna play.

Ikudayisi   It nice.

He mimics the song and tries to sing along.

Yemi   Shut up, man. It's not nice. (*To* **Shopkeeper**.) How
do we know it isn't some Islamic chant that you're playing?

Shopkeeper   It's prayer music.

Yemi   You only saying that cos we don't understand it.
Furthermore, how do I know it ain't a bomb factory you got
back there? That why you ain't tryna let me in.

Shopkeeper   I NO BOMBER, I NO SUPPORT
TERRORIST!

He moves towards **Yemi***, waving his hands in his face.*

Shopkeeper   I LOVE THIS COUNTRY. I NO
TERRORIST. NO BOMB IN MY SHOP, NO BOMB IN
MY SHOP.

Yemi   Don't start coming nears me now, you might try blow
me up –

Shopkeeper   You mutta mutta, you lie, no bomb in my
shop –

Yemi   Look at the way you acting. You see, you see, that's
why you of all people shouldn't judge, cos you're not liking it
when you're getting judged.

Shopkeeper   I NO EVER SAY BAD THING ABOUT
ENGLAND.

Yemi   Calm down, man, I was just making a point. Just cos
I got a hood on my head don't mean I'm tryna rob nobody.
Same ways *I know* just cos you're Indian don't mean you're a
BOMBER!

Shopkeeper   I TELL YOU ALREADY I NO BOMBER!
I PROUD TO BE ENGLISH. NO TROUBLE, NO
TROUBLE. SHOP CLOSE, SHOP CLOSE.

The **Shopkeeper** *goes inside and closes the door.* **Yemi** *tries to open the door but it is locked.*

Yemi   Let me in! Don't you understand English? I was just making a point.

Shopkeeper (*from behind the door*)   Go away! I will call police now. You trouble.

Yemi *begins kicking on the door.*

Yemi   That's what I can't stand bout you Indians! Smelling of curry, coming over here, taking up all the corner shops, and man can't buy nothing. What da fuck you got a shop for if you're not tryna sell nothing? Call the police, call the police, I ain't doing nothing.

Ikudayisi   This is stupid, let's just go.

Yemi   I ain't going nowhere. Let the police come. (*To* **Shopkeeper**.) YOU HEAR ME? CALL THE POLICE. What can they do me for? It's more like they'll come and search up your shop. I just need to tell them you got a bomb in there. I bet *you* get arrested before I do!

The **Shopkeeper** *has now turned off his Islamic music and is playing the England World Cup song: 'Three Lions on the Shirt'.*

Ikudayisi   Let's just go, it not worth it at all, you are just scaring him.

Yemi   Scaring him? I should be scared of *him*. He is strange man!

Ikudayisi   It's not worth it.

Yemi   And what would you know? You wasn't even here on July the seventh when *his* people blew up bare heads last year.

Ikudayisi   What has that got to do with you wearing your hood in the shop? And you are lying – I heard about the July story. Not all Indian people are the same, and one of them was even black. Look at you, you should not judge like that.

Yemi   You're so backwards! Don't you know nothing at all? That how they look at us. Dem people are racist, they don't like black people, and I don't like dem either.

Ikudayisi   It's not cos you are black that he shut the door.

Yemi   You have a lot to learn.

Ikudayisi   I don't need to learn rubbish. You have to pick your battles well. Taking your hood off is nothing. You could have put it back on when we have finished.

Yemi   Shut up!

He pushes past **Ikudayisi** *and starts banging and kicking the door.*

Yemi   Let me in, you bloody Paki. You're going on like I ain't got money. I got bare dough.

Ikudayisi   He is not going to open de door when you are acting like a baboon.

Yemi *stops and turns to* **Ikudayisi**.

Yemi   Baboon! You're one to talk. You da one who lived in da jungle.

Ikudayisi   Your head is not correct.

Yemi *tries to punch* **Ikudayisi** *but misses.*

Ikudayisi   You are foolish, you don't know yourself.

Yemi   You eediate, you so dumb. I wish you would just go back to where you belong. You get on my nerves.

Ikudayisi   I am here to stay so you better digest it well well.

Yemi   Why don't you just piss off and die?

Yemi *pushes* **Ikudayisi**, *who falls to the ground.*

Ikudayisi   OK, I'll go home.

He turns to leave and **Yemi** *stops him.*

Yemi   NAH NAH NAH, you can't.

Ikudayisi   Now you want me to stay eh, ehh? Why?

Yemi   I'm sorry innit, I didn't mean it.

Ikudayisi   You meant it. Oh, you are evil! I'm going back home. Let the police come and catch you here.

Yemi   I'm not going to beg you, you nah.

Ikudayisi   I don't care. You are crazy.

Yemi *stands in his way.*

Yemi   Use your head. If you go home without the milk, *we* will get in trouble.

Ikudayisi   NO! *You* will get in trouble. I will just tell her you are misbehaving.

Yemi   And *I* will tell her you tried to steal somink.

Ikudayisi   That's a lie! You are the one causing trouble outside here. I was not part of it, I never did anything.

Yemi   SO! But how will she know dat?

Ikudayisi   Cos it a lie.

Yemi   Who has she known longer? Trust me, blud, don't test me.

Blackout.

Scene Three

Ikudayisi *and* **Yemi** *have now walked to a different part of the estate.*

Ikudayisi   We have been walking for long-oh.

Yemi   Stop your complaining.

Ikudayisi   So, how far are we going to go before we go back home?

Yemi   She said not to come back without the milk. What about *dat*, don't you understand?

Ikudayisi   But all the shops are closed.

Yemi   You always point out the obvious, innit. Indian shops are always open on a bank holiday in this country. They are money-orientated people, they will do anything for money.

Ikudayisi   What, like the other shopkeeper did? Have you forgotten he didn't care if you had money, he didn't want you in his shop.

Yemi   No! It was *me* who didn't want to go into *his* shop.

Ikudayisi   Your memory is short.

Yemi   Whatever.

Ikudayisi   So where is this other shop? I'm tired! We have been walking, walking, and I cannot see de shop. I don't want to walk no more, I want to go back home.

He sits down.

Yemi   I don't know what you are complaining bout. Don't you have to walk miles in Nigeria to get water? And now you're in England you going on like you can't even walk. We haven't even gone far. That's the problem with you people straight from the bush, you get to this country and want bare luxuries. What, you think, a horse and carriage is gonna come and carry you around? I was raised in these ends so I know where I'm going.

*He starts walking but **Ikudayisi** remains seated.*

Yemi   GET UP! You know how Mum stays, so why do you act all dumb? If we go back empty-handed, what do you think she will do?

Ikudayisi   I don't care. You are de one dat is scared of punishment.

Yemi   I'm not scared.

Ikudayisi   So let's go back home then ah ah now.

Yemi   No. We've been stuck inside da house for a week and now we are out, you want to go back in. Are you mad? You GO! I'm not going till I get this stuff, and if that means going to bare different shops, I'm going.

Ikudayisi (*looking around*)   It's only now you are saying I should go. Do I know where to go? We have been walking, walking, walking . . .

Yemi   Boy! If you don't know the way – I guess you got to stay den, innit!

Ikudayisi   *Ah ah koda now.* [That is not good.]

Yemi   WHAT DID YOU SAY?

Ikudayisi *starts laughing.*

Yemi   I SAID, WHAT DID YOU SAY?

Ikudayisi   You are Nigerian, you should know.

Yemi   What are you talking about? You know I don't understand.

Ikudayisi   It's not my problem.

Yemi   I hate it when you speak dat language.

Ikudayisi   Why, are you ashamed of being Nigerian? You can't change what you are.

Yemi   I'm not. I SAID I'M NOT!

Offstage there is giggling, then two girls come onstage. **Yemi** *notices them and runs up to them.*

Yemi   What's up, Armani, Paris?

Paris   Hi, Yemi.

Yemi   You're look Chung today, Paris.

Paris   Thanks!

Yemi   So where you lovely ladies going?

Paris   Nowhere, we were just about –

Armani   None of your business.

Pause.

Yemi   So, Paris, when are we gonna link up?

Armani   She's not! (*To* **Paris**.) Come, man, let's go.

Paris   I can talk for myself, you nah.

Armani   Why would you . . . ?

Ikudayisi *has bopped up to* **Yemi** *and is profiling behind his shoulder. He looks at the girls in admiration.*

Ikudayisi (*in a dodgy American accent*)   Yo, Yemi, you're not gonna introduce me to your friends?

Armani   Whoo's dis?

Yemi *shrugs* **Ikudayisi** *off.*

Yemi   I don't know him.

Ikudayisi   Ah ah . . . Oluyemi Adewale, so you are going to pretend we are not bruddas?

Paris   You got a brother? I never knew dat.

Yemi   No, he's my brother, but not my –

Armani   I never knew you was African.

Paris   You don't look African.

Ikudayisi   I don't look African?

The girls laugh.

Armani   No, *you* look African. Yemi don't look African.

Ikudayisi   *Ori e o pe.* [Your head is not correct.]

Armani   Wat did he say?

Yemi   I don't know, I don't speak dat language. What does an African look like? What is it you're tryna say?

Armani   You come from his country – what did he say?

Yemi   What does an *African* look like?

Armani   That's not what he said.

Yemi   No, *I* said what does an African look like.

Armani   I don't care!

Yemi   Well, I do. What does one look like?

Armani   An African, innit. Now what did he say?

Paris *nudges* **Armani**.

Paris   Lauw it, Armani.

Yemi   Nah, tell her to say what she mean.

Paris   She doesn't mean nothing.

Yemi   Let Armani speak.

Paris   It's just –

Armani   *Forget* it, man, I was only saying you don't look African, innit. What your problem? It's a compliment.

Yemi   *Compliment?*

Armani   You should be happy you don't look like dem. Be grateful you don't have big lips and big nose.

Yemi   What?

Paris   Armani!

Armani   It the truth, why am I going to sugar-coat it for? You're lucky you're not black black.

Ikudayisi   All of us are black. We are all from Africa-oh.

Armani   Nah, later, I'm from *yard*, bruv.

Ikudayisi (*laughing*)   D' backyard? (*To* **Yemi**.) *Werre.* [Crazy.]

He continues laughing.

Armani   What did he say now?

Yemi   What is wrong with having big lips?

He begins to feel his lips.

Armani   Why you covering up for him for? Dat's not what he said.

Yemi   I told you before, I don't speak dat language.

Ikudayisi   *Omo iranu koti e mo kun ko.* [Stupid girl, don't even know nothing.]

He laughs again.

Armani   But *you're* African –

Yemi   I was *born* here!

Paris   He is laughing hard dough. Seriously, Yemi, what did he say?

Yemi   I don't know.

Ikudayisi (*to* **Yemi**)   Backyard. *Omo jaku jaku.* [This silly girl.]

Armani   Yemi, are you tryna take da piss?

She moves towards **Yemi**.

Yemi   Back up, man. I ain't the one saying or doing anything, he's the one speaking. Speak to him.

Armani *moves still closer to* **Yemi**.

Yemi   You're starting to get on my nerves now. Just duss –

Armani   Are you taking the piss?

Ikudayisi   *Omo girl e omo jaku jaku.* [This silly girl.] *Oti so ro so ro ju.* [She talks too much.] *Werre.* [Crazy.]

Armani   Listen, Adebabatunde, or watever your name is,
yeah, we are in England so tell ya people to speak fucking
English if they got something to say.

Yemi   IS THE WORDS EVEN COMING OUT OF
MY MOUTH? I TOLD YOU I DON'T SPEAK THAT
LANGUAGE. GET OUT MY FACE.

Armani   AND WHAT YOU GONNA DO, YOU
AFRICAN BUBU?

Yemi (*starts squaring up into her face*)   Who da fuck you talking
to like that?

Armani   I'm talking to *you*!

Yemi   You better watch your mouth, yeah.

Armani   What what what, what are you gonna do?

Yemi   Just watch your mouth.

Paris   Yous lot, man . . .

Ikudayisi   Please, let's not fight –

Armani   Nah, later, man, chatting like he gonna do
something. Make him come and do something. (*To* **Yemi**.) If
you're gonna do something, do something, innit.

Yemi   Move. I ain't got time for you.

He turns to leave.

Armani   See, you're just a pussy, all you African people
dem are. Jus go home and eat your jelly and rice.

Yemi   WHAT?

Armani   What, you got problem understanding English
now? (*She puts on an African accent.*) EH EH, do I need to speak
in your language –

Yemi *goes for* **Armani** *and pokes her in the head.* **Paris** *tries to stop
him and gets pushed to the ground.*

Paris   No, don't . . .

Armani   AHH . . .

Ikudayisi   No no no, Yemi, you cannot hit a lady. (*To* **Paris**.) Yo, mammy, you OK?

Paris   Yeah, I'm cool.

Armani   Oh my God, oh my God, you just touch me, you just touch me! Nah nah, I ain't having dat.

She tries to go for **Yemi** *but* **Ikudayisi** *holds her back.*

Ikudayisi (*to* **Armani**)   Yo princess, you gotta calm down.

Armani   Don't touch me, don't touch me! Move, man, don't come near me.

Ikudayisi   Let's go, Yemi.

Yemi   Shut up, man. (*To* **Armani**.) You started this. I ain't going nowhere.

Armani   Just watch, yeah, fink sey you can touch mi and get away with it. Watch wen my man hears bout this, you think you're gonna be alive? My man gonna have you up, he is gonna slash you up. You think you're a bad now, yeah, yeah, yeah. Watch, yeah, watch.

Yemi   I'm watching.

Paris   Please, you two –

Armani   Is it, is it. Mans don't lay their hands on me and live to see the next day, you know. People like you get taken and buried where no one can't find you. Even your mum's gonna be searching for your body, she not even gonna know where to look, yeah, yeah.

Yemi   Ohhh, *gangsta* now, is it?

Armani   I ain't tryna be gangsta, I'm just telling you how it is. You made the worst mistake of your life today, the worst mistake. This is the beginning, blud, this is the beginning. Living on this estate is gonna be the hell from today. Everywhere you go you're gonna have to watch your back. You see, you see, you forget, yeah, I know bare people on these ends. Once everyone knows what you tried to do today, what, you're done for. You better pack your bags and go back to Africa now.

Yemi   SHUT YOUR MOUTH. SHUT UP AND DUSS. GO GET YOUR MAN. THINK MANS LIKE ME IS SHOOK?

Paris   Yemi, please –

Armani   Nah, don't beg babatunde for nothing, let him talk, cos everything he is saying now my man's gonna hear bout it. (*To* **Yemi**.) Just watch you, bubu.

Yemi *goes for* **Armani** *again.*

Blackout.

Scene Four

Yemi *and* **Ikudayisi** *have moved to another part of the estate.* **Yemi** *is sitting down with his legs up on a bench and his bum on the top half. He is still very angry about his run-in with* **Armani**. **Ikudayisi** *watches him and when he registers that* **Yemi** *is not moving he too sits down on the bench.*

Ikudayisi   Yemi, next time you should not hit a woman-oh.

Yemi   She's not a woman, she's a yout.

Ikudayisi   You should try and talk it out.

Yemi You saw her – I didn't even get a word in. She is always running up her mouth. And for the record, I never hit her, I only *revered* her. And if it wasn't for you this wouldn't have happened in the first place.

Ikudayisi I didn't do anything.

Yemi You were talking in that language that nobody *understands*! I told you already I didn't like it – see what you started.

Ikudayisi She was talking nonsense.

Yemi She is *such* an idiot.

Pause.

And so is her man too, bout she saying she gonna get him on to me. Make him come, I'm ready for him, blud. I'm not afraid of no one.

Ikudayisi Just calm down. Don't go looking for trouble.

Yemi I ain't looking for no trouble. All I'm saying is, if it comes I'm ready! Come, man, get up – we ain't got time to sit down.

Ikudayisi But . . . you . . . please let's just stay here for a minute, all that punishment I have been doing today has hurt my legs. I am tired-oh.

Yemi So? So am I.

Ikudayisi So let's rest. What is the big hurry?

Yemi Look at the time. It getting late.

Ikudayisi I don't have a watch.

Yemi Like that should stop you – can't you just look at the sun and know the time?

Ikudayisi Ah ah, Yemi, what *nonsense* are you talking? You are so ignorant! *Kí lo she e?* [What is wrong with you?]

Yemi Why do you always mix English with Nigerian?

Ikudayisi   It's not called Nigerian – the language is Yoruba.

Yemi   I don't care what it is.

Ikudayisi   *Kini problem e?* [What is your problem?]

Yemi   You don't listen. See, that what I mean. Don't you know when you speak nobody round here understand a word you're saying.

Ikudayisi   You can learn if you want.

Yemi   Dat's long.

Pause.

Ikudayisi   What was that jelly and rice she was talking about?

Yemi   Who?

Ikudayisi   Dat girl.

Yemi   Oh, dat idiot. She was tryna say *jollof rice*, innit.

Ikudayisi   How can jollof rice be jelly?

Yemi   Exactly!

Ikudayisi   *Omo jaku jaku.* [Silly girl.]

Yemi (*laughs*)   That word is funny. Dat's what you called her innit? Did you see her face when you said that?

Ikudayisi   Of course now, she looked like this.

He mimics **Armani***'s face and they both laugh.*

Yemi   What was the other word you used?

Ikudayisi   Which one? I used a lot.

Yemi   That word beginning with 'w'.

Ikudayisi   Oh, *werre*.

Yemi   Yeah, dat one is funny too. I heard Mum saying that on the phone a few times. What does it mean?

Ikudayisi   It means crazy.

Yemi   For real. *H*ow do you say it?

Ikudayisi   *Werre.*

Yemi   *Warrri.*

Ikudayisi   No, *way* as in 'way' and *ray* as in 'ray'.

Yemi   *Way-ray.*

Ikudayisi   Yes, that's close.

Yemi   I guess that word is alright. Teach me ano – Nah, forget it, man.

Ikudayisi   Stop fighting it – you want to learn Yoruba.

Yemi   I don't.

Ikudayisi   It's easy.

Yemi   No man, I don't want to know.

Ikudayisi   Why?

Yemi   What is the point? When in Rome do as the Roman.

Ikudayisi   What do you mean?

Yemi   Meaning, what is the point of learning to speak *your* language when I don't even live in *that* country. We are in England. I only need to know how to speak English.

Ikudayisi   It's a nice language.

Yemi   No, it's not, it's not like it's Spanish or anything – now *dat's* a sexy language, I'll learn dat *any day*.

Ikudayisi   Yoruba is sexy too. Back home when I use it on the girl Kai! They come running, and I have to beat them away with a stick.

He moves towards **Yemi** *and demonstrates.*

Ikudayisi   Come here and let me show you. *Omo ge ki lo ruko e?* [Sexy girl, what's your name?]

Yemi   Move, you batty man.

Ikudayisi   Stop your shakara. Don't try and fight it. Yoruba can hypnotise you. When it does, there is nothing you can do. Come here, stop trying to resist it. *Omo ge, omo ge.* [Sexy girls, sexy girls.]

Yemi   Move, I'm not convinced. There is nothing sexy bout the language.

Ikudayisi   It bad-oh.

Yemi   What's bad?

Ikudayisi   That you are not embracing your culture. What does Mum say when you talk like this?

Yemi   She don't say nothing. She don't care bout speaking African either.

Ikudayisi   Ah ah, that not true, she speaks *Yoruba* all the time.

Yemi   No, she only started when you came. Before, she was forever speaking English. I never knew she could even speak in that language. Don't you hear, when she is on the phone she acts more English than me?

Ikudayisi   Come here, let me teach you Yoruba. Try it – *omo ge, omo ge.*

Yemi   Get lost!

Ikudayisi   You can use it on dat girl's friend. I saw da way you were looking at her, your mouth touch the floor.

Yemi   Shut up! Move, man.

Ikudayisi   I know you have never kissed a girl –

Yemi   What?

*An **Old Lady** enters with some shopping bags. She is halfway across when she notices **Yemi** and **Ikudayisi**. She stops in her tracks and contemplates turning back, but is too afraid to move.*

Ikudayisi   Before, you can use Yoruba on her, she will lie down at your feet, treat you like a king!

Yemi   See, that's why I can't stand you, you're going on like you know everything bout me – you don't know shit.

Ikudayisi   I'm only playing. I know you have kissed plenty of girls.

Yemi   Shut up, man! You don't know nothing about me . . . You going like –

Ikudayisi *notices the* **Old Lady** *now and jumps off the bench.*

Ikudayisi   Ma, sorry, don't you want to sit down?

Yemi   Ahhhhhh –

He rolls his eyes, takes out his phone and starts playing with it.

Old Lady   No no no no. I'm OK!

Ikudayisi   I can see you are tired – please come and sit down.

The **Old Lady** *stays still, scared.*

Ikudayisi (*to* **Yemi**)   Move now.

Yemi   What? NO! What for?

Ikudayisi   For this lady – she needs to sit down.

Yemi   What is wrong wid you?

Old Lady   I'm not looking for trouble. (*To* **Ikudayisi**.) I'm OK, I just wanna go home.

Yemi   Exactly. Let her go.

Ikudayisi   No, it's not OK. (*To* **Yemi**.) You're going to have to move your feet.

Yemi   She don't need a seat.

Ikudayisi   Yemi, where is your manners?

He snatches **Yemi***'s phone and the* **Old Lady***, frightened, drops her shopping.* **Ikudayisi** *goes to help.*

Yemi   Give it back.

Old Lady   Please don't touch me – I told you, I'm not looking for trouble.

Yemi   Give me the phone back – the battery low.

Ikudayisi   Ma, let me help you.

The **Old Lady** *starts edging backwards, raising her voice.*

Old Lady   Stay away! Stay away.

Yemi (*to* **Ikudayisi**)   What wrong with you?

Old Lady   Please . . .

Ikudayisi   I'm only helping.

Old Lady   Please, I just wanna go home.

Yemi   Go.

Ikudayisi   We can't let her go – her bags have broken.

He tries to help her gather up the things that have fallen on the ground.

Old Lady   OH GOD!

Yemi   Are you blind? She don't want you to come near her.

Old Lady   I know what you're trying to do, you can take it.

Yemi   What you talking about?

Old Lady   Anything, have anything.

Yemi   Oh my Dayz, see what I'm saying?

Old Lady   Please, please, I just wanna go home.

Yemi   DAYISI, JUST MOVE AWAY FROM HER!

Old Lady   Have it, have it, anything you want.

Ikudayisi *moves away from the bag.*

Yemi   Stop making noise, man, no one is near you.

Ikudayisi   Ma, I'm sorry, I only trying to help.

Old Lady   Stay away from me! STAY AWAY!

She picks up her bag but is too frightened to move.

Yemi   Go, blud!

The **Old Lady** *scurries off the stage.*

Yemi (*to* **Ikudayisi**)   You're so dumb.

Ikudayisi   What are you talking about? You shouldn't talk so harsh to her – she is not your mate.

Yemi   What?

Blackout.

Scene Five

It is late afternoon, around five o'clock. **Razer**, **Flamer**, **Armani** *and* **Paris** *are hanging around on another part of the estate, drinking and making noise.*

Armani   . . . and then he tried to get rude, can you believe it? He put his hand on me, you nah.

Paris   To be fair, he only revered you in the head.

Armani   So what, he's your man now.

Paris   NO!

Armani   You meant to have my back.

Paris   I'm just saying what happened.

Armani   You calling me a liar?

Paris   No . . .

Armani   So what you saying?

Paris   Nothing, forget it.

Armani   Nah man, I'm not forgetting it. You been like this all day. Say what you got to say, Paris, say what you got to say.

Paris   Nothing.

Armani   It better be.

Paris   What better be?

Armani   I'm just saying, innit. You're meant be my friend. And friends always have each other's backs, no matter what. Know whose side you're on.

Razer   Stop talking to her like dat – Paris is your girl, man.

Flamer   She's always got your back.

Armani   Not today she didn't. Anyway, back to the story . . .

A big boy with a hood start is slowly walking towards them.

Paris   I wonder who that is.

Armani   ERHH UM! Hello!

Flamer *and* **Razer** *ignore* **Armani**, *turn round and draw out their knives.*

Paris   What is wrong with you? What's that for? Put them away.

Flamer   Mans can't be too careful on the ends. We can't let our guards down just cos we are home.

The figure is still walking towards them suspiciously.

Mans better identify themselves before they reach any closer, you know.

Blazer   What's up, my youth?

Everyone recognises the voice immediately and lets their guard down, except **Armani** *who kisses her teeth.*

Razer *and* **Flamer** *burst into the song and start dancing. They put their knives away.*

Razer *and* **Flamer**   Who you calling my yout, my yout?

Armani   I'm not anyone yout but my mother's.

Blazer   Shut up.

Armani *kisses her teeth and rolls her eyes.* (*To* **Razer** *and* **Flamer**.) You should have seen you mans' faces, you were shook.

Flamer   Nah man, we were prepared.

Flamer *shows* **Blazer** *his knife.*

Blazer   Nice, nice, it's good to see you mans are following rule number one.

Razer   Yep! You always got to watch your back –

Flamer   – cos your enemies are always closer than you think.

Blazer   Ahhh, my youts are learning fast.

He nudges **Flamer** *and* **Razer**.

Armani   Oh please, you ain't teaching anyone anything worthwhile.

Blazer   Every time I see you, you always got something to say. I am the preacher on these ends, so you better listen.

Paris   Preacher! You're funny.

Armani   He is not funny, Paris!

Blazer   Whatever. (*To* **Flamer** *and* **Razer**.) So what's popping, my soldiers?

Flamer   Nothing – Armani was just telling us bout her run-in wid Yemi.

Blazer   Which Yemi?

Paris   The one who lives on Farnborough Way –

Armani   Oh yeah, before we got rudely interrupted. As I was saying, *dat babatunde*, yeah –

Blazer (*to* **Flamer**)   I thought you said Yemi?

Flamer   Yeah –

Armani   Excuse me, I'm talking now –

Blazer   Hold on. Armani, are you trying to take da piss?

Armani   As I was saying –

Blazer   What, *all* African are called *babatunde*, yeah?

Razer   Blud, she ain't saying dat.

Blazer   So, what she tryna say? Cos I swear Flamer said she was talking bout Yemi and now she calling him *babatunde*!

Flamer   It's just a figure of speech.

Blazer   Nah, it's rude. (*To* **Armani**.) When you're in my presence you got to speak properly. If you talking bout Yemi, call him Yemi. If not –

Armani   Oh my God, yeah, why are you longing everything out? I just want to finish my story.

Blazer   Nah!

Armani   But I'm talking.

Blazer   No, I'm talking now. Listen and understand. If you talking bout a specific person say their name.

Armani   Cha, man, I'll do whatever I wanna do.

Blazer *moves towards* **Armani** *and stands really close to her face.*

Blazer   No, you do as I say. You're talking bout Yemi, his name is Yemi.

Unafraid of his presence, **Armani** *moves away and continues talking.*

Armani   His name can be called Kunta Kinte for all I care. I don't give a shit.

Blazer   You need a lesson in history then, cos Kunta Kinte is from Gambia.

Armani   I don't care, I don't care. I wasn't even talking to you in the first place. I know all history I need to know, you ain't got to teach me anything new. All I need to know is, I'm from yard!

Blazer   I've seen your mum – she's *white*!

Armani   So my dad is black.

Blazer   And?

Armani   And he is Jamaican. So dat makes me Jamaican.

Blazer   Have you *even* seen him? Probably don't even know what he looks like.

Razer   Lauw it, blud, you don't have to bring her dad into this.

Blazer (*to* **Armani**)   I've never even seen you set foot outside this estate, let alone go to another country, so how can you say you're Jamaican? Do you have a passport? Do you even know what a passport looks like?

Flamer   Blazer, man, it's not called for.

Blazer   Nah, blud, she's too rude and needs to learn her place. If her mum doesn't know how to teach her bout respect, I'll teach her. (*To* **Armani**.) When someone older is talking to you, you keep your mouth shut. Speak only when spoken to. Know your place. Respect your elders.

Armani   You're not even related to me.

Blazer   SHUT UP! I said speak *only* when you're spoken to.

Armani   What are you talking about? You *are* speaking to me.

Blazer (*to* **Razer**)   Tell your girl to mind out, you know.

Armani   I should mind out, I should mind out. (*To* **Razer**.) You not gonna say nothing? Look how I've been quiet when this boy been shouting at me. When are you going to step in?

Razer   He's only playing. (*To* **Blazer**.) Ain't you, Blazer?

Blazer   Blud, I'm not! Your girl needs to mind out.

They sit in awkward silence.

Paris (*to* **Blazer**)   I thought Kunta Kinte was a made-up name.

Blazer   Nah, he was real.

Paris   How do you know that?

Blazer   Cos I read. (*Staring at* **Armani**.) Unlike some people. And does anyone have a problem with dat?

Razer   Lauw it, blud, man, this is not a history class.

Flamer   Yeah, let's just keep the peace.

Blazer   So what, *you two* got a problem with me?

Razer   Course not, blud, you know I'm easy. I don't want no trouble, innit. We're one big fam out ere.

Flamer   Yeah, man, just take it easy.

Armani   He ain't my family.

Razer   Armani!

Armani   Look, yeah, I don't know why you lot are begging it with him for. (*To* **Blazer**.) You wasn't even invited to this conversation, *Blazer*!

Blazer *stares at* **Armani** *and* **Razer** *jumps in.*

Razer   Armani, man, please.

Armani   Why can't I talk? No, I'll speak when I want to.

Razer   Just lauw it, man. Sometimes you really need to know when to keep your mouth shut.

Armani   What, like you?

Razer   We were having a good time before.

Armani   And am I the one who was spoiling it?

Razer   Ahhhh, man.

Armani   I don't know what you making noise for. I swear you people forgot this is a free country. And in a free country people can talk freely. We are not in no third world. I can do what I want. I ain't afraid of no one.

Razer   ARMANI!

Flamer *and* **Paris** *start laughing at* **Armani** *and* **Razer** *arguing.* **Blazer** *gets up to leave.*

Flamer   You gone already?

Blazer   Yeah, man, this is too childish for me. And before I do something I might regret –

He looks long and hard at **Armani**.

– it's best I'm off. When you mans are done here meet me up at frontline. There is something I need you two to work on.

Flamer   Yeah, fam.

Blazer   One.

He nudges the boys.

See you later.

Paris   Yeah, see you later.

Blazer *exits.*

Armani *looks at* **Paris** *and gives her a dirty look.*

Armani   I hate him, you nah.

Razer   He can ruin the mood sometimes.

Flamer   So can your girl, you know.

Flamer, **Razer** *and* **Paris** *start laughing.*

Paris   I like Blazer, I think he is cool.

Armani   Yeah, you would.

Flamer   Nah, she right, most times he is alright. But he likes to talk a lot. We all know it shit, but it don't matter. When he talks just let him talk, innit.

Armani   Why? He not my dad. I'm not gonna shut *my* mouth cos he's around. He don't control me. No one does.

Flamer   But you ain't got to stir things up.

Armani   Stop sitting on the fence and defending him. You don't have to worry, your *boss* is gone, he can't hear me. You can now tell the truth bout what you really feel, speak your mind. You won't get arrest for it, you know. This is a *free* country.

Flamer   That's your problem, Armani, you don't listen. Didn't you hear me? I'm agreeing with you, and he ain't my boss.

Armani   You could have fooled me. When he comes around you lot start shaking.

Razer   Not me.

He nudges **Flamer**.

Armani   Whatever! He rules you too. Cos you chat different bout him when it just me and you. Den when he is in your face you're nuff quiet like a likkle biatch! I'm surprise you ain't following him around on a leash.

Razer   It's not like dat man – shut up.

Paris   I think he chats nuff sense. He is cool with me. He got a nice way about him, I love the way he proud bout where he from.

Armani   What, like being so fucking proud to be African but then calling himself Blazer? I bet you don't even know what his real name is.

Razer *laughs.*

Razer   She's right you nah. I can't remember his real name. Do you, Flamer?

Flamer   Yeah, course I know.

Armani   What is it?

Flamer   It's one long ass-funky name like Oluade . . .
Oluwaye . . . ahhh, I can't remember it.

Paris   Why does dat matter doe? He may not like people
knowing his real name. Most people never know how to
pronounce African names properly anyway. It probably
frustrates him. Anyways, Blazer is only his street name. (*To*
Razer *and* **Flamer**.) Not dat many people know yous lot
names either, do dey?

Armani   You're so stupid – that's not the reason.

Paris   What the reason, then?

Armani   *He is ashamed!*

Paris   He's not, he always talking bout Africa. How can he
be ashamed?

Armani   *So* why doesn't *he* hang around his people den?
Everyone *I* see him with is West Indian.

Paris   Dat don't mean nothing.

Armani   Look, Paris, yeah, you're always sticking up for
dem people. I told you once already today – know your sides!
You forget back in da days they sold us off as slaves, you nah.

Flamer   I ain't no slave. My nan told me she was invited to
this country, you get me?

Razer   Yeah, same here, fam.

Flamer *and* **Razer**   WINDRUSH!

They nudge each other.

Armani   You two are so dumb. We are all slaves, all of us
from the West Indies. Dat why I don't like African, cos they
sold us off to da white man, and den stayed in Africa living
as kings and queens, while all my ancestors had to work hard.

Razer, **Flamer** *and* **Paris**   WHAT?!

Armani   Nah, blud, I'm not happy with dat and I'm not having it either. You can go around loving off your African people but I stick with my own.

Paris   You have it so messed up. Everything you're saying don't make no sense. It doesn't even go like dat and furthermore you're half white . . . so . . . do you hate white people as well?

Armani   No, eh, my mum's white, *hello*!

Paris   You're not making any sense, Armani. You can't just be one-sided. How can you hate African people but not the white people who were also involved in slavery?

Armani   Cos slavery started in Africa.

Paris   But white people *went* to Africa and took them from their land.

Armani   So, what, *you* love African but hate white people now?

Paris   I didn't say dat.

Armani   Well *that's* what I'm hearing.

Paris   No, that's what you want to hear. You're not getting my point.

Armani   Yeah I am, yeah I am, it's all coming out now.

Paris   You're still not understanding me –

Armani   I'm getting exactly what you're tryna say.

Paris   You're not.

Armani   Yes, I am. It's all coming to light now. Now I understand the way that you been acting towards me. I'm so stupid, I should have seen it before.

Paris   What are you talking bout?

Armani   You're a *racist*, Paris.

Paris   What?

Razer   No she's not, man.

Flamer   She is far from racist – Paris is the nicest person we know.

Armani   Yes she is, YES SHE IS – she said it with her own mouth.

Paris   Said what? I never said anything.

Armani   Oh my God, you're a liar too.

Paris (*to* **Razer** *and* **Flamer**)   You two woz here. Did I say I hate white people?

Flamer *and* **Razer**   No.

Armani   I don't care, you can't backtrack now, I know you're a racist.

Paris   But if I'm racist you're racist too, then.

Armani   No, far from it.

Paris   Yes, you are. Hating African is *just as* racist as hating white people. So if you're calling me a racist, you're racist too.

Armani   That's not even the same.

Paris   Why – is it one rule for you and another for me? You can't have it your way *all the time*, Armani.

Armani   At least I know why you don't like me now.

Razer   How can she not like you? You been friends for years.

Armani   That's just a cover-up.

Paris   You really don't know what you are talking bout.

Armani   Yeah, I do. Things like this happen all the time. That's why I hate being friends with girls.

Paris   But I've never had a problem with you before *or* now.

Armani   I know where this hatred comes from anyway. It's jealousy.

Paris   What are you talking bout *now*?

Armani   Dark-skinned girls always have problems with light-skinned girls.

Flamer   Ahhh, come on.

Armani   It's the truth. All dark-skinned girls are like dat, they are forever hating –

Flamer   Paris is not like dat – why would she hate, she pretty herself –

Armani   They forget us light-skinned girl are not to blame, you nah. We don't get to pick our parents.

Paris   First I'm a racist and now I am hater. Make up your mind, Armani.

Armani   Ask Razer – he knows what I'm talking bout.

Razer   What?

Paris   What's she talking bout, Razer?

Razer   Don't get me involved in dis.

Paris   What, Razer, you think I hate light-skinned girls?

Razer   I've never said dat.

Armani   Don't lie now.

Razer   I'm not, don't get me involved in yout madness.

Paris   Well, everything you say is wrong. I haven't got any problems and never had one either.

Armani   You're such a liar. At least everyone here gets to know it now.

Paris   Stop talking rubbish, Armani.

Armani   I'm not, it's the truth!

Paris   It's not me that tryna be something dat I'm not.

Armani   What you saying?

Paris   Exactly what I just said!

Flamer   Take it easy, girls.

Paris   Nah! I'm fed up of being quiet. If you want me to get everything out in the open, *I'll* be real with you.

Flamer   Paris, lauw it, it's not worth it.

Razer   Girls, man, you're meant to be friends.

Paris   No, I'm fed up of this. It's my time to speak now.

Armani   Speak then – ain't no one holding you back.

Paris   I think it's *you* with the big problem.

Razer   Keep the peace, man, keep the peace.

Paris   But it not your fault cos *all* mixed-raced girls are confused.

Flamer   Paris!

Paris   I said girls.

Armani   Nah, later. Not me.

Paris   Especially you! You don't know what to identify yourself with. Should you be on the white side, should you be on the black side – *you don't know.* You try and act like you're blacker dan anybody else, but then you contradict yourself cos you go on like it's a bad thing for me to look black, or anyone else at that. I've always been cool with myself and even cooler wid you. When other *light-skinned* girls have chatted shit bout you, I've been the one to defend your ass. But I'm the hater – cos I'm dark-skinned! You just don't get it. You are *so* confused!

Flamer   Ooohhh, see what you started, Armani. I bet you thought Paris never had no mouth.

Armani   Oh my God, you're so funny – is that what you think?

Paris   No, it what I know. You forget sometimes how long I've known you and what you *used* to be like. How would you know about the black-hair shops if I didn't take you there? Cos your *mum* never knew what to do with your hair. You were walking around with a picky Afro *until the day I met you*! I've still got pictures in my house! I'm the one who still braids your hair! And who taught you about the dance moves that they did in Jamaica, cos Blazer's right – you ain't never been there, or anywhere else apart from *here*. And furthermore, I been to your yard and the *only* food your mum showed you how to cook was beans on toast! Remember – I introduced you to rice and peas. So don't get it twisted!

Flamer   You got told!

Armani   WHAT? SHUT UP! She is such a liar. She never taught me nothink. Come say that to my face. COME SAY THAT TO MY FACE.

Armani *tries to go for* **Paris** *but* **Razer** *and* **Flamer** *hold her back.* **Paris** *stands her ground.*

Paris   If it's a lie why you acting all mad for? It shouldn't be bothering you. You should just be cool. You're the big bad Armani. You're always right – right?

Armani   How can you try and say you taught me bout hair? Look at my hair and look at yours. (*To* **Razer**.) Look, Razer, look.

Paris   *So*, as I said, it's my influence.

Razer *and* **Flamer** *start laughing.*

Armani   What, come say that to my face.

Paris   I am. The truth hurts, doesn't it?

Blackout.

Scene Six

Yemi *is on another side of the estate,* **Ikudayisi** *is offstage, trying to catch up with him and calling his name.* **Yemi** *does not respond and goes and sits down on a wall, playing with his phone.*

Ikudayisi (*off*) Yemi, Yemi, Yemi!

He comes onstage and is shocked to see **Yemi** *sitting down. He walks over to him.*

Ikudayisi   So is this where you have been all this time?

Yemi *ignores him.*

Ikudayisi   So, did you not hear me calling your name?

Yemi *still ignores him.*

Ikudayisi   Yemi! Can you not hear me asking you questions?

Yemi   JUST LEAVE ME ALONE.

Ikudayisi   No – what is your problem?

Yemi   AHHH, MAN!

Ikudayisi   Are you having some kind of breakdown?

Yemi   JUST LEAVE ME ALONE, leave me alone.

Ikudayisi   No, we need to talk about what happened before. You shouldn't have talked to that old lady like dat.

Yemi   What, are you dizzy?

Ikudayisi   She is as old as our grandmother and you were rude.

Yemi   She was *scared* of you! Why can't you just go away?

Ikudayisi   No, I'm your brother, I'm here to stay.

Yemi   Why did you have to come? Why couldn't you just stay in Nigeria. Ever since you come . . . I liked it how it was!

Ikudayisi   Why are you being like this?

Yemi   Why can't you just go away?

Ikudayisi   No, I'm here to stay. I couldn't wait to come, just to see you. To see my younger brother and this is de way you are treating me. If this was Nigeria –

Yemi   This is not Nigeria. Why do you think you could just come over here and take over?

Ikudayisi   I'M NOT TRYING TO TAKE OVER. I just want to be a part of your life.

Yemi   You come here and act the way you do, and think . . . and think . . . everyone should just accept that. All these stupid things you keep on doing like speaking in that language and trying to be friendly to everyone does not work here. People don't want you to be nice to them. YOU NEED TO UNDERSTAND THIS IS NOT NIGERIA, things are different here.

Ikudayisi   What do you mean?

Yemi   You can't do what you do there, *here*.

Ikudayisi   I can't be friendly?

Yemi   NO, you can't! This country is not like dat. People will look at you like you are crazy. You just need to mind your own business. Don't watch no one else.

Ikudayisi   That's nonsense. You are lost.

Yemi   NO, you're lost. You think being the way you are is cool. It's not! You're a joke. People in this country laugh at people like you – they find your look and your accent funny. They think you're a joke. But you can't *even* see dat.

Ikudayisi   That's nonsense. Since I have been here people have been nice to me – it's you that has been having problems.

Yemi   Are you stupid? You almost gave an old lady a heart attack. She thought you were robbing her.

Ikudayisi What?

Yemi If you stopped living in la-la land for once, you would see that. Stop being stupid and look around you.

Ikudayisi You this silly boy. See what? What is there to see? You are not thinking straight. Your mind-set needs to change.

Yemi You're the one who needs to change, not me! Stop all the 'we are the world' shit you keep on doing, and understand that in order to get along on this estate, in this country, you need to stop being you, Dayisi!

Ikudayisi I can't change – being a Nigerian is what I am.

Yemi I can't help you then, cos you're never gonna fit in.

Ikudayisi That's a lie. I fit it well, I get on with everyone.

Yemi Look! Take some good advice: you're not going to get far how you are right now – trust me, I know this.

Ikudayisi You are strange-oh, you talk too much rubbish.

Yemi No, I'm chatting sense and it best you listen to me, cos

Ikudayisi No, you listen to me. You are trying to educate someone who is already educated. I know who I am and what I stand for. I will not change for anyone. Ahhh, you disappoint me-oh, I didn't know your problem run so deep.

Yemi You're buzzing. I ain't got time for this.

He turns to walk away.

Ikudayisi Dat's your problem – you don't want to face up to nothing. You talk so much nonsense, but the minute someone else has something to say, you want to go.

Yemi Shut up, man. What would you know? You don't even know me, man. What! WHAT! You been here two months and you think you can tell me bout me. I don't expect you to understand coming from a backward country.

Ikudayisi   Take that back! Nigeria is not backward.

Yemi   Uhhh, yes it is. Don't get it twisted, blud, just cos I
ain't been there don't mean I ain't heard the stories. Duh!
Mum's always talking bout you lot not always having
electricity. How can you tell me dat not backward?

Ikudayisi   You don't understand . . . It's only when Nepa
[*Nigerian Electricity Board*] takes the light. We have generators.

Yemi   But the lights are not on 24/7, are they? I bet you
ain't even got traffic lights – how can you, with no electricity?
Is there even cars in Africa? Do you even have houses?

Ikudayisi   You dis one who has never set foot in Nigeria
and is now talking like you discovered it. You are de one that
is backward and confused, talking bad about your mother
homeland like that. Be careful God does not strike you now.

Yemi   Shut up. I don't even know why you getting offended
for. You don't live there any more, you couldn't wait to come
here. So everything you're saying is rubbish. Work on
changing yourself and leave me out of it.

Ikudayisi   No, I'm proud of who I am.

He sings.

> Green white green on my chest,
> I'm proud to be a Nigerian!
> Green white green on my chest,
> I'm proud to be a Nigerian!

Yemi   Oh my dayz!

Ikudayisi
> Green white green on my chest,
> I'm proud to be a Nigerian!

Yemi   Do you not see how stupid you look?

Ikudayisi
> Green white green on my chest,
> I'm proud to be a Nigerian!

He falls to his knees with his hands in the air.

> Proud to be a Nigerian,
> Proud to be a Nigerian,
> Proud – to – be – a – Ni-ge-ri-an,
> Proud – to – be – a – Ni-ge-ri-an!

Yemi   But then you put on a fake American accent when you talking to other people.

Ikudayisi *stops singing.*

Ikudayisi   That is just my accent, it is always changing.

Yemi   No. (*He mimics* **Ikudayisi***'s accent.*) This is your accent. (*He mimics* **Ikudayisi***'s fake American accent.*) And this is you when you're trying to be American. They are two different accents.

Ikudayisi   I'm still proud to be Nigerian.

Yemi   You're telling me I'm lost, but what bout you? You can stand here all day going on bout how proud you are, but the truth is in your action, not just your word.

Ikudayisi   Jo, leave me.

Yemi   Ohh, did I hit a raw nerve? Don't worry – as I said, your accent a joke, everyone understands why you want to get rid. It's no big ting. No one ain't gonna hate you if you change – I've already told you, I think you need to!

Ikudayisi   You are so young, you don't understand anything at all. I was once like you. As I keep on saying, I just wish you went to Nigeria. The way you are talking you will see –

Yemi   I don't *wanna* go there.

Ikudayisi   That's your problem, and why I personally feel sorry for you. You are telling me I need to change, but I'm not the one with the problem, it's you. You are a lost puppy. One minute you feel you don't fit in here because people are racist but then you don't want to be a Nigerian. Then you want to be left alone, but you complain you have no friend. Do you know who you are, Yemi?

Yemi   Yes, I'm a free person.

Ikudayisi   Nobody is free-oh.

Yemi   You might not be, but I am.

Ikudayisi   How can you be free when you deny your own heritage? You don't like your name, you are ashamed of your language. If you are *so* free you won't care what people think about Nigerian and you will just be what you are.

Yemi   Do you think I care what people think? It's not other people that make me hate Nigeria, it's Nigeria that makes me hate it.

Ikudayisi   *But you have never been there.* How can you judge? Nigeria is a nice place.

Yemi   Forget it, man. You're not going to make me change my mind overnight. Let's go.

Ikudayisi   No, ah ah.

Yemi   I don't give a shit bout Nigeria. Why can't you just leave it?

Ikudayisi   YOU NEED TO LEARN TO RESPECT IT! What are you going to teach your children?

Yemi   THAT THEY ARE FREE LIKE ME.

Ikudayisi   And when they want to know about their family?

Yemi   This is long, man, lauw da chat.

Ikudayisi   No. Will you even give your kids Yoruba names?

Yemi   I don't care.

Ikudayisi   WELL, YOU SHOULD!

Yemi   Why? Why should I? I'm not you, I'm my own person. Stop trying to force your views on me. I'm sick of this. I just wanna be me. Don't wanna be no one else. Let me be me. Why do you care what I think?

Ikudayisi   You *really* don't understand. Despite all its problem, Nigeria is a great place. YOU HAVE TO BE PROUD OF WHERE YOU ARE FROM.

Yemi   If it's so great, why do you *all* wanna come here?

Ikudayisi *remains silent.*

Yemi   *Exactly!* No matter how bad this country is, I bet it better than there!

Ikudayisi   *Ironi yen.* [A lie.]

Yemi *cuts his eye at* **Ikudayisi** *and kisses his teeth.*

Ikudayisi   I don't understand you at all. If people saw us now they would not even know we are from the same mother. We are brothers, and you act like we are from different countries, different worlds.

Yemi   We are.

Blackout.

Scene Seven

It is early evening, and **Yemi** *and* **Ikudayisi** *are still out on the estate. They have finally got the milk and are heading home. They have been to a chicken-and-chips shop, too, and are eating on the way.*

Yemi *spots* **Blazer** *and pushes* **Ikudayisi** *behind him so it looks like they are not walking together. He quickens his pace and tries to act cool.*

Blazer   What's up, blud?

Yemi   I'm cool, man.

Ikudayisi (*in dodgy American accent*) Yeah, what's poppin?

Yemi   AHHH, MAN!

He gives **Ikudayisi** *a dirty look.* **Blazer** *laughs.*

Blazer   Who is dis?

Yemi   Erm . . .

Ikudayisi (*dodgy American accent*)   His older brother.

Blazer   I never knew you had a brother.

Yemi   I wish I never.

Blazer   What?

Yemi   Long story – he just come from Nigeria.

Blazer (*to* **Ikudayisi**)   *Ba wo ni.* [Hi.]

Yemi   What?

Ikudayisi (*goes to nudge* **Blazer**)   Fellow Nigerian, how now?

Yemi   You're Nigerian? I thought –

Blazer   Course I'm Nigerian – one hundred per cent. (*To* **Ikudayisi**.) *Se en gbadun ilu oyinbo?* [Are you enjoying England?]

Ikudayisi   *Ko bad now.* [Not bad.]

Yemi   What you two saying?

Blazer   Don't you understand Yoruba?

Yemi   No.

Ikudayisi   *Ko gbo nkan nkan.* [He doesn't understand anything.]

Blazer (*to* **Ikudayisi**)   Why ain't you teaching him?

Ikudayisi   I've tried-oh.

Yemi   Tried what?

Ikudayisi   To teach you Yoruba. (*To* **Blazer**.) But he said he don't give a shit about Nigeria, he telling me I need to change, forget about my heritage, be *free* like him.

Blazer (*to* **Yemi**)   Did you say dat?

Yemi   Nah, I never.

Ikudayisi   *Iro ti fo ori e.* [Lies are filled in his head.]

Blazer *laughs.*

Yemi   What did he say?

Blazer   Dat's why you need to learn to speak Yoruba, you nah.

Yemi   Uhhh.

Blazer   So dat you know what people are saying bout you.

Yemi   True dat, true dat. I never thought of it like dat.

Ikudayisi   What! True what? (*To* **Blazer**.) Before he was saying dat he don't want to have anything to do with Nigeria. He was talking nonsense, saying dat he is free, dat we are from different worlds.

Yemi   So? He tries to act like he is American.

Blazer   You *both* got something to learn.

Ikudayisi   I'm one hundred per cent proud of being Nigerian.

Yemi   Ehh, you think you're American.

Blazer (*to* **Ikudayisi**)   Blud, what is that all about?

Ikudayisi   When I put on the accent I'm only playing. I know who I am and where I'm from.

Blazer   Good, cos that LA Lagos shit pisses me off.

Yemi   Me too.

Ikudayisi   Me too what? You still don't know yourself.

Yemi   Shut up, man, you're chatting shit.

Blazer   Don't talk to your brother like dat, man. I swear he said he is older than you.

Yemi   So?

Blazer   So you need to learn to respect him, you nah. You can't go around talking to him like that. That's what makes us different.

Yemi   What does?

Blazer   Respect.

Yemi   From who?

Blazer   Da West Indians.

Yemi   See, that what I was trying to tell Dayisi bout us being different –

Ikudayisi   You were not talking about respect, you were talking rubbish.

Yemi   No I wasn't, I was saying –

Blazer   You two should know this already. Respect is something you shouldn't play wid. My mum taught me that years ago.

He begins to sing.

Money, power, respect is what you need in life.

Yemi *joins in.*

Yemi
Money, power, respect is the key to life.
You see in life, it's your given right.

Blazer   See, you know the song.

Yemi   Course, blud!

Blazer   Every word is the truth, mate.

Pause.

You see me, yeah, on the street I get bare respect, but don't get it twisted, it never came easy. I had to earn that shit. From when I learnt at home to show my family respect I came out on the road and showed mans respect. It like a chain reaction. You give respect to get respect, you get me?

Yemi   Yeah, man, I understand.

Ikudayisi   Hey-oh. God is listening to my prayers. (*To* **Yemi**.) You need more friends like this-oh.

Yemi   Shut –

Blazer   Yemi! I thought you understood. Come on, man, you couldn't have just forgotten what I *just* said.

Yemi   Sorry.

Blazer   It's important for you to respect him, man. He your older brother.

Yemi   I'm gonna try.

Blazer   It's not bout trying, you got to. He gonna show you tings no one can teach you.

Yemi   Nah, blud, *I'm* da one that teaching him tings.

Ikudayisi   It's a lie.

Blazer   If you were in Nigeria you would be calling him uncle, you nah.

Yemi   What?

Ikudayisi   It's true-oh.

Yemi   I'm not sure bout dat one – he is not my uncle, he is my brother.

Ikudayisi   You should even be bowing down to me.

Yemi   Please!

Blazer   He right. Even *now* I don't call my sister by her name and she is only two years older than me. I call her auntie.

Yemi   Even in the street?

Blazer   The streets, at home, everywhere. *Blud*, I don't play when it comes to being respectful, you nah.

Yemi   Don't you care what people think?

Blazer   Fuck what people think. You think I care? What da fuck can they try say to me? I'll have up any mans if they try to disrespect my tradition.

Pause.

You see me, yeah. I ain't ashamed of nothing.

Pause.

When I was younger, people used to take the piss out of me cos I had an accent. And it used to get me *mad*, but I never used to say nothing. But then one day I had enough and every man who tried to take the piss – got knocked out. Straight!

Yemi   I remember hearing your fight stories, but I never knew the reasons behind it. You kept it real, blud.

Blazer   So what, you think now people will try take the piss with me now?

Yemi   No.

Blazer   Exactly. It's not going to happen. They can say what they want behind my back, but to my face, mans have to be careful what they say. And that's the way I like it. Gone are da days when mans take the piss out of this African! Cos I run this estate now. And you know, I know they don't like it. But what can they do? The roles have reversed now.

Yemi   Rahh, I like it! I like it.

Blazer   I'm not saying to you, go around testing people. You just need to learn how to stand your ground, but keep it real at the same time. It's not a bad thing to be African. Be proud to be different.

Yemi   I will man . . . I mean, I am.

Blazer   Make sure you start to learn Yoruba from your brother.

Yemi   Yeah, course.

Blazer (*to* **Ikudayisi**)   Make sure you teach him.

Ikudayisi   *Mo gbo.* [I understand.]

Blazer (*to* **Yemi**)   Even if you want, blud, come round to mines, I will teach you. It's easy once you get started. (*To* **Ikudayisi**.) And make sure you don't put on that fake accent again.

Ikudayisi (*in dodgy American accent*))   No problem.

Blazer   Oi.

Ikudayisi   I told you, it was joke I'm playing, I'm playing –

Blazer (*to* **Yemi**)   What's your full name?

Yemi   Oluyemi Adewale.

Blazer   Do you know what it means?

Yemi   Nah.

Ikudayisi   I know.

Yemi   Tell me.

Blazer   Don't tell him. Let him find it out himself – it would be a good lesson for him. That's your first assignment.

Yemi   Why? What does it mean?

Blazer   It's your mission. You need to investigate it yourself.

Yemi   OK.

Pause.

Blazer   So what's this I'm hearing bout some mad run-in with Armani?

Yemi   How do you know? . . . I never done nothing to her – is that why you come to chat to me?

Blazer   No, calm down, Yemi man, it's a question.

Yemi   Oh, she is just a fool who talks too much.

Blazer   You don't got to say that twice.

Yemi   So how did you know about my run-in with her?

Blazer   I heard her telling Razer.

Yemi   So, what, he's proper looking for me now? Man ready for war, you nah?

Blazer   Nah, blud, calm down. They weren't even paying attention to her anyways.

Yemi   *Dey?*

Blazer   You know, Razer and Flamer are always together.

Yemi   So dey must be looking for me den.

Blazer   Nah, man, don't worry.

Yemi   I'm not. I telling you, I'm ready for dem mans if they wanna start something.

Blazer   Calm down. So for the last ten minutes you ain't heard a word I said.

Yemi   I did – you said to stand your ground.

Blazer   When needed!

Pause.

Dem youth are my soldier, man. They can't make any movement without my say so. I don't want you to get into no madness. I will talk to dem if you want.

Yemi   If mans come, I just know to be prepared, innit.

Blazer   Stop talking like dat, man. You got to pick your battles wise, you know. Look, I'm having a word with dem. You're too young to be getting into madness.

Yemi   Nah, it cool.

Blazer   Seriously, I don't mind to chat to dem. Us Nigerians need to stick together. (*To* **Ikudayisi**.) Innit.

Ikudayisi   Of course now.

Yemi   It cool.

Blazer   OK. But don't do nothing stupid. One.

He nudges **Yemi** *and* **Ikudayisi** *and exits.*

Ikudayisi   I like him-oh.

Yemi *stares after* **Blazer**.

Ikudayisi   I said dat I think he is a cool guy.

Yemi *still ignores him.*

Ikudayisi   YEMI, are you listening?

Yemi   WHAT?

Ikudayisi   Your friend, he is a cool guy.

Yemi   Yeah, he is alright.

Ikudayisi   What wrong now?

Yemi   Nothing. I can't believe he is Nigerian. I can see it now but I never saw it before.

Pause.

Do you know, that the first time he has ever proper stopped and chat to me? Usually it's just hi and bye.

Ikudayisi   And so?

Yemi   Don't you think it's strange with all that been happening today?

Ikudayisi   Stop over-analysing everything. Did you not hear a word he was saying?

Yemi *is still looking into the distance.*

Ikudayisi   Yemi, you are reading too much into it.

Yemi *is still silent.*

Ikudayisi   Snap out of it.

Ikudayisi *clicks his fingers in front of* **Yemi**'s *face.*

Yemi   What does my name mean?

Ikudayisi   Now you want to learn.

Yemi   Stop being silly, just tell me.

Ikudayisi   Give me a hundred pound, and I'll tell you.

Yemi   Yeah, right! Just tell me, man.

Ikudayisi   OK, fifty pounds.

Yemi   This is why you get on my nerves.

Ikudayisi   OK, OK . . . it means 'God suit you'.

Yemi   'God suits me'! That's crap, man.

Ikudayisi   No, I mean, it hard to change it from Yoruba to English. It is better in Yoruba. Oluyemi is a big name.

Yemi   Whatever. Why did he go on like it was important for me to find out? What was he talking bout I need to know what it mean? That don't mean shit.

Ikudayisi   Nigerians believes names hold power.

Yemi   Why?

Ikudayisi   Cos they think that people will live up to it, they have special meaning.

Yemi   What does your name mean?

Ikudayisi   'Death spared me'.

Yemi   WHAT?! I should have got that name.

Ikudayisi   I came first.

Yemi   But that type of name don't suit you. You ain't no warrior. It suits a fighter like me!

Ikudayisi   Dat not what it means.

Yemi   What does it mean then, if it's not a warrior name?

Ikudayisi   It means that when Mum was having me she may have had some complications – you know, cos she had me young, and death spared me. I survived!

Yemi   *I don't care*, I should have had that name.

Ikudayisi   Look at you – now you want a Nigerian name. Anyway, I'm happy-oh.
    Green white green on my chest,
    You're proud to be a Nigerian.

Ikudayisi *starts to sing his song and notices* **Yemi** *bounces his head.*

Ikudayisi   Eh, eh, so now you are proud.

Yemi *pushes* **Ikudayisi.**

Yemi   Move. Shut up, man!

They begin to play-fight and **Yemi** *gets* **Ikudayisi** *in a head load.*

Yemi   You may be older than me, but I'm stronger. See, that why I should have had your name.

Ikudayisi   Let go of me.

Yemi   Who's your daddy?

Ikudayisi   Olakunle Adewale.

Yemi   No, you fool, say I'm your dad.

Ikudayisi   No.

Yemi   Say it and I'll let go.

Ikudayisi   No.

Yemi   Who's your dad?

Ikudayisi   You are squeezing my neck. I can't breathe.

Yemi   Say I'm your dad and I'll let go.

Ikudayisi   I can't breathe!

Two **Police Officers** *come onto the estate.*

Police Officer 1   Oi, can I have word with you?

Yemi *lets go of* **Ikudayisi** *as* **Police Officer 1** *walks up to him.* **Ikudayisi** *begins rubbing his neck.*

Ikudayisi (*to* **Yemi**)   You play too ruff, you dey hurt my neck-oh.

Police Officer 2 (*to* **Ikudayisi**)   You OK, son?

Yemi   Course he alright.

Police Officer 2   You will get your chance to speak in a minute, mate.

Yemi   We were just playing.

Police Officer 2   That's what they all say.

Yemi   What's that suppose to mean?

Police Officer 1   Watch your mouth, lad!

Yemi   What?

Ikudayisi   It's true, we were just playing.

Police Officer 2 *moves* **Ikudayisi** *away from* **Yemi**.

Police Officer 2 (*to* **Ikudayisi**)   Don't worry. We're here now, you ain't got to be scared anymore. Are you OK?

Ikudayisi   I'm OK . . .

Yemi   I told you we were just playing.

Police Officer 2   And I said *that's* what they all say.

Yemi   Are you buzzing, blud? What's your beef?

Police Officer 2   Who do you think you're talking too? I ain't your pal or your mate. Does it look like we are from the same blood? Show some respect and talk properly.

Yemi *heads to confront* **Police Officer 2** *but* **Police Officer 1** *gets in the way and they both crowd over him.*

Yemi   Man is speaking English.

Police Officer 2   You're not a man, you're still a boy.

Police Officer 1 (*to* **Yemi**)   So where you heading off to now?

Yemi *remains silent.*

Police Officer 1   You deaf, *boy*? I'm asking you a question.

Yemi *still remains silent.*

Police Officer 1 (*holds* **Yemi**'s *face*) I said, *where* are you going?

Yemi   NOWHERE. I ain't got to speak to you if I don't want to.

Police Officer 1   Do you wanna be answering these questions at a police station? If not, start talking.

Yemi   Is there something you're looking for?

Police Officer 2   Is there something *you're* tryna hide?

Yemi   You got time on your hands. I know my right. Why don't you go and fight real crime.

Police Officer 1   Black-on-black violence *is* a crime.

Police Officer 2 *laughs.*

Ikudayisi   Please, what's the problem, sir?

Police Officer 1   We're just trying to find out what the problem is here, son.

Yemi   There is no problem – we were playing. Mans like you is just tryna harass us.

Police Officer 2 (*to* **Police Officer 1**)   You understand what he saying?

Police Officer 1   Kids find it so hard to speak English nowadays.

Police Officer 2   All that seems to come out their mouths is bumba clat this, bumba clat that, and innit man, yeah man.

Police Officer 1   Such a disgrace. Schools really ain't teaching them anything.

Police Officer 2   I think I should start up my own school.

Police Officer 1   Oh yeah, what would you call it?

Yemi   You two are nuts. Let's go, Dayisi.

Yemi *begins to walk around them and* **Police Officer 2** *grabs his hand.*

Yemi   Let go of my hand.

Police Officer 1   We have not finished here.

Yemi   Man, best let go.

Police Officer 1   *Oohh,* is that a threat?

Police Officer 2   Sounds like one to me. You getting ready to assault a police officer?

Yemi   You don't know me – when I make a threat, *you will know*!

Police Officer 2   Oohh, I think the Yardie is getting mad.

Police Officer 1 (*in a dodgy Jamaican accent*)   Bumba clat, we may need some backup, man, up in de place.

Police Officer 2   And request for the drug squad.

Police Officer 1 (*in a dodgy Jamaican accent*)   SO man may start shooting up de place, he na care, him gangsta.

The two **Police Officers** *begin to laugh at their own jokes while* **Yemi** *still struggles.*

Yemi   Shows how much you know. I'm not even Jamaican. I'm Nigerian.

Police Officer 1   Stop being silly, you're not from Africa, he is.

Ikudayisi   We're both Nigerian.

Police Officer 2   He don't act African. He lied to you, son, he is a Jamaican.

Yemi   Yeah, I am Nigerian.

Police Officer 2   Let me see your passport.

Police Officer 1   You mean his photocopy?

Yemi (*to* **Ikudayisi**)   You hearing this now. I told you they treat you different when you are black.

Ikudayisi   Yemi, shh.

Yemi   What? Why should I be quiet, you blind?

Ikudayisi   Please, sir, we are just coming from de shop.

Police Officer 1   Don't worry, we know how to deal with him. We handle situations like this on a daily basis.

Yemi *still struggles with* **Police Officer 2** *but his grip on him gets tighter.*

Yemi   Stop tryna take the fucking piss.

Police Officer 2   Watch your language, son.

Yemi   I ain't your son.

Police Officer 2   Glad you ain't. If I had a child I'd teach him to have a lot more respect than you.

Yemi   Look – what do you want?

Police Officer 1   For you to show some manners and respect.

Yemi   But I'm not even doing nothing.

Police Officer 2   You're causing a scene.

Yemi   You're the one's who is *harassing* me. Touching me for no reason. You know you ain't got nothing on us. (*He gets free. To* **Ikudayisi**.) Let's go!

Police Officer 2   He is not going anywhere with you.

Yemi *attempts to grab* **Ikudayisi**'s *hand.* **Police Officer 1** *holds him back again.*

Yemi   STOP TRYNA FUCKING TOUCH ME UP. YOU BATTY MAN!

Police Officer 1   Ohh, bad mistake!

He starts to bring out the handcuffs.

Ikudayisi   Please, sir, he doesn't mean it.

Police Officer 2   Just stand over here, son.

Yemi   You can't hold me against my will.

Police Officer 1   We can if we suspect you being under the influence.

Yemi   Under the influence of what?

Police Officers 1 *and* **2**   Cannabis.

Yemi   Dat's how I know you're chatting shit. Can you even smell anything on me?

Ikudayisi   Sir, please, how much do you want.

He begins searching in his pockets.

Yemi (*to* **Ikudayisi**)   Dayisi, are you mad, you don't got to pay for nothing.

Ikudayisi   How much do you want? I will go and get it and you can let him go.

Yemi   Stop talking!

Police Officer 2 (*to* **Ikudayisi**)   Son, we're not corrupt officers, we don't take bribes – just sorting out this little dispute for you, OK?

Ikudayisi   Please, we don't want trouble.

Police Officer 2 (*to* **Ikudayisi**)   Don't worry, it's not you that's causing the problems. (*He gets out his notebook. To* **Yemi**.) We will try this again. What is your name?

Yemi   I really ain't got time for this. Arrest me, innit.

Police Officer 1   Well, disturbing the peace is a big offence.

Yemi   Disturbing the peace, disturbing the peace – you're disturbing *my* peace. You came up to me with nothing to say, nothing! Just tryna force me to get mad. TO GET MAD SO I WILL DO SOMETHING, SO YOU CAN DO ME FOR SOMINK. That's how I know you people are corrupt. When you should be out doing something constructive. You're bugging me cos I'm black.

Police Officer 1   Don't try and use the race card here, boy, and keep your voice down.

Police Officer 2   There is nothing racist about us, stop tryna make a scene.

Yemi   You're stopping me from going home.

Police Officer 1   Home?

Police Officer 2   If you were willing to say that in the first place, of course we would have let you go home. Go on then.

Yemi   What?

Ikudayisi   We are sorry, sir.

Yemi   SHUT UP, DAYISI, WHAT YOU SAYING SORRY FOR? These mans are taking us for dickhead. Are you blind?

Yemi *goes to push him and the* **Police Officers** *hold him back.*

Yemi   The only reason they acting nice now is cos there are bare people around, looking at them, knowing they are being racist!

Police Officer 1   Oi, leave him alone.

Police Officer 2 (*to onlookers*)   This is why, people, we're here. Just looking out for *his* best interest. (*To* **Ikudayisi**.) We wouldn't want anything to happen to you whilst you're in this country.

Ikudayisi   Uh?

Yemi (*to* **Ikudayisi**)   This is what I've been telling you all day, all day, but you never wanted to listen to me. What did I tell you bout this country?

Police Officer 2   Stop causing a scene.

Yemi   Nah, people need to hear what's going on.

Police Officer 1   Stop trying to be a smart alec.

Yemi (*begins shouting while being held*)   The only reason why these mans are holding me is cos I'm black. I ain't done nothing and they tryna arrest me.

A message comes in on the police radio about a more important case.

I'm being harassed, I'm being harassed!

Police Officer 2   Today's your lucky day, son.

Yemi *and* **Ikudayisi** *start to move, but get stopped again.*

Police Officer 1   No, you go that way and we will help him out.

Yemi   But we live *that* way.

Police Officer 2   There is still a chance of you getting arrested.

Ikudayisi   Please, he is my brother, sir.

Police Officer 1   You don't have to *pretend*, son, he won't trouble you again.

Yemi *kisses his teeth and heads off to the right. The* **Police Officers** *stay and watch till he goes offstage.*

Police Officer 1   Off you go then.

Ikudayisi   But –

Police Officer 2   Don't worry, son, we got you covered.

The **Police Officers** *stay and watch as* **Ikudayisi** *walks off to the left. He glances backwards once or twice, but the* **Police Officers** *stand their ground till he is out of sight.*

Blackout.

Scene Eight

On the other side of the estate, **Razer** *and* **Armani** *are walking down the street.* **Razer** *has his arms around* **Armani**.

Razer   You need to be more nicer to your friend, you nah.

Armani   Uh.

Razer   Paris, man, she is the only friend you got.

Armani   What? Whose side are you on? You saw the way she tried to speak to me.

Razer   Ah, don't worry. You two will be talking by the end of tonight.

Armani   I won't. She gets on my nerves and I'll let her know dat. I'm not fake – if I don't like someone I make dem know.

Razer   She's cool, man. How come she ain't got a boyfriend?

Armani   Cos she ugly.

Razer   Stop being silly. I'm tryna be serious.

Armani   Why are you interested for?

Razer   I'm not, it's for Flamer.

Armani   So let Flamer find out for himself. I'm never talking to her again.

Razer   You kinda messed up his flow.

Armani   How?

Razer   By making her storm off.

Armani   He needs to forget bout dat then.

Razer   Why?

Armani   Cos she tried to take me for an eediate, and I ain't no fool, and we are no longer friends.

Razer *lets go of* **Armani**.

Razer   You're so childish.

Armani   No, I'm just real.

Razer   No, you're just silly.

Armani   I don't know why you care. She is frigid, man. Anyways, Flamer don't stand a chance.

Razer   You're a hater, do you know that, Armani?

Armani   *No*, I'm not.

Razer   You are.

Armani   WHY ARE YOU SO FOCUSED ON TALKING BOUT PARIS FOR?

Razer   Forget it. Sometimes you get on my nerves. Man can't even have a civilised conversation with you without you running up your mouth.

Armani   I'm sorry. It's just today been a mad day. Everyone is trying to have a go at me. This is suppose to be a free country and people are not even allowing me to speak my mind.

Razer   Don't take it out on me.

Armani   Paris never even had my back.

Razer   You told this story already.

Armani   And you're my man, so don't you think you should have stood up for me when that dickhead African Blazer was shouting at me?

Razer   If you kept quiet Blazer would have left you.

Armani   And even when Paris tried to tell all those lies you never even said anything.

Razer   Aaaah, man.

Armani   Its true, dough – you could have said something.

Razer   Armani, you started most of these argument. What do you expect me to say?

Pause.

Armani   You gonna sort that Yemi out den?

Razer   Why?

Armani   Because these Africans are forgetting their place and you need to show him.

Razer   I'm not involved in this African war ting you're tryna start.

Armani   But he tried to attack me.

Razer   So? You tryna say you never done nothing to provoke him?

Armani   No – you know Africans are animals, man. He just went mad on me. He hit me in the head and he called you a dickhead, saying you can't do shit to him. You can't let him get away wid dat.

Razer   I'm not troubling nobody. If I get in trouble one more time I'm getting locked down, and I ain't going jail for no chick.

Armani   But –

Razer   Listen! I told you I'm not getting locked down for stupidness. Didn't you hear anything I said before? No chick gonna be the reason I get locked up, including you, Armani.

Armani   Then maybe you shouldn't be my man. I need a man who can look after me, one who is not afraid.

Razer   Go then.

Armani   A man is supposed to look out for his girl – he is meant to protect her no matter what.

Razer   I said, go then. Go fine a man better dan me.

Armani   That's why I should have gone out with Flamer. He's is not afraid of no one.

Razer   FUCK OFF!

Armani   You don't have to be so rude. What's your problem?

Razer   WHAT IS YOURS? You giving me a headache, man. I'm telling you to stop talking and all you do is talk. Can't you just be quiet for once, man? That's what gets you into trouble – your mouth. And you want me to get involved in your bullshit. I only fight battles that worth fighting. I'm tryna make changes and you're tryna force me to go down the wrong road.

Armani   Are you on your period or something?

Razer   Piss off, man.

Razer *puts up his hood and walks off, leaving* **Armani** *speechless.*

Blackout.

Scene Nine

It is now around eight in the evening, and **Flamer** *is walking on the estate by himself when* **Ikudayisi** *runs onstage.*

Ikudayisi   YEMI, YEMI, WHERE ARE YOU NOW?

He bumps into **Flamer**.

Flamer   You idiot.

Ikudayisi   I'm sorry-oh, I didn't see you.

Flamer   So, what, I'm too black now?

Ikudayisi   Don't be stupid.

Flamer   You calling me stupid?

Ikudayisi   No, you don't understand. I'm saying how can I not see you, you are not that black.

Flamer *looks down at his trainers and sees one has a mark on it.*

Flamer   Look at my trainer, blud. Are you on a hype ting?

Ikudayisi   I'm sorry.

Flamer   What, is *that* all you're gonna say?

Ikudayisi   What do you want me to say now? It was only an accident. I didn't mean it.

Flamer   So what you gonna do about it then?

Ikudayisi   What do you want me to do? You can go home and clean it.

Flamer   Blud, do you think I'm a dickhead?

Ikudayisi   Please, I don' have time for this, I have to look for my brother.

Ikudayisi *start to walk off but* **Flamer** *catches hold of him.*

Flamer   Did I say we have finish?

Ikudayisi   What is wrong with today-oh? Why is everyone stopping people from walking? All I want to do is go home. I have said I'm sorry. What else do you want me to do?

Flamer   Sorry ain't gonna pay for it. I want my fifty pound!

Ikudayisi   Fifty pound for dis dirty trainer. Kayi! I don't have that kind of money-oh.

Flamer   Is this man dizzy? You steps on my foot and now you're tryna take me for an eediate. Are you buzzing?

Ikudayisi   I beg your pardon? I don't understand what you just said.

Flamer   What? All of a sudden you don't understand English now? Man better start understanding what I'm saying.

Flamer *brings out a knife.*

Ikudayisi   Ahhh, ARMED ROBBER! (*He raises his hands in the air.*) Be careful-oh. *Jo ma pa me! Ma pa me-oh!* [Don't kill me.]

Flamer   Speak English.

Ikudayisi   I don't have anything on me – please don't kill me.

Flamer   I'm not playing around! Give me my money.

Ikudayisi   I beg-oh. I don't have no money with me.

Flamer   Empty out your pockets.

Ikudayisi   Ah ah, now you don't believe me. Why will I lie? Look, I live on this estate. Give me your trainer and I will go and wash it for you now.

Flamer   I have never seen you round here before, so don't take me for an eediate. Empty your pocket.

Ikudayisi *empties out his pockets.*

Flamer   Where is your phone?

Ikudayisi   I don't have one.

Flamer   You ain't got a phone? What type of . . . ?

He looks **Ikudayisi** *up and down from head to toe.*

Flamer   Take off your trainers.

Ikudayisi   Ah, ah, I can't give you the trainers, I said I will clean your shoe for you.

Flamer   I said, take off the trainers.

Ikudayisi   It's not mine. Please, it's my brother's.

Flamer   Take off the fucking trainer, now.

Ikudayisi   Please, I didn't mean to step on your trainer.
It was an accident, ah ah –

Flamer *moves closer to* **Ikudayisi** *with the knife.* **Ikudayisi**
quickly takes off the trainers.

Ikudayisi   What is happening to this country? Why are you
behaving like dis?

Yemi *enters and sees what is happening. He shouts over.*

Yemi   Oi!

Flamer *takes the trainers and runs.* **Yemi** *runs over to* **Ikudayisi**.

Yemi   Why you letting people push you around? This is
what I mean bout you need to change.

Ikudayisi   Just leave me. *Awon olori buruku.* [These horrible
people.]

Yemi   What happen, man?

Ikudayisi   This London *babanla problem lo wa fumi* [This
London is nothing but trouble for me.]

Yemi   I don't have time for this – what happen?

Pause.

Where is your – I mean *my* trainers?

Ikudayisi   He took it now.

Yemi   You got *jacked*!

Ikudayisi   No!

Yemi   So what happened?

Ikudayisi   I stepped on his trainer –

Yemi   You let someone take your trainers and you never
even fought back? What the hell is wrong with you? See, see, I
thought everyone was nice to you! You just made a man take
you for an eediate and you couldn't do nothing.

Ikudayisi   I tried now.

Yemi   Tried! Tried! I swear in African you train with lion.

Ikudayisi   Yemi, don't start that . . . In Nigeria people die over things like this all the time-oh. I value my life. He had a knife.

Yemi   So?

Ikudayisi   What did you want me to do?

Yemi   NOT TO GET ROBBED!

Ikudayisi   I said he had a knife.

Yemi   If that was me, I would fight him same way. Do you think I care? You just made a man take you for an eediate and you didn't do nothing? And you were saying I don't know what I'm talking bout. I DON'T KNOW WHAT I'M TALKING ABOUT! Do you *now* see what this country is like? Do you see?

Ikudayisi   Where were you, eh?

Yemi   What! You tryna switch this on me? Was you not there when the police told me to walk? If you had any sense you would have followed me, instead of just standing around with them.

Ikudayisi   They told me to wait.

Yemi   Why did you listen?

Ikudayisi   Why didn't you stay?

Yemi   So is it my fault? You're a big boy and you got rob – I would never let that happen to me.

Ikudayisi   It wasn't my fault, it wasn't my fault. I beg him not to take it, he didn't listen. I'm not going to get killed because of trainer.

Yemi   You pussy.

Ikudayisi   I don't like this country. *Babalan* [enormous] problem.

Armani *enters, looking for* **Razer**.

Armani   Razer, where are you? RAZER!

She sees **Yemi**, *cuts her eye at him, then quickly runs off the other way.*

Yemi   Come on, let's go.

Ikudayisi   Where are you going to go?

Yemi   I'm going to settle this once and for all.

Ikudayisi   I don't have shoes on.

Yemi   We are going after the shoes.

Ikudayisi   You don't know where it is.

Yemi   Do you think it a coincidence that that girl is looking for her man in the same place you got robbed? Open your eyes.

Ikudayisi   Who?

Yemi   Armani. You blind? Did you not just see her come round da corner?

Ikudayisi   I don't want trouble. Let's just go home. We already have the milk. Mum will be worried.

Yemi   In this country you ain't got to look for trouble before it finds you. Can you not see dat? If you don't go for what is yours, they will always think you're a dickhead. If you don't stand your ground.

Ikudayisi   Who?

Yemi   Dem. That crew, it was dat Armani chick that told dem to come for you. We need to show them that they can't take us for eediate.

Ikudayisi   Please, let's just go home.

Yemi   Didn't you hear what Blazer was saying before?

Ikudayisi   Oh, please, eh, I don't like this.

Yemi   He said, yeah, we have to demand respect. I'm going to teach you how to stand your ground.

Ikudayisi   Listen to me, Yemi, I'm standing my ground now. Going after somebody who has a weapon is not good-oh. Yemi, I don't want to be a part of this. Let's go home.

Yemi   I ain't going nowhere till I sort this out. I have let this go on for too many years now. Mans ain't gonna take me for a dickhead *no more*!

Ikudayisi   Forget about years ago. You have to learn to choose your battle. There are more important things to fight over. Believe me.

Yemi   *Yes*, and this is one of them.

Ikudayisi   No, it's not – please, look, this is why you need to go to Nigeria and see. Things like this is small, small.

Yemi   Shut up! *Shut up!* Now is not the time to start talking your Nigerian shit.

Ikudayisi   Then what is it you are going to fight for? You are running to go and prove a point, but you don't know what point you are making.

Yemi   I'm doing this for me. I'm gonna make people know who I am.

Ikudayisi   Please, Yemi, this is not a good idea.

Yemi   Move out my way, Dayisi.

Ikudayisi   No, I can't let you do this. You have been telling me all day I need to change, but now it's time for you to stop and think. You make me laugh, you go on like your life is so hard. Believe me, you have it easy. Once you stop thinking dat the whole world has declared war on you, you will see how great your life is.

Yemi   Why don't you care about the fact that you just got robbed?

Ikudayisi I told, I told you, it's not important. Do you think I have never had to make choices? I told you I was once like you. Is it the first time I got robbed? *No!* In Nigeria it happens all the time – even the police have robbed in broad daylight. I used to put up a fight but I told you, you soon realise thing like this is not important. As long as I'm alive, I'm happy. Friends in Nigeria have died over nonsense like this. I want to enjoy my life – those are the changes I have made. Don't waste your life away like this.

Yemi Move. You ain't got to follow me. You can go off home.

Ikudayisi *tries to hold him back.*

Yemi Get off me. This is going to be sorted with or without you!

Blackout.

Scene Ten

Armani *has caught up with* **Razer** *and they are walking together when* **Yemi** *comes round the corner, followed by* **Ikudayisi***.*

Yemi Oi, RAZER! Yeah, you, I'm talking to you. Give me my shit back.

Razer *(looks stunned)*   What? *(To* **Armani***.)* What's he talking bout?

Armani Move, you dickhead, who do you think you're talking to like that?

Ikudayisi It wasn't him.

Yemi Blud, why are you tryna take man for a dickhead?

Razer What? What's wrong wid you people?

Yemi I want it back now.

Armani Are you crazy? Go talk your gibberish elsewhere, man.

Yemi You think it is a coincidence my brother got robbed five minutes ago and then the only people I see on road – is you two?

Razer Your brother?

Yemi Yes, my brother. Don't think I'm stupid. You messed with the wrong person now.

Razer Shut up, man. Move.

Armani YEAH, DUSS.

Yemi (*to* **Armani**) You shut up.

Armani That's what I'm saying, Razer. Look, he is tryna get rude. Put him in his place. You see I wasn't lying. Look how he is acting like an animal.

Razer Blud, just go home. I'm not in the mood.

Razer *tries to walk off but* **Yemi** *holds him back.*

Ikudayisi Yemi, I told you it wasn't him.

Yemi Only mans like him like to take advantage of people who can't defend themselves.

Armani Be quiet, you bubo.

Yemi I will knock you out.

Ikudayisi *Omo girl e.* [Oh this girl.] Shut up your mouth.

Armani SPEAK ENGLISH.

Razer *moves towards* **Ikudayisi**.

Razer Don't talk to my girl like dat.

Yemi He will talk to her any way he wants. Don't try to take him for an eediate and think he will sit down bout it. Give me my shit back.

Razer Blud, don't get rude.

Yemi   What, you think you can pick on him cos he is African, but you can't deal with me?

Razer   I'm being nice – go home.

Yemi   Give me my tings and I'll go.

Armani   Razer, you're good, why don't you just thump him in his mouth, maybe then he will start making sense.

Yemi *moves close to* **Armani**.

Yemi   Thump who?

Ikudayisi   Yemi, leave her, it's not worth it at all. (*To* **Razer**.) We don't want trouble.

Razer   He seems to be asking it for it dough. You need to speak to your brother, cos I don't know what he is talking about.

Ikudayisi *tries to move* **Yemi**.

Yemi   DON'T TOUCH ME! I'm doing this for you. If you let people treat you like shit they will walk over you all your life.

Ikudayisi   Stop lying to yourself – I have already told you I'm not asking for this.

Yemi *pushes* **Ikudayisi** *and moves to* **Razer**.

Yemi   I just want my tings back.

Razer   Don't try and start something you can't finish.

Yemi   What dat suppose to mean?

Razer   This is da last time I'm going to tell you to go home. Don't try and get too big for your boot. Lauw da hype ting.

Yemi (*moves real close to* **Razer**)   I'm not on no hype ting – I just want my FUCKING TRAINERS BACK!

Armani (*to* **Razer**)   Why are you letting him talk to you like dat? This boy is a waste, man. DO SOMETHING.

Yemi *goes for* **Razer** *and* **Razer** *pulls out a knife.*

Razer LOOK, I TOLD YOU GO HOME. Why are you making me do this?

Ikudayisi Oh God, oh . . .

Razer I'm trying, yeah, I'm trying. I don't wanna do this.

Yemi You're making me mad and I don't want to get mad.

Razer I DON'T WANNA GET MAD EITHER. Now I've told you I don't know what you're talking bout. So leave. NOW!

Ikudayisi Please put it down.

Yemi (*to* **Ikudayisi**) Stop BEGGING PEOPLE. (*To* **Razer**.) I ain't scared of you, bruv. If you're gonna wet me then wet me. But I don't care, I'm not going anywhere till you people understand I ain't a dickhead. I ain't a dickhead.

Ikudayisi Please, let's go.

Armani Just wet him up, man, he deserves it.

Razer Shut up Armani, man.

As **Razer** *gets distracted* **Yemi** *goes for the knife. They get into a scrap and* **Yemi** *gains control over it.*

Yemi Who is bad now, who bad now?

Ikudayisi Yemi, put it down, you going to hurt somebody. It wasn't him.

Armani Yeah, listen to your brother.

Yemi BE QUIET. YOU'RE ALWAYS FUCKING TALKING. Don't you know when to keep your mouth shut, uh? You really think you're bad, innit.

Armani No.

He waves the knife at her.

Razer Yemi, I swear – put it down.

Armani   No, please!

Yemi   See, you're scared now. I thought you were a bad girl. African this and African that. You're not better than me now, are you? Carry on running your mouth, see if you don't get wet.

Ikudayisi   Why can't you listen to me? I keep telling you – what you are fighting for is not worth it.

Yemi   Don't you get it? I don't care. These lots go on like they run this fucking estate. It about time people sees who really runs this estate. These jams think they are better dan us Africans. Dat we ain't shit. That's why they robbed you. It something they do all the time. They treat Africans like they are beneath them. I AIN'T BENEATH NO ONE.

Razer   Look, I'm tryna stay out of trouble, I ain't robbed no one in time.

Yemi   Well, you messed with the wrong person.

Ikudayisi   I didn't come from Nigeria to be a part of this. We are all BLACK! WE ARE ALL BLACK AND YOU ARE ACTING LIKE WE ARE ALL DIVIDED! It needs to stop now. We need to stop this nonsense. Why are we always fighting each other? Why can't we just get along? I just want everyone to get along. Yemi, you tell me you are free, be free to make the right choice. Don't go down the wrong road. It's your choice, make the right choice. GIVE ME THE KNIFE.

Ikudayisi *goes for the knife and struggles with* **Yemi**. *In the process the knife falls and* **Razer** *picks it up again.*

Yemi (*to* **Ikudayisi**)   Why do I bother listening to you – look what you done.

Ikudayisi   He doesn't want no trouble, he is going – leave him.

Razer *starts to walk.* **Yemi** *grabs him.* **Ikudayisi** *tries to stop him and as he gets in between his arm gets cut by the knife.*

Ikudayisi   Ahhhh!

He falls to the ground.

Yemi   IKU, IKU!

He grabs **Ikudayisi** *and holds him.*

Armani   Razer, look what you done, look what you done.

Razer   I didn't mean to, it was just in my hand. It wasn't my fault, it wasn't my fault. Ah fuck man! Yemi, it wasn't my fault.

Blackout.

Scene Eleven

Two weeks later. **Yemi** *and* **Ikudayisi** *are in their bedroom.* **Ikudayisi** *is in traditional African attire and is struggling to put on his hat because his arm is in a sling.* **Yemi** *is putting the agbada over his head and is profiling in front of the mirror.*

Mum *(offstage, shouting)*   You two children, what is taking you so long? We were supposed to be at the party from seven o'clock. Look at the time now.

Ikudayisi *and* **Yemi**   I'M WAITING FOR HIM!

They point at each other, look and begin laughing.

Mum *(off)*   People already think I don't have any control of you, that I leave you to gallivant and act like animals. What are they going to be thinking when we show up late, eh? . . . People always tell me that I'm –

Ikudayisi   LUCKY TO HAVE BIG BOYS!

Yemi   We are coming, Mum.

Mum *(off)*   I'M ONLY GIVING YOU TEN MORE MINUTES!

Ikudayisi *(turns to* **Yemi***)*   You're waiting for me? I've been ready for an hour now and I'm the one that is handicap.

Yemi   Stop rinsing that line, it's played out now.

Ikudayisi   I know, I know, I just like making you feel guilty.

Yemi   Badmind.

Ikudayisi   I will never forget the look on your face that day when you thought I died.

Yemi   It wasn't funny, you nah. My heart skipped a beat.

Ikudayisi   And that Razer, I've never seen two boys cry as much as you two.

Yemi   Why do you have to keep on telling the story like that?

Ikudayisi   Cos that is how it happened. Iku, Iku, don't die, don't die.

Yemi *punches him in the arm.*

Ikudayisi   Ow.

Yemi   Oh shit, oh shit. I'm sorry, I'm sorry.

Ikudayisi *(starts laughing)*   You are so gullible. At least I know you really love me.

Yemi   Shut up.

Ikudayisi   Come on, say it, you love me.

Yemi   Leave me.

Ikudayisi   Not until you say you love me.

Yemi   No! Stop acting gay.

Ikudayisi   Just say it.

Yemi   No.

Ikudayisi   I can't hear you.

Yemi   Cos I never said it.

Ikudayisi   Why are you being so –

Mum *(off)*   YOU THESE CHILDREN, I HAVE BEEN NICE TO YOU SINCE THAT DAY – OH, BUT I WILL STOP BEING NICE IF YOU DON'T LISTEN.

Ikudayisi   *Mon bo, Ma.* [I'm coming, Mum.] *(To* **Yemi**.*)* Just hurry up before she starts breathing fire and smoke comes out her nose.

Yemi   Yeah, OK.

Ikudayisi *turns to leave.*

Yemi   Ikudayisi.

Ikudayisi   Yeah?

Yemi   You have forgiven me, right?

Ikudayisi   For what?

He turns to leave again.

Yemi   Dayisi.

Ikudayisi   Yes?

Yemi   I'm sorry.

Ikudayisi   I know, I guess you now know what's important, right?

Yemi   Yeah, yeah I do.

Ikudayisi *goes to give* **Yemi** *a hug.*

Ikudayisi   Don't beat yourself up, we're brothers.

Yemi   Yeah, brothers.

Ikudayisi *exits.*

Yemi *picks up a basketball cap but then decides on the traditional hat. As he starts to put on his shoes he changes his mind and goes for his trainers. Once he has them on he stands in front of the mirror and checks himself out.*

Yemi   Yeah, I look heavy, man.

He begins singing and dancing around the room.

Green white green on my chest,
I'm proud to be a Nigerian!
Green white green on my chest,
I'm proud to be a Nigerian!
Proud to be a Ni-ge-ri-an!
Proud to be a Ni-ge-ri-an!

Simon Stephens

Pornography

Simon Stephens began his theatrical career in the literary
department of the Royal Court Theatre where he ran its
Young Writers' Programme. His plays for theatre include
Bluebird (Royal Court Theatre, London, 1998 directed by
Gordon Anderson); *Herons* (Royal Court Theatre, London,
2001); *Port* (Royal Exchange Theatre, Manchester, 2002); *One
Minute* (Crucible Theatre, Sheffield, 2003, Bush Theatre,
London, 2004); *Christmas* (Bush Theatre, London, 2004);
Country Music (Royal Court Theatre Upstairs, London, 2004);
On the Shore of the Wide World (Royal Exchange, Manchester,
and Royal National Theatre, 2005); *Motortown* (Royal Court
Theatre Downstairs, London, 2006); *Pornography* (Deutsches
Schauspielhaus, Hanover, 2007, Edinburgh Festival/
Birmingham Rep, 2008, and Tricycle Theatre, London,
2009), *Harper Regan* (Royal National Theatre, 2008); *Sea Wall*
(Bush Theatre, 2008, Traverse Theatre, 2009); *Heaven*
(Traverse Theatre, 2009); and *Punk Rock* (Lyric Theatre
Hammersmith and Royal Exchange, Manchester, 2009). His
radio plays include *Five Letters Home to Elizabeth* (BBC Radio 4,
2001) and *Digging* (BBC Radio 4, 2003). Awards include the
Pearson Award for Best Play, 2001, for *Port*; Olivier Award
for Best New Play for *On the Shore of the Wide World*, 2005; and
for *Motortown* German Critics in *Theater Heute*'s annual poll
voted him Best Foreign Playwright, 2007. His screenwriting
includes an adaptation of *Motortown* for Film Four; a two-part
serial *Dive* (with Dominic Savage) for Granada/BBC (2009)
and a short film adaptation of *Pornography* for Channel 4's
Coming Up series (2009).

Pornography was originally translated into German by Barbara Christ and was first presented in a co-production between the Deutschen Schauspielhauses, Hamburg, and the Festival Theaterformen and the Schauspielhannover in Hanover. It received its world premiere in Hanover on 15 June 2007 and transferred to Hamburg on 5 October 2007. The cast was as follows:

Sonja Beisswenger
Christoph Franken
Peter Knaack
Angela Muethel
Jana Schulz
Monique Schwitter
Daniel Wahl
Samuel Weiss

Director Sebastian Nübling
Designer Muriel Gerstner
Lighting Roland Edrich
Music Lars Wittershagen
Costume designer Marion Münch
Dramaturgs Nicola Bramkamp, Regina Guhl, David Tushingham

This play can be performed by any number of actors.
It can be performed in any order.

I am going to keep this short and to the point, because it's all been said before by far more eloquent people than me.

But our words have no impact upon you, therefore I'm going to talk to you in a language that you understand. Our words are dead until we give them life with our blood.

Images of hell.
They are silent.

What you need to do is stand well clear of the yellow line.

Images of hell.
They are silent.

Seven

I wake up and I think he's drowning. I can hear the sound of him in his cot. His breath is tight and he's gasping. I go into his room. Stand there. Every bone is as small as a finger. He's not drowning. Of course he's not drowning, he's on dry land. It's Saturday morning. He's still asleep. I watch his chest rise and fall. It would take only the lightest of forces from an adult's arm to crush the bones in his ribcage. I feel so much love for him that my heart fills up. I can feel it filling up. Like a balloon.

It's six thirty.

I go back into my bedroom. I crawl under the covers. Jonathan, my husband, is lying on his side. When I get back into the bed he lays his arm across me. It's incredibly heavy. Like it's made out of leather.

I wait for Lenny, for my son, to wake up.

He does.

I turn the radio on downstairs. I put the kettle on. I put Lenny in his chair. He's grumpy this morning. I make a pot of three cups of Jamaican Blue Mountain coffee. And slowly, methodically, I sit and drink all three cups myself.

I let Jonathan sleep.

I don't remember any news story that was on the radio that day. Apart from everybody's talking about, there's a concert. A man's talking about this concert. And exactly what it is going to achieve I must admit I find a little unclear. But he's deeply passionate about the whole affair. And the singer's passion, and Lenny's grumpiness, the little tiny whining noises that he makes, and the taste of the coffee and the feeling of wood on my table means that I find, to my surprise, that there are tears pouring down my face and falling onto the newspaper which the boy, some boy, a boy I think, at least I think it's a boy, delivered, must have delivered at some point this morning.

I go shopping in the afternoon and in my head I'm already getting prepared for work next week.

I push Lenny in his pushchair. He's got one of those three-wheeled pushchairs. It has fabulous suspension. It makes it ideal for city street life. I buy myself a pair of sandals which are pink and they have this golden strap with a little pink flower on. I think in the shops everybody's got the concert on. It's that man I like. He's singing the song about looking at the stars. Look at the stars. See how they shine for you. Maybe today is the most important day that there's ever been. And this is the biggest success of human organisation that we've ever known. And everybody should be given a knighthood of some description. There should be some kind of knighthood which is given out to all of the people there. To the people who sell the ice creams even. They should get an ice-cream seller's knighthood. For the important selling of ice cream at a time of organisational urgency. I'd like to watch the Queen knight the boys selling ice cream in Hyde Park today. She wouldn't even need to walk far from her house. She could go on a bike. It would take her five minutes. This is a day of that level of importance.

I'm pushing him so much that he falls to sleep in the end. You bump up and down. I want to walk home. I could duck south of Euston Road. I could head through Bloomsbury. Today is a day for heading through Bloomsbury with a new pair of summer sandals, ideal for the beach, on a Saturday.

I don't.

I start off.

And then I get the bus from Holborn.

And I get home and Jonathan's not there. He should be there. He should be at home. I don't have the slightest idea where he is. I try not to think about it. The house is quieter without him.

Where were you? Where were you? Which shops? What were you doing? What were you doing there? What were you buying? What are you going to paint? I want to know what you need paint for. I want to know what you want to paint. I want to know where you've been. Do you like my sandals? I bought some sandals, do you like them? I bought them for the beach. For the summer.

Sunday's Jonathan's day with Lenny. He takes him to buy newspapers. I sleep in. But Lenny starts crying when Jonathan's putting his shoes on. He's putting his shoes on wrong. His socks are bunched up over his feet. He's put his little socks on and not pulled them up properly and they're all bunched up so the shoes are uncomfortable and he starts to cry. I say to myself I am not getting up out of bed to help him. I am not getting up out of bed to help him. I am not getting up out of bed to help him.

They leave. I have no idea what I'm going to do today. I sit still for up to half an hour at a time.

I don't know where he takes him. He's windswept when he comes back. Windswept and scruffy and Lenny's crabby but happy. When Jonathan's hair is like that. When his hair is all over the place and there's a sense that he's been outside because his cheeks are all pink. I look at him and there's something about him which is enough to make me smile.

We eat our tea in front of the television when Lenny's in bed. I want Jonathan to touch me. If he were to reach out and touch me. Just rest his hand on my neck and stroke the back of my hair. If he were to do that now. Right now. Right this second.

I drop Lenny off at Julia's and he squeaks with happiness.

The tube is full of people and nearly all of them nowadays have iPods. I can't remember when that happened.

I head into work.

The Triford report is nearly finished. It's nearly ready. When it's ready. If we get it right. If David gets it right then the implications for the company are, well, they are immense. We actually did have to sign a contract that forbade us to speak even to our spouses about what was going on. It's a legally binding contract. There are rumours that Catigar Jones are working in a similar area. But David thinks they're months behind our work. Their R&D is flawed. R&D is the key to these things. David doesn't smile at me. He doesn't wish me good morning. He doesn't ask about Lenny. Or about my weekend. He asks me if I'm feeling ready. This is a big week.

I take my lunch break in Russell Square. All I ever seem to eat any more is duck hoisin wraps. I ring Julia. Lenny's fine. Everything's fine.

Jonathan doesn't ring.

At the end of the afternoon, there's a man in the square who's taken his top off and started doing press-ups. On my way back home I watch him. I watch the muscles down his spine. I watch the rivulets of sweat on the back of his neck.

At home, I am very tempted to explain to Jonathan exactly about the Triford report. To tell him in complete detail about the nature of the report. Explain it to him meticulously. Encourage him to sell the details to Catigar Jones.

He's watching the news. There's been another car bomb in a market in Baghdad. There's always a car bomb in a market in Baghdad. I don't watch. I try to read my magazine. I'd rather watch *Sex and the City*. *Sex and the City* is on. Can we watch *Sex and the City*, please?

I want to go on a long-haul flight. I'd like to take Lenny on a long-haul flight. I like the screens, the in-flight maps on the backs of the seats in front of you. They allow you to trace the arc of the flight. They allow you to see the size of the world. They allow you to imagine the various war zones that you're flying over. You're flying over war zones. You're flying over Iraq. You're flying over Iran. You're flying over Afghanistan. And Turkmenistan. And Kazakhstan. And Chechnya. On your long-haul flight. On your way out on holiday. With the sandals that you bought with the gold strap and the plastic pink flower.

When Lenny sleeps he sticks his bum in the air. He sleeps on his knees. He wraps his blanket around himself. He's incredibly sweaty. It's Monday night and I get up again and get out of bed to check he's all right. Jonathan doesn't notice I've gone. I lie down on the floor next to his cot. Watch him breathe. Fall asleep on his floor. I go back to bed at about five o'clock and can't sleep. What did he want to buy paint for? Where did he go to buy his paint?

In the morning I can't decipher all of the different news stories on the radio.

Jonathan comes downstairs in a suit and he's so clean. His hair is clean. And his skin. He's had a shave. He grabs a banana and runs out of the door.

The freezer needs defrosting. There's a crust of ice that sits on everything. It takes a while to open the drawer and chip away at the cubes. They always make the same sound when you drop them in the glass. And their frost is settled by the whisky.

My hand is shaking. It's eight in the morning. It's Tuesday. It feels fucking amazing.

I manage to get a *Metro*. I enjoy the cartoons in the *Metro*. And the photographs of pop stars on marches. All of them. Hundreds of pop stars walking hundreds and hundreds of miles. All the way through the fields of East Scotland.

Politicians have immense respect for pop stars that walk hundreds and hundreds of miles through fields in East Scotland. Their eyes light up when they see one.

There are seventy-two unread messages in my inbox. Nearly all of them relate to the Triford report.

David hasn't slept, he says. He was working on a polish. On two polishes actually. He completed one polish at about eight thirty. He went out for a Chinese meal and afterwards instead of going home he came back and worked all night on another polish. That makes two polishes in one night. The polish is the key stage, he tells me. The polish and the R&D are the key stages of any report. He asks me to print off a copy of the conclusion. I print it off on the wrong type of paper. I print it off on photographic paper. There's photographic paper in the machine and I don't check and he roars at me. Don't I realise what I've done? Don't I realise how much more difficult it is to shred photographic paper? Why didn't I check? Wasn't I thinking? Don't I think? Don't I ever fucking think?

In the afternoon it's like David has been for a shower somewhere. Maybe over his lunch break he went for a swim and got himself a shower after his swim. He doesn't talk to me. I tell him I'm sorry. He says well. You know. There are some people for whom this report means something and some people for whom it clearly doesn't mean so much. He asks me what time I'm working until tonight. I tell him I'll be there until nine. Maybe ten. He doesn't think he'll make it that long. He needs to crash he says. His work is done.

He leaves at six thirty.

Jonathan's picking Lenny up from Julia's tonight because I have to stay late because of the report. I'm on my own. In the office I'm on my own. I recheck the report. I run the figures another time. I double-check the statistics. I become indescribably bored. David has a photograph of himself on his desk. This is surprising to me. I look for jokes on Yahoo. There are images of Sebastian Coe who is getting ready for the announcement in Tokyo tomorrow. All of the people there will wear the same coloured jackets, it says.

I take the report from David's desk. It's nine thirty at night. It's a Tuesday night. There's nobody else in the office. Maybe there's nobody else in the whole building. Maybe tonight there's nobody else in the whole city. I turn on the photocopier. Warming Up. Please Wait. I turn each page individually face down onto the glass. I go to the fax machine. I find the number for Catigar Jones. Fax/Start. Set.

At midday the next day, I went to see what had happened. And the BBC website said London. For about three minutes I couldn't believe it. I had to check it and check it and recheck it again.

Are you laughing or crying?
What?
I said are you laughing or are you crying?

I don't go in on Thursday. They don't want me to go in on Thursday.

I was the only person in the office on Tuesday night.

I won't take Lenny to see Julia today.

I pick him up and bring him into bed with me. I tickle his tummy. I blow raspberries on his tummy. What did he need paint for? I daren't ask him where he goes for his lunch breaks. Who is he on the phone to on his lunch breaks?

I can feel his ribs underneath his tummy and he's giggling and when he giggles his legs kick up into the air.

I look into his eyes and he looks right at me. Like he knows I was the only person in the office on Tuesday night and he finds it immensely, immensely funny.

The radio's on. Somebody's calling into a phone-in show. He's just been woken up by a friend of his phoning him from just south of Russell Square. There's a bus in Russell Square, he said.

Images of hell.
They are silent.

Six

I wasn't born here. They tell me I was born here, it's not true.

'What the fuck are you talking about, Jason, eh? What the fuck are you like?'

I'm Italian, I'm half Italian. How can I be half Italian if I was born around here?

My mum and dad live here. They live in this house. They've got one room. My sister's twenty-three. She's got one room. I've got one room.

They're completely the same to me. They have exactly the same skin and exactly the same structure of their face. And exactly the same hairstyles. Their clothes are exactly the same. I can't even tell the fucking difference between them half the time.

Dad comes home. Mum's watching the television.

What have you been doing?
You what?
While I've been at work all day. What have you been doing?
I cleaned the house.
You did what?
I cleaned the house. The house. I cleaned it.

Did you?
I did as it goes.
It doesn't fucking look fucking clean.
You what?
I said it doesn't fucking look fucking clean.

Every day.

I don't even like them.

I don't act like them.

You should have seen my sister at school. And I get there and everybody tells me that they taught my sister.

I bet you did.
I'm sorry, Jason?
I said I bet you fucking did.

Sometimes I go into her bedroom and I lie under her bed.

One time she came in. She didn't know I was there. She moved around. She took something from out of a drawer. Closed the drawer. Left the room. My heart was beating so loudly I could feel the blood pressure in my ears.

I got out from under her bed. I got to the drawer that she opened. Ran my hand through her clothes.

I picked up a stick of lipstick. It was a dull, pink lipstick. I lifted it to my nose. Smelt it. I opened it up. Licked it a little bit. I put some on. I was preparing in some ways. I was getting myself ready in a lot of ways.

The first time I saw her in school I didn't really notice her. That's quite funny. If you were to say to me, the first time you saw her in school you didn't notice her. Or the first time you see her you won't notice her. I'd look at you – I'd give you my look like –

I don't like it. The school. It's not a good school. Don't believe anybody who tells you that as schools go it's not a bad school.

Because that's a lie. And we have enough lies in the world,
I think.

The rules here are the rules of the insane.

Don't walk on the left-hand side.
Don't chew gum.
Don't drink water in the corridor.
Don't go to the toilet.
Tuck your shirt in.
Don't stand up.
Unless in Assembly.
Then don't sit down. Ever.

The teachers stand in front of a class and they can't control it.
They stand there. Their eyes going this way and that way.
Their arms flapping about. They can't control their eyes.
They can't control their arms let alone a –

Will you be quiet please?
I asked you to be quiet.
I won't ask you again.
I'm going to count to five and if you're not quiet.
One. Two. Three. Four. Five.

On the days when she wears a grey skirt it's like everything
has come together at once. Did you ever get a day like that?

I found out that her name was Lisa. I wrote it down.

I wanted to do a BTEC in computers. I don't suppose I'll get
the chance now.

There are things wrong with this world. I think when you look
at the power that Pakistani people have. And the money they
make. There are black people up London and they have meat
cleavers. They'll properly kill you. There are Gypsies out by
Goresbrook. They take your bike. You'll be going past them
on your bike and they'll stop you and they'll say to you – get
off your bike. Give it to us. Give us your phone. Give us your
trainers. Say you have a nice pair of trainers. Say you saved
up or your mum saved up and bought you a nice pair of

trainers. They'll just take it. I don't think that's right. Don't tell me you think that's right because it's not.

And white people. The white people round here are left with nothing to do. The women wear clothes that only have one real purpose really. I am part of an Aryan race. I came out of nowhere. It didn't used to be like this. Why do you think it's like this now?

I ask her. Why do you think it's like this now?
She gives me a smile that I swear I've never seen before on any other human being and she says to me, 'I have no idea Jason, you tell me.'

I'm going through the Heathway and I only see one of them at first. He walks towards me.
Aright, Jason?
Pushes into me. Pushes me around.
And before I notice it there's been another one comes up behind me.
You stood on my toe.
I didn't.
You stood on my fucking toe, you fucking retard cunt.
I didn't mean to. It was an accident. I –
Are you calling me a liar?
Are you calling him a liar, Jason?
Don't call him a liar.
There's a third.
I'd cut his face off if I was you.

I think one of them has a screwdriver.

I'm running across the Heathway into the mall there.
I don't turn round to see where they are.
There's a railing on the side of the Heathway and it slows me down and they catch me.
And they push me to the ground.
And one of them stamps on my face. He holds my face there with his foot.
The other has a screwdriver pressed against my cheek.
You fucking pikey thick fucking cunt. You are dead. You call

me a liar. You are so fucking dead.
Don't. Don't. Please don't. Please don't. Don't. Don't.

What happened to your face?

There's blood on my face.
On my shirt. On the pavement. I go into the toilets of the
shopping mall and wash it off.

I don't tell my mum anything.
I don't tell my dad anything.
I don't tell my sister anything.
I have my tea like nothing happened.

I used to deserve this.
I used to be really mouthy in class.
I have the capacity to be really horrible to people.
I have been really horrible to people.
I have been horrible to people about their mothers.
I'm not any more.
This kind of thing used to happen to me all the time.
I don't deserve it any more.

There are ways of smoking cigarettes that I've experimented
with. You can smoke a cigarette like this. Or you can smoke a
cigarette like this. You can light a match like this. Or like this.
Or like this. If you're smoking draw, which is another name
for marijuana, then you should probably smoke it like this.

Lisa smokes Marlboro Lights. Which is about as fucking
obvious as you could ever get.

I go downstairs and my sister's watching Coldplay. They're
singing that song about looking at the stars. I want to kick the
television screen in. Sometimes you think about kicking things
in like that. Stomp on his teeth.

When's Snoop Dog on?
Half five.
You gonna watch him? You gonna watch him? You watching
Snoop Dog?

She says nothing. I go out.

I found Lisa's name in the phone book. I found her address in the phone book. You wouldn't have thought it would be so easy, would you? I go to her house. I stand outside her house. There's nobody there. Nobody's home. Nobody comes in. Nobody goes out. There's a pub on her corner and they've got the concert on while I'm waiting.

Madonna brings this coon onstage with her.

Are you ready, London? Are you ready to start a revolution? Are you ready to change history?

I go back the next day and the house is still empty. Maybe she's gone away for the weekend. Maybe she's gone to see some relatives or something like that. I have a cigarette while I'm waiting. I keep a packet of ten cigarettes in the lining of my blazer. After a bit I go right up to her window. I wonder which of these rooms her bedroom is. I can only see the front room. I imagine her in her front room. Watching the television. With the curtain closed. I could come round. Watch the television with her.

Miss.
Yes, Jason?
How are you today?
I'm good thank you, Jason. How are you?
I'm all right. Did you watch *Live 8*?
I watched bits of it.
Did you enjoy it?
I did, yes.
Who did you enjoy best?
I don't know.
Did you like Snoop Dog?
I didn't see him.
Do you think we'll get the Olympics, Miss?
I'm not sure. I think Paris might get it.
It'd be better there, don't you think?
I don't know.
I think it would. It would be better in Paris than in London.
London stinks, I reckon. Don't you think, Miss? Don't you

think London stinks? I think it does. I think it stinks. I think it stinks of dead people.

Monday night. I get home. I think Dad's started hitting Mum. I'm not sure. There are bruises across her face. I ask her. She tells me not to be so ridiculous.

Tuesday morning. Lisa's wearing a red blouse and a grey skirt. Her hair has come loose at the end of the day. She asks me if she can get past. I let her pass. She's being rude to me. I think she's being rude to me. Why's she being rude to me today? How come she's started being rude to me?

And later she starts talking to the head of maths. It makes me want to cut his throat open.

Next day. Next maths lesson. This is hilarious. I won't stop talking. He sends me out. I won't move.

You can't make me.
You can't make me move.
You can't touch me.
You touch me and I'm going to the police.
Sir, you touch me and I'm going to the police.
Sir, do you fancy Miss Watson?
Sir, do you know where she lives? She lives on Parsloes Avenue, doesn't she? Have you been round there?

I could buy a knife. That wouldn't be difficult. I could buy a gun. I could get really fucking drunk and get myself a gun.

How did you find out where I live? Jason, this is serious. It's in the phone book, Miss. It's not difficult. Do you want a cigarette?
What are you doing here?
I'm just sitting here.
Can you move please?
You were wrong about the Olympics, Miss.
I was what?
I can't fucking believe it myself. I think they must all be insane. Did you see them? Don't you think they're insane? Don't you think Lord Sebastian Coe is insane, Miss? And

David Beckham.
Jason, can you move away from my house please?
Where were you at the weekend, Miss?
Where, what?
Where were you at the weekend? You weren't in all weekend.
Did you go away for the weekend?
Jason, get off my wall this instant.
Or what?
If you don't get off my wall this instant then I swear I will call
the police.
Are you worried about losing your job?
Am I what?
Because teachers and students aren't really meant to fall in
love with each other. I'd look after you though. If you did.
Jason, what on earth are you talking about?

There's a fizzing sound. Sometimes with an ashtray or a wall
or something you have to rub and rub the cigarette in. It's not
like that this time.

Let me say this. Now. After everything that's happened. I
would cut out her cunt with a fork. I would scrape off her tits.
I would force a chair leg up her arse until her rectum bled.
I would do these things. If I was forced to I would do all of
these things. Don't think I wouldn't because I would.

On my way up Oxlow Lane there's this guy. He stares at me
like he's seen something in my eyes. He's drunk. I think drunk
people are the worst. I didn't know if he was going to hit me
or kick me or what. He looked at me as though he recognised
something. And then he started smiling.

I get home and I go to my room and I put a CD on. I can't
stop thinking about the way it made a fizzing sound. It
shouldn't have made a fizzing sound. That was a complete
surprise to me.

I'd like to go on a roller coaster. Right now that's what I
would like. To go to Chessington or Alton Towers and ride on
a roller coaster.

Downstairs I can hear Mum and Dad. I don't go down.

I go into my sister's room. I lie down under her bed.

The phone goes. Please don't answer it. Please don't answer it. Please don't answer it.

I go to bed at eight o'clock. I don't even watch much TV.

In the future people will look at me and they'll know I was right about all this. In the future people will do what I say. I'll be like a Führer. Do you think I'm joking? Do you think this is some kind of a joke?

I watch the TV with my sister all morning. She comes back from the tube station. She can't get to work. The images are from CCTV cameras close by to the scene. They change every thirty seconds. I watch them. I keep thinking something is going to happen. The people keep talking but the images only change every thirty seconds or so. I wonder what it's like down there. I wonder what it smells like. I think about the rats. It's such a hot day that I have to close the curtains to stop the sunlight glaring on the television.

I wish she was on the tube. Lisa. I wish Lisa had had a training day and happened to find herself sitting on a tube bound for the centre of town when a young man with a backpack climbed on.

The way the images move, I think the word is tantalising.

I look at my sister.

Are you laughing or are you crying?
What?
Are you laughing or are you crying?

Images of hell.
They are silent.

Five

Have you got any cigarettes?

I'm sorry?

Have you got a cigarette I could have?

Sure. Here.

Can I have the packet?

What?

Can I have your packet of cigarettes?

No, don't be –

Please.

How long are you staying?

Long enough. Don't worry.

I wasn't worried. Believe me.

You're looking well.

Thank you.

You've lost weight.

I have a bit.

You look rather dashing.

Dashing?

But you need to clean your house.

I know.

What room am I staying in?

In here. You can fold the sofa out.

Can't I sleep in your room?

Fuck off.

You could sleep on the sofa.

—

Put some music on.

What music do you want to hear?

You decide. Have you seen Mum and Dad?

Last month. I went up.

How are they?

They're fantastically well. Dad's taken up jogging. Mum keeps buying things. She's bought an array of electronic goods the like of which I've never even heard of.

Good Lord.

I know. Are you going to go and see them?

I might do. I might not. I might have other things to do. Have you got any booze?

No.

Get some.

Alcoholic.

Now.

*

You wanna know my favourite bit? This always happens. It's always hilarious. You'll see them talking about their loss. Maybe their child has been abducted. Or they lost a lover in a terrorist attack. Or a natural disaster. Or just, you know, in the general course of, of, of, of –

Life.

Of life, precisely. And they always do this! They'll be talking
perfectly normally. They'll be talking with real grace and often
they'll be, they'll be, it's like they'll be –

Happy?

Happy, yes. But then the thought of their lost one, of their
child or their lover or their colleague, hits them like a train.
And their voices catch in their throats and they can't carry on.
Tears well up in their eyes. And what we do is, we stay with
them. Every time. We hold them in our gaze for a good
twenty seconds before the cut. It has become a formula. That,
for me, is one of the highest achievements of our time.

Do you ever get tired?

And I love the way that certain phrases in our language have
become like a kind of intellectual Pepto-Bismol. Language is
used to constipate people's thinking. Yob Culture. Binge
Drinking. What do these things fucking mean? What do they
fucking mean exactly? We're losing all sense of precision. Or
accuracy. We're losing all sense of language. And at the same
time some of the fundamental rights and fundamental
privileges of our culture have been removed from us.

Such as?

Simple joys.

Such as?

The simple joy of beating up your lover. The feeling you get
when you molest your own child. The desire to touch the
physically handicapped. Or a burn victim. Or the blemished.
That recoil you get, instinctively.

–

What?

–

What have I said?

*

How did you sleep?

I slept incredibly well. I slept really deeply. I didn't have a single dream. I closed my eyes. Opened them up again. Eight hours had passed. It was fantastic.

Would you like some breakfast?

Yes I would, please.

What would you like?

I have absolutely no idea. Surprise me.

You look like you slept well.

You what?

You look rested.

Thank you.

You look great.

Thank you.

It's really good to see you.

Yeah. You too.

You were absolutely mad last night. But it is.

—

What do you want to do today?

Go out.

Where do you want to go?

*

She was a cleaner at St Pancras, at the train station. She found out she was pregnant. This was a hundred years ago. She came here. She spent all her money on getting a room. Threw herself over the side of the stairs. All the way down into the lobby. I've never seen her. People talk about her all the time. That's why they built the handrail.

How did you find out you could get in?

I was persistent.

It's amazing.

People reckon they've seen Roman soldiers marching through the basement. Or there's the man in Room 10.

Who's that?

There's a man who lurks around the back of one of the rooms here. Room 10. If you approach him he runs away. I've seen him. Loads of people have.

Did he run away from you?

Yeah.

He must be mad then.

—

—

They'll open this up. If the Olympics come here. They're gonna build the extension for the Channel Tunnel here. Join us all up to Europe. You'll be able to go anywhere. They'll re-open it. It's mine until then.

*

Keep your eyes open.

I am doing.

Any second.

—

—

—

There!

Wow!

It's for the British Museum. It's not been used for sixty years.

Fucking hell.

I know! They closed it because there was no need of it any more. With Holborn and Tottenham Court Road.

You can imagine the people.

I know.

Standing there.

—

—

The whole city's haunted. Every street there's something disused. There are forty tube stations, closed for fifty years. There are hundreds of pubs. There are hundreds of public toilets. The railway tracks. The canal system. The street map is a web of contradiction and complication and between each one there's a ghost.

—

People disappear here in ways they don't in other cities. People get buried in rooms. They get walled up in cellars. They're dug under the gardens. All of these things happen. What? What's funny? Don't you believe me?

Of course I believe you.

What then?

I'm just happy.

What are you happy about?

Seeing you. You idiot.

*

We didn't watch it.

No.

Any of it.

I know.

I bet it was fucking dreadful.

I would have liked to have seen Pink Floyd.

I would have rather cut my eyes out with a spoon.

I'm extremely drunk.

Me too.

—

—

Where were you?

What?

You never told me. All this time.

I was all over the place.

Tell me where.

No.

Why? Why won't you?

—

Were you all right?

—

Were you?

Not really.

Why not?

—

What happened?

You don't need to know.

I'm sorry.

What for?

I'm sorry you weren't all right. I would have done anything to have stopped you from getting hurt.

—

Come here.

—

You smell nice.

Thank you.

You smell like you. Nobody else smells like you. Why is that?

I have no idea.

*

In Moscow all the black marketeers and prostitutes were evacuated from the city centre to create an archetypal image of the dignity of Soviet communism. In Munich the Israeli wrestling went to the theatre to watch *Fiddler on the Roof*. Moshe Weinberg, their coach, got so drunk with the actors afterwards that when the kidnap started he attacked one of Black September with a fruit knife. In Atlanta they flew the flag of the Confederacy from the roofs of most of the venues. In Barcelona trackside officers carried sub-machine guns. I fucking hope London doesn't get it. It'll rip the heart out of the East End. It'll be a catastrophe.

Shut up.

What?

Shut up. Stop fucking talking.

—

Here.

What?

Feel this.

—

Stop talking and feel this.

Where?

Here.

What about it?

It's soft, isn't it?

*

We shouldn't do this.

I know.

It's against every rule that has ever been written by anybody in the whole history of human culture.

I know.

You're my sister.

I know.

This is.

What?

I can't.

Come on.

I can't.

Please. For me. There. There. It feels good. Doesn't it? Well, doesn't it?

*

Oranges.

Oranges?

Yeah. Or apples. Kiwi fruit, a bit.

I didn't know kiwi fruit *had* a smell.

It's a very subtle smell. You smell of it. Very subtly.

You smell of grass.

Grass like draw grass or grass like freshly cut grass?

Freshly cut grass.

Can I ask you something?

Of course.

Are you all right?

Yeah. I am. I'm fine.

—

You look about fifteen. In a good way. There's something about the light on your face.

Can I tell you something?

Go on.

I've wanted to do that for fucking ages.

Have you?

Years.

God.

I know.

What do we do now?

We could get something to eat. We could watch a video. Have you got any porn? We could watch some porn. I'd quite like to watch some porn, I think.

I don't.

We could download some.

Fuck off.

We could go for a walk. Go to Brick Lane and buy a bagel. Get a bottle of wine from the pub next door. I'll put your jeans on and go next door and get a bottle of wine and bring it back here and lie in bed and drink it with you. We could do that. What? Why are you smiling?

Cos I'm happy.

*

Do they know you watch them, do you think?

I've no idea.

Do they ever watch you?

I don't know.

I wonder if they do.

They might do.

They might turn the lights off and lie in the dark and watch you work.

They might do.

Have you ever spoken to them?

No.

I wonder what they're like.

I bet they're cunts.

Don't say that. They might be lovely. What do you think they'd say?

If what?

If they saw us here.

They'd think you were my girlfriend.

What if they knew?

I don't know.

I am kind of your girlfriend, aren't I? A bit.

Kind of.

—

What did they say? At work?

They didn't say anything.

What did you tell them?

I told them you had food poisoning.

*

If I set you a task to do would you do it?

It depends what it is.

It shouldn't.

Well, it would. Don't push it.

If I set you one you could set me one.

Are you sure?

Absolutely.

I might set you a really terrible one.

I wouldn't care.

Or a really rude one.

That wouldn't matter. That would be good.

Go on then.

Take your top off.

Here?

Yeah.

There.

Drop to the floor.

To the floor?

To the ground. I want you to do some press-ups for me.

You what?

I want you drop to the ground and do ten press-ups for me.

—

Thank you. That was lovely.

My turn now.

*

I'm not telling you.

You have to.

I don't.

We made a deal.

It doesn't count.

Yes it does. Of course it does.

That wasn't what I was talking about.

I don't care. I did my press-ups for you. People watched me.
Strangers. You made me. You made those rules up. I make
the rules of what I want you to do.

I'll do anything else.

I don't want anything else. I want you to tell me what happened.

No.

What happened to you?

No.

What happened to you?

I'm not –

What fucking happened?

Nothing happened. I went away. I thought things would be better than they were. They weren't. I did some jobs. I got my passport stolen. I came back home.

What kind of jobs?

Normal jobs. Jobs. Jobs for money. It was nothing. It wasn't the jobs. It was the disappointment.

–

–

I don't think I understand you.

No.

–

Come to bed with me.

–

We can fuck all night if you want to. I'm not tired. Are you tired? I'm not tired at all. You could tell me all the things you ever wanted to do with me and we could do them and nobody would ever know. I love you so much it's like my body is bursting out of my skin and all I want is for you to love me in the same way and for it to be like this forever. I know that it won't be.

No.

But that's what I want.

*

I should go to work today.

Don't.

I don't want to. I have to go back. There are things I need to do.

What things?

There's a report we need to finish. By next week. Everybody else'll be working their arses off trying to finish it.

Are you not tired?

I'm all right.

Did you sleep?

I did a bit.

Did you see?

What?

London got the Olympics.

Fucking hell.

I know. The French are apoplectic.

We missed it.

I know.

How did we miss that?

I don't know.

It's awful.

I know.

—

Would you like some coffee?

I would please.

—

—

What would I have to do to stop you from going in?

Don't.

What would I have to promise you?

Nothing you promise me will make any difference.

Wouldn't it?

No.

I'll wait for you.

OK.

I'll stay in all day and watch TV and wait for you to come home.

OK.

I'll have your tea ready for you. I'll cook you something nice. I'll go to the shops and get something nice to cook. I'll get your Pink Floyd records out so you can listen to them to make up for the disappointment because everybody says they were brilliant according to this.

Right. That'd be nice.

Can I ask you something?

Go on.

Are you getting a bit frightened now?

*

I was worried about you. You're really late.

I know.

I was terrified. I tried ringing you but all the mobile phone lines were down.

I know. I'm sorry.

You're safe.

Yeah.

Where were you?

They cancelled all the tubes. I had to walk home.

Fucking hell.

What?

Just fucking hell. Fucking hell. Fucking hell.

—

I thought you were dead.

I wasn't.

No.

It's mad out there. Everybody's walking. All the pubs are packed.

—

You need to go.

—

I'm really sorry. You do.

What are you talking about?

You need to go. You need to leave. You can't stay here any more. This is awful. This is all awful. We have to stop doing this. There are some things which you just can't do and fucking hell did you not see the news at all?

Of course I did.

Did you not see what's going on?

What's that got to do with anything?

I can't do this any more. This is all wrong. It's terrible. What are you even doing here? I look at you and all I can see is your stupid fucking horrible fucking face.

Stop it.

I walked home and the place has been destroyed. And I come home to this. And I can't bear it any more and I want it to stop.

I'll kill myself.

I don't believe you.

*

This isn't the last time I'll see you. I will see you again. We will see each other again.

—

I'll tell Mum and Dad you had to go. That it was good to see you. You asked after them. You wanted to see them and then you had to go.

I don't know what I'm going to do without you.

You'll be – People survive. You'll be all right.

You've completely broken my heart.

There are some things that people don't recover from but sadness is never one of them.

It's not about being sad. It's not that I'm sad. For Christ's sake!

No. Sorry.

How long do you think we should wait?

You what?

Until we see each other again. How long do you think we should leave it?

I have no idea.

How long do you think it'll take?

Hundreds and hundreds and hundreds and hundreds of years.

Yeah.

I think about you all the time.

—

I close my eyes and all I ever see is you and your hair and your face and that's not a healthy thing for anybody.

—

You're my sister.

Yeah.

—

—

Have you got everything?

Yes. I think so.

—

—

If you've left anything where should I send it? Is there an address I could send it to?

Throw it away. Put it on eBay. Keep it.

Images of hell.
They are silent.

Four

It's dark. It's still dark when I leave my house.

I kiss my children goodbye. I kiss my wife. I promise that I'll call her.

There's nobody around.

There's the sound of my feet on the gravel of my driveway. The metal on my front gate is cold to touch. My bag slices into my shoulders.

The bus driver turns his face to the road. He's the only vehicle on the road at this time of the morning. He's the only person here.

A young Bangladeshi boy with a Walkman slumps in the middle of the bus towards the right-hand side. Stares out of the window. His feet are rested on the seat in front of him. I sit on the other side. Behind him. I watch the back of his head. I watch his gentle movements to the sound of his Walkman. I take aim. I release the safety catch. I stare down the barrel, down my arm, rigid, straight. I squeeze. I pick up a copy of the morning *Metro*. I look for my horoscopes. I've always looked for my horoscopes.

As we bore into its heart, though, the traffic thickens. There are more buses. Heavy goods vehicles pack up after midnight deliveries. Rumble away again. Lone drivers with no passengers understand the idea of the car pool. They admire the idea of the car pool. They are determined to get involved in a car pool.

They rub eyes with hands balancing coffee in paper cups. Warning. Contents are extremely hot.

We swing round the turnings of the one-way system. I send psychic signals to the bus driver. Drive through the red lights. Turn right on the left turn only. Drive up and over the pavements. From today, from now on you can do, you have it in you to do whatever it is that you want to do. Here is where the rules end. Today is the day when the law stops working.

I thank the bus driver when I get off the bus. I always thank the bus driver when I get off the bus. He doesn't say anything. He stares out of his windscreen. His eyes don't move at all.

I turn out of and away from Piccadilly Gardens.

I climb up the hill towards the railway station.

I could do with a coffee.

I really need a cup of coffee.

Can I have a cup of coffee please? Thank you. Great. Thanks. Thank you.

All of a sudden, as if by magic, there are people everywhere. Turning away from train platforms. Suited and smart and elegant and crisp. Weary-eyed and bloated. Breakfasting on McDonald's or Breakfast Bars or Honey and Granola. Lugging their laptops. Clicking their heels. Pulling their shirt cuffs. Pressing their phones. They've been working all night on a polish. They've been driven by the R&D. Their attention to detail and their R&D is breathtaking.

We have reserved seats in different carriages.

We don't check that each other is here. We don't need to check that each other is here. We trust one another. We're here.

The train arriving on Platform 5 is the 5.43 for London Euston. Calling at Stockport, Macclesfield, Stoke-on-Trent, Milton Keynes Central and London Euston only.

We will take the train to Stoke and get off at Stoke.

From Stoke we will take a train to Derby and change at Derby.

From Derby we will take a train to King's Cross St Pancras.

At King's Cross St Pancras we will each travel on a different tube line. At King's Cross St Pancras one of us will take a Piccadilly Line to Heathrow. One of us will take a Victoria Line to Brixton. One of us will take a Hammersmith and City Line train to Hammersmith. At King's Cross St Pancras I am going to take a Circle Line train via Liverpool Street. We won't speak. We won't signal with one another. We will not communicate with one another in any way. We will, however, each send one text.

I think the weather is warming up. I think we're going to have a beautiful day today. Today the sun will shine all throughout England.

The luggage racks are spacious. They have space for my backpack. There's plenty of room.

This is the first train. There are only a handful of people on my carriage.

And when the second of our number comes into my carriage and sees me he walks right through the carriage and away from me into a carriage further down the train. And we don't speak. And we don't look at one another. We don't say anything at all.

A man sat across the table from me has removed his tie. He furrows his brow at an early-morning anagram, seven across, eight letters, second letter E. He looks like –

I drink bad black coffee from Upper Crust. I am very much in need of mineral water. There are no almond croissants. I want an almond croissant. Where the fuck are your almond croissants, you fucking bewigged, myopic, prurient, sexless dead?

A man down the carriage from me. A young man. He is dressed smartly. He is handsome. He won't stop picking his nose. He burrows around in his nose, removes something from it and surreptitiously, imagining that nobody can see him, slips it into his mouth. Toys with it between his teeth.

By the sides of the tracks as we pull out of Manchester and Stockport there is a mass of containers. There are corrugated-steel industrial units.

I look into the eyes of the woman sat across the seat from me. I think for a second that she's been crying. She hasn't. It's my imagination.

The sunshine through the window of the train is burning up my arms. I want to take my jacket off. Can I take my jacket off please?

I close my eyes for a time. I can sleep now. I try to sleep.

I wake up and panic about how far we've come. I look out of my window as we pull out of Macclesfield.

I've forgotten to do something. There is definitely something that I've forgotten, I've forgotten, can you help me, is there something that I've forgotten? I think it's a word. Is it a word?

I honestly have no memory of changing trains at Stoke. I must have changed trains at Stoke.

East. Out towards Derby.

Disused Jet garage forecourts sit side by side with double driveways. Here there are food-makers and the food they make is chemical. It fattens the teenage and soaks up the pre-teen. Nine-year-old children all dazzled up in boob tubes and mini-skirts and spangly eyeliner as fat as little pigs stare out of the windows of family estate cars. In the sunshine of mid-morning in the suburbs of the South Midlands heroin has never tasted so good. Internet sex contact pages have never seemed more alluring. Nine hundred television channels have never seemed more urgent. And everybody needs an iPod. And nobody can ever get a *Metro* any more.

If I had the power I would take a bomb to all of this. To every grazing horse and every corrugated-metal shed and every wind-blasted tree and every telephone mast and every graveyard. Wipe it all off the skin of the world. Scratch it away.

The only thing I remember about the station at Derby, as we wait at four different points, staring in four different directions, is the oddness of a unisex hairdresser's being there, at the station. Nobody today is having a haircut.

I climb on the third train. Try to close my eyes again. I daren't.

The land rolls on.

I'd like to listen to some music. I'd very much like to listen to the music of Pink Floyd. There's a woman across the aisle from me. She is dressed in a black business suit. She is wearing black tights. I'd very much like to lie in her bed on a Sunday morning eating oven-heated croissants and listening to the music of Pink Floyd.

The teenage girls in the counter of Boots didn't even check the signature on my card. Five hundred bottles of peroxide for hair dye. Fifty bottles of nail varnish remover. I'm making a movie. I'm the runner on a movie.

I want some chewing gum. I want to read the sports pages of a national newspaper.

We're getting closer now. You can tell it. In the shape of the land here.

Glass and concrete and grey metal tubes pepper platforms, punctured by yellow paint at Luton Airport Parkway. Aeroplanes fly throughout the whole of Europe. Don't forget the tax. Don't forget the air tax. Don't forget the consequence. An array of suburbs all throughout Europe have been re-energised by the possibility of cheap flights. There is a legacy of incremental deep-vein thrombosis and an explosion of ramp attendants. Asian boys from suburbs the whole of Europe over have become ramp attendants. Juggling the matrix snake of the luggage hold. Perfecting the ergonomics of bags on wheels. Their mothers package sandwiches in airtight silver foil. Their sisters spray perfume. Their fathers drive buses that move you from one car park to another. Welcome to England.

London rises. It takes you by surprise. Cut out of the edges of bomb blasts. And a thousand years of fire. This is a city that is always on fire. This is a city that is forever under attack.

Nobody checks my ticket. The ticket guards stare at one another's shoes, giggling

St Pancras Hotel is spectre from another time. The whole of the city looms up and over us through the St Pancras Hotel. A metal stairway and the sweep of elegance. Haunted by women who have walked down the stairwell.

There are things I need to say. There is a sequence of words that I've been told I must say. But I can't remember what order it goes in. I want to phone home. I want to tell my wife to wake up and take our children to school. I want to ask her what order the sequence of words is meant to go in.

There is a panelled walkway from St Pancras to the Underground. There are blue arrows telling me to go this way only. I can't seem to feel the weight of my bag any more and I'm terrified that something has gone wrong. Something has gone wrong here. Something terrible has gone wrong.

I follow the blue lines in that way only.

They apologise for any inconvenience that anything may have caused. There is a constant state of apology for any inconvenience that may have been caused.

They have dug up the floor tiles. They are rebuilding everything. They have no choice but to rebuild everything. When the Olympics get here this place will have the newest floor tiles you'll be able to imagine. All of the newspaper headlines, each after the other after the other, are roaring with delight. They cannot believe what happened yesterday. Nobody can believe what happened yesterday and what that will mean.

I pay £2.20 for a single ticket to Zone 2 via Zone 1 stations.

I smile at the man who holds the gate to the platform open for me so that I can get through with my bag. But he doesn't smile back. He doesn't check my ticket. He doesn't even look at me. He looks away from me.

The second of our number sends me a text message. The third of our number sends me a text message. The first of our number sends me a text message. I reply to them all.

I follow the signs for the Circle Line. The platform is busy. The platform is busier than I expected it to be. I find the space for the busiest carriage. At the heart of the train. I have to push my way on with my bag. People are complaining about the size of my bag.

Suddenly I feel lighter than I have ever felt in my whole life.

We move past Farringdon. Where the platform is open and sunk in the grey blue light of morning. And red-brick Moorgate. Liverpool Street is white with sugar and pace and desire. Smoke blue, blood red, ghost white.

The train pulls out of Liverpool Street and moves towards Aldgate.

Three

You look just like him.

That's not true.

You've got the same eyes. You've got exactly the same hair. How old is he?

He's twenty-five.

He's very handsome.

I worry about him constantly.

What do you worry about?

I worry that he won't achieve the things he has the potential to achieve. I worry that nobody will ever fall in love with him.

That he won't get out of bed. Ever. That he'll die before me. Things like that.

Solipsist.

He is incredibly vulnerable. He has absurdly soft skin, for a man of his age. Did you call me a solipsist?

You are.

I'm not in the least bit solipsistic. I'm not a solipsist at all.

You're projecting onto him. Mercilessly.

That's not true. It's the opposite of that.

Would you like another drink?

I'm not sure now.

Are you all grumpy and cross now?

I'm just not sure if I want to be insulted by you.

It's incredibly good to see you.

I was going to say that it's good to see you too. Until you started insulting me.

You're looking fantastic. You funny little man. You've lost weight. Your skin's cleared up.

My skin?

I remember your skin being kind of blotchy. We used to stare at it during your seminars.

Did you?

It isn't now.

Who stared at me?

All of us. It looks fresh now. You look good.

Thank you.

That's my pleasure.

I think I would like another drink. I think I'd like another Merlot.

I bet you would.

Will you buy me another Merlot please?

It's funny, isn't it?

What is?

People's faces. When people get older their faces don't change. They just decay a little bit. The shape is the same, though. The shape of their eyes. You recognise them completely. They send off little messages through your synapses.

Your face has changed. Your eyes have got smaller. How did that happen?

I have no idea. It's the same with voices, by the way. The speed with which we recognise one another's voices when we pick up our telephones is staggering to me. Human beings are so fucking clever that sometimes it makes me want to fall over.

Should I go myself, to get my drink?

Don't you think I'm funny?

No.

I am. I think I am. I make myself laugh my head off. Wait here.

*

I went to America.

Good thinking.

I got myself a job in a faculty in Minneapolis.

What was Minneapolis like?

It was fantastically cold. You go outside in winter and after seconds, literally seconds, your nasal hairs freeze over. That was unusual.

It sounds it.

The students were banal. They all had the same haircut, which disconcerted me. And everybody was fat. You had to walk for twenty minutes to get any fresh fruit. Even then it was coated in genetically modified chemical additive.

How long were you there for?

Two years. I found it difficult to get the energy to leave. I blame the diet.

And how long have you been back?

Four years.

Four years?

Yeah.

Jesus.

What?

When did you graduate?

Eight years ago.

I'm nearly literally twice your age.

Yeah.

That makes me feel terrible. That makes me feel like I'll probably die soon.

You might.

Well, yes. I might. We all might. Anybody might. But I probably will. Is my point.

I enjoyed the teaching.

Did you?

I want to teach again.

—

—

That's where I come in.

No.

No?

I mean maybe. I mean yes. Really I mean yes.

You don't sound like you enjoyed the teaching.

I did. I just didn't enjoy the students. I hankered after British students. I kept imagining how great British students would be.

They're not.

I bet they fucking are. I need a job.

Yeah. We all need a job.

I can't work in bars again. I'm far too old to get a bar job. It would be so humiliating.

You can't even remember to get people drinks.

No.

I'll see what I can do.

—

I'll talk to the Dean. I have no idea if there's anything available.

Thank you.

That's OK.

This is my grateful face. This is my excited face. This is my excited and grateful face.

They're remarkable.

I know. Have you eaten?

What?

Supper. Have you had any supper?

No.

No. Neither have I.

*

It gets to a point in a marriage where the house is full of these horrible psychic forces. You can feel the anger. I'd come into the house and look at her standing in the living room or in our bedroom and there would be part of me that would want to cave her head in with a brick. That's quite an unnerving feeling.

You should have left each other earlier than you did by the sound of things.

There was Mark. I didn't want to leave while he was still living there.

No.

—

—

—

Have you lived round here since?

Yes. I have. I've got a flat. It's got two bedrooms. I don't have a television. Mark comes to see me if he's in town but he never stays the night even though the reason I got the spare room in the first place was for him. Fucking ingrate.

You don't mean that.

No. I enjoy seeing him. I like taking him to the pub and talking to him about work and about football as though we were mates. I talk to him about his mum. Make sure she's all right.

Is she?

She's having a ball. She's living with the father of one of Mark's school friends. A gentle, decent, intelligent man who I still occasionally bump into and who, despite my best intentions to the contrary, I can't bring myself to dislike.

Cunt.

I know.

–

–

Do you like living on your own?

I do. You know? I do. I do. I do. I really do. I like shopping for food. I like discovering food shops in odd places and going there. I like eating out occasionally on my own. Going to the cinema and not worrying about being back in time. Going to the pub and staying there. Working all night if I want to. Naked. At my desk. Scratching my balls.

Lovely.

I know. And I've started running.

Have you?

I've taken up jogging.

I thought you'd lost weight.

I love it. Round the park. I did four laps on Saturday. I'm going to enter the Olympics, I think.

You should.

I will.

–

What do you think that it be like?

What?

The Olympics.

I have no idea.

Don't you think it'll be rather brilliant?

I'm not sure.

I was in my car this afternoon, when they announced it. I had
the radio on. And the hosts of the Olympic Games in 2012
will be . . . London! I punched my fists in the air. I nearly
punched the roof off the car. I honked my horn in celebration.
Other people did too. It was like we were having a big party on
the road, in our cars. Everybody was grinning at each other.

I didn't really know what to think.

Oh come on! You know? Life is so short.

*

Are you not cold?

No.

Would you like to borrow my scarf?

—

What?

Nothing.

—

I used to come here when I was a child. To the museum.
Have you ever been in there?

No.

You should go in. There are dolls in there from four hundred years ago. Other dolls, porcelain dolls from the nineteenth century with three faces. They're terrifying. I'll take you.

Will you?

You get me a job and I'll bring you to the museum and show you the dolls with the three faces.

Would you like some coffee?

I'm sorry?

Would you like to come in and have a cup of coffee with me?

*

It's from Jamaica.

Right.

From Blue Mountain. It's the most exclusive coffee in the world. How do you like that?

Very flash.

What do you think?

It's lovely. Thank you.

Good. Good. I'm glad.

I like your flat.

Do you?

I do. It's simple. It's spare. It's minimalist.

There's nothing here, you mean.

It feels deliberate.

It isn't.

That's not the point. I like the view. You can see the Gherkin.

Yes. I rather like that. Would you like to stay?

I'm sorry?

Here. Tonight.

—

I don't mean to 'stay' stay. I mean. I've got the room. And it's late. It'd be difficult for you to get back now. You'd have to get the night bus. And the night bus from here is like one of the lower circles of hell. You'd never survive it.

—

I'd make you breakfast.

—

It's been very good to see you. I'm sorry. I shouldn't have asked.

—

—

You had no idea, of course, at the time. But you were everything to me. You were my teacher. I was completely besotted with you. I wanted you, what I wanted you to do was, I wanted you to notice me. Of course you never did. You shouldn't have asked me. No. You probably really shouldn't.

*

The sheets are completely untouched. They're practically brand new.

Thank you.

Have you got some pyjamas?

Pyjamas?

You can borrow some. If you need to. I've got piles and piles of the things.

Thank you.

What time do you need to get up in the morning?

I don't really need . . . I'm not working at the moment.

I get up absurdly early. I have completely lost the ability to sleep any more. So I'll wake you up at any time you want.

Nine o'clock. How's nine o'clock. Is that all right?

A lie-in!

Kind of.

—

—

It'll be quite funny wearing your pyjamas.

Funny?

I've not worn pyjamas for years. Not since I was a little girl.

—

What?

Can I ask you something?

Of course.

Will you dance with me?

—

If I put some music on. Would you dance with me?

*

Are you crying?

What?

I couldn't tell if you were laughing or if you were crying.

Shhhh.

Hey. Hey. Don't cry.

I'm not.

Hey.

—

—

—

Don't.

Shhhh.

Don't, please.

Shhhhh.

Please don't.

Come on.

—

I can feel you breathing.

Please don't.

You know exactly what you're doing to me. You've known all night what you've been doing to me.

—

What knickers are you wearing? Tell me.

Be quiet.

Are you even wearing any?

Christ.

Come on. I'm noticing you. This is me noticing you.

–

Ow.

–

Ow. You fucking. You. That fucking hurt.

–

I should beat the crap out of you for doing that.

–

Don't tell me that you didn't want exactly what –
Is there a lock on that door?
What?
Is there a lock on the bedroom door?

–

Can it be locked from the inside?
Yes. Of course it can.
I need to sleep somewhere.

–

–

–

You're quite little, aren't you?
Little?
I've never noticed before.

*

I'm very sorry. For what I did last night. I was awful.
It's not enough.

No. Of course not.

—

I made you some breakfast. I cooked bacon and everything.
Will you stay for breakfast? Will you stay for breakfast, please?

—

—

I need to get to Edgware Road. Can I get the train to
Edgware Road from near here?

I dreamt about you last night. It was horrible. The dream was
horrible.

—

I woke up. I thought my wife was there. I thought she was
sleeping next to me. She looks like Mark when she's asleep.
She wasn't. I was on my own. I'm fucking cracking up is the
thing. I'm completely losing my fucking mind.

—

These things, they're not bruises. They don't fade. They're
scars.

Two

You never get bus conductors any more. On some tube lines
now you don't even get drivers. The machines have started to
run themselves.

I like this.

I have absolutely no interest in speaking to anybody.

In the free newspaper there is talk of the events of the weekend.
They write, in this paper, without any editorial bias. I hate the
fucking thing. They've removed any semblance of perspective
or personality.

This was not music. What they did on Saturday was the opposite of music. It was everything I wish I had the strength to rip down and destroy. I'd take a pickaxe to the lot of them. They manifest charity masquerading as action. They are driven by a singular spirit of self-congratulation. It makes me want to bite the throats out of their domestic pets.

I have an article to deliver.

I take the bus to the entrance of the faculty. Walk up Gower Street. The university brackets the road with the hospital. Right through the northern heart of central London. One starts in one bracket. Crosses. Returns.

I haven't worked there, properly, for fifteen years now. They look at me with a mix of bewilderment, pity and an odd kind of rage. I leave my article for Dr Schults. He'll call me.

I go back home.

There was a time when I'd walk. Gower Street to Hammersmith.

I couldn't do it any more. I can barely fucking breathe half the time.

Wait for the bus. Get the bus. Get home. Drink tea. Try not to spend too many hours staring out of the window. If you stare long enough into a mirror, of course, you begin to hallucinate. My entire life has the feeling of that nowadays.

I watch television with a mixture of awe and horror.

Sometimes I forget if I've eaten or not. It is as likely that this will lead to me eating two meals of an evening as it is that I'll end up eating none. I wouldn't be at all surprised if I became enormously fat.

I don't see anybody. I don't speak to anybody. And God, the fucking horror if I were forced to. I wouldn't know what to do with my hands. Occasionally letters are delivered. Letters from abroad that may require a signature. I go to the door. I swear that they can see it in my eyes. The blank shivering terror.

Where do I sign?

Do you need a date with that?

Do you need the time of delivery to be recorded?

Would you like to come in for a cup of tea?

There are few things that have caused me more pleasure in recent years than the coverage of the war in Iraq. This offers me the same kind of thrills as do exciting video games. There was a time when I played video games quite often. The feeling I get watching war coverage is the same.

In the evenings I wear my husband's robe. Most of his clothes were wrapped by his sister into black bin liners and taken away to a variety of shops. His robe was saved. I pull the blinds down. And I turn the computer on. Sometimes I don't pull the blinds down. Sometimes I like the idea that in the middle of the night, in the heart of west London, all of the neighbours can see me. His gown is, it's this red, silk gown. I let my hand fall beneath it.

I watch the trailers. Every trailer follows a genre convention. There's a moment, at the end of every film, where the girl is waiting for the boy to come. Kneeling below him. Looking up. She asks him to come on her face. And at that moment she looks tired and worn out and the good years, when the work was flying in, have taken their toll. And you do kind of think.

Dr Schults doesn't ring me. He doesn't ring me to tell me he got the article. He doesn't email. He doesn't acknowledge it in any way.

I lose complete track of when I go to bed.

I have the same thing for breakfast every day. I have a hundred grams of muesli mixed with fifty grams of fresh berries and milk and honey and yogurt. I have some fresh orange juice and some coffee. And then I go up to my desk and I start to work.

And in between jobs. When an article is finished and there are no new commissions waiting to begin I can sit at my screen and I simply have no idea what to do. And the pull, my God, the pull towards the world that is there, on the other side of my screen!

I have to leave in the end. To go shopping. To buy ingredients to make some food. To go into town. To go to a museum. To do anything I possibly can to get away from my computer.

I hate shopping for my own food. I see other people in food shops and they fill me with the deadness of real despair. What is the point of buying aubergines when there are people in the world who dress like that? And who have faces like that? And talk with accents like that? And treat their children like that?

In town everybody's talking about the possibility that the Olympic Games might be coming to London. I'm struck by the irony of this. Because the people of London, palpably to me, are universally obese and under-exercised. Fat fuckers. Gibbering about athletes. The lot of them.

London in summer is a horror story. The Underground is a cauldron. The shopping centres are brutalised. There is no such thing as air conditioning.

She's dressed in a baby-doll nightie. With a red eye mask over the top of her face. And she asks him if he's her daddy. Call me Daddy. Will you call me Daddy? And it doesn't bother me. It doesn't matter to me how old she is.

Two days pass like this.

There are images of things that I have seen seared onto the inside of my skull.

And then on Wednesday lunchtime the news comes in that London's bid to host the Olympics in 2012 has been successful. And now people smile. Transistor radios broadcast the events over and over. We go live to Trafalgar Square. We go live to Tokyo where Lord Coe is speaking. We go live to the derelict battered crack dens of Stratford where residents there can barely contain their glee at the prospect of Kelly Holmes racing madly around the peripheries of their houses.

Cars do little dances. Drivers toot their horns at one another with idiot inane grins on their faces. Shocked by their own daring. Epileptic with thoughts of how old they'll be in 2012.

And when I get back Dr Shults has called. He's left a message for me on my phone. This is BT Call Minder 1571. The person you are calling is not available. Please leave a message after the tone.

I listen to the message three times. Put some music on. Pour myself a whisky. Pour myself another. I smoke an entire packet of cigarettes in one sitting.

What I realise now is that I won't die. I'm going to live on and on.

He wants me to see him the next day. He wants me to go in and see him the next morning to talk about things.

I don't sleep.

At three o'clock in the morning I go outside into the garden. This city is never silent. At this time of morning it hums and roars in the distance. It has a throb and a pulse of its own. It feels latent. It feels charged. It feels sprung. As though something remarkable is going to happen.

I go back to bed eventually. I have no idea what time it is.

I am eighty-three years old next month.

I get up. Measure out my breakfast. Get dressed. Get on the tube. Go and see Daniel.

But it's clear by the time I get to the tube station that something is going wrong. Nobody says anything. But Hammersmith tube station is closed. Both stations actually. For all three lines. On each side of the roundabout.

The traffic into town has stopped completely still.

Posters warn me not to make any journeys unless they're completely necessary.

I walk.

I walk through Hammersmith up towards Shepherd's Bush. Up Holland Park Road on to Notting Hill Gate. Down Notting Hill Gate up to the corner of the park. Down Oxford Street to Tottenham Court Road. Up Tottenham Court Road towards Gower Street. I'm very late. There's nobody there. Nobody came in today. Nobody at all came into the centre of London today. Nobody rang to let me know.

On my way back my feet, I think, start to blister and it feels like they might start bleeding.

There are masses of people waiting at bus stops. I see one man. He does look like my husband. Just for a second I was thrown. But he's far too young. He can't be more than forty. Did he see me looking at him? Did I frighten him? Did I frighten you? Were you frightened? I didn't mean to frighten you.

It's on days like this that I realise how intelligent my decision to talk you out of having children was. I mean, can you imagine? Really. Can you imagine what would have happened?

And tonight, I think, everybody in London walked home.

It's getting dark by the time I get back. As I approach my house the streets get smaller and they are quieter. I can't feel my feet any more. I think my socks have stuck to the soles of my feet.

It's a warm evening. There is the noise of music coming from one of the houses. People are listening to music of some description. And somebody close by is having a barbecue.

I can smell chicken. I can smell barbecued chicken cooking. It smells good.

It's nine o'clock.

I find the house where the chicken is being cooked and I knock on the door.

Hello.

– Can I help you?

I, I, I, I'm sorry.

– Can I, is there anything – ?

I walked past your house. I could smell chicken.

– What?

It smells delicious.

– We're having a barbecue. I'm sorry. Can I help you?

Can I have some?

– Can you – ?

I just wanted you to know that I think your chicken smells delicious.

– Thank you. You said.

And I wondered what would happen if I just knocked on your door and said, your chicken smells delicious, please can I have some of it?

– Ha.

Don't laugh.

– That's quite funny to me.

Don't laugh at me.

– How old are you?

What?

– You're completely fucking retarded, sweetheart, aren't you?

Don't laugh at me.

– Here.

What?

– Wait here. Don't come in.

–

–

–

–

–

–

–

– Here.

Thank you.

– I don't have any napkins. I'm sorry.

No. No. No. No. This is fine. This is kind of you. This is lovely. Thank you.

– I'd have brought you a beer but I decided not to.

No. I don't want a beer. I just wanted some chicken. I just wanted – This is lovely. Thank you.

I walk home. The chicken tastes good. I let myself in. I can't feel my feet any more. I can't understand why there are tears pouring down the sides of my face. This makes absolutely no sense to me at all.

On the evening of 7 July 2005 many of the working people of London walk home from their workplaces in the centre of the city.

Images of hell.
They are silent.

One

1 A church deacon, he was a man known for his deeply held Christian faith and tolerance of other religions.

2 She usually drove to her PA job while her boyfriend preferred to cycle from their home in Tottenham, north London.

3 He had just moved in with his boyfriend of three years but also spent much of his time looking after his widowed mother, who suffers from multiple sclerosis.

4 Her daughter had just arrived in London from Poland on the day her mother was killed.

5 He was passionate about two things: his family and sport.

6 If he was known for anything, it was for his sense of fun. If there was a party to go to or on occasion to celebrate, he would always be the first and the loudest there.

7 Even in this time of sadness, friends tend to laugh when discussing his life. It happens when they talk of his passionate defence of all things Arsenal, should anyone have dared mock his much-loved football club.

8 She came to Britain five years ago from Mauritius.

9 One of three sisters from a distinguished Italian family, she was preparing for a great celebration in Rome which would have united Catholic and Muslim rites.

10 She was making her daily journey to University College London Hospital where she worked as an administrator in the neuroradiology department when she boarded the Piccadilly line train on 7 July.

11 He was on his way to the Royal Borough of Kensington and Chelsea, where he worked as a human resources systems development officer.

12 He was on his way to a one-day course at the Kensington branch of Jessops, the camera chain. He sent a text

message to his mother twenty-one minutes before the first blast, and that was the last his parents heard from him.

13   The twenty-six-year-old, an engineering executive from Hendon, was killed on the number 30 bus after he was evacuated from King's Cross.

14   His hit calypso is still played on local radio station ZJB, many years after it was recorded. But calypso was merely his hobby, albeit a highly acclaimed one.

15   When he was a teenager, his father caught him putting on his sister's heavy black mascara. He was going through a goth phase and had dyed his hair to match.

16   She was due to leave London on the evening of 7 July for a romantic long weekend in Paris with her boyfriend. The day before she died, her dad was wallpapering the kitchen, and she scrawled the words '06/07/05 we got the Olympic bid 2012 on this day' on the bare wall.

17   His hobbies included waterskiing, quad-bike riding and skiing. He had a lifelong love of music and met his fiancée, seven years ago, in a rock club.

18   He helped to set up the Ipswich and East Suffolk hockey club nine years ago.

19   She had taken leave from her job with a Turkish textile company to improve her English.

20   He was former chairman of the Polish Solidarity Campaign of Great Britain, vice chairman of the Havering branch of the Humanist Society, chairman of the H.G. Wells Society and a long-standing supporter of the Anti-Slavery Society among other charities.

21   She had just sent text messages to friends telling them she had safely been evacuated from the tube. As well as travelling and socialising she loved music, and recently went to see Coldplay in Thailand.

22   She worked for BBC Books and the *Sun* for a short time.

23   She had lived in Luton for twenty-five years.

24   She attended the mosque every Friday, but loved Western
     culture and fashions and regularly shopped for designer
     clothes, shoes and handbags. She worked as a cashier at
     the Co-operative Bank in Islington.

25   She was evacuated from the Underground at Euston and
     decided to catch a bus to work.

26   Deciding that university was not for her, she moved to
     Salamanca for a year to learn Spanish. Her first job was
     in the wine trade, which took her abroad again, to
     Australia, where she lived in Melbourne for a year.

27   He travelled all over Europe as a product technical
     manager for the clothes manufacturers Burberry.

28   She had a successful career as an accountant in Glasgow
     and later the City, but she was as happy helping out at
     homeless hostels as she was discussing the financing of
     management buyouts.

29   Her taxi-driver husband described her as a 'devoted and
     much-loved wife and mother of two sons'.

30   He survived fleeing Vietnam as one of the boat people
     when he was less than a year old.

31   She was born in Auckland, New Zealand.

32   He was born in Vietnam, the son of a South Vietnamese
     soldier killed in the conflict when he was just five months
     old.

33   On a normal day, a politics graduate from Warwick
     University, he would have used a completely different
     route to his place of work.

34   There, on a website he helped create, hundreds of people
     have posted almost 18,000 words of tribute.

35   She was born in Tehran but made her home in London
     twenty years ago.

36 One of the last tasks she completed, with her usual
    cheerful verve, was promoting a new rose at Hampton
    Court flower show, named in honour of the Brownies on
    their ninetieth anniversary.

37 She was an optimist. Her mother is certain she would
    have taken comfort in the compassion and caring shown
    to her family over the past fortnight.

38 She had lived in London for eighteen years and was
    nervous about visiting her native Israel because of the risk
    of suicide bus bombings.

39 She missed London; the people, the lifestyle, the pubs. So,
    after completing a two-year dental technology degree at
    the Los Angeles City College, she turned down an offer to
    continue her studies at the prestigious UCLA and
    returned to her adopted home town.

40 On any given Thursday night, she could be found at
    Chiquito in Staples Corner, the Mexican restaurant of
    choice for nights out with her friends Nell Raut and
    Andrea Cummings.

41 He was the kind of man people went to with their problems.
    'He always had time to listen,' said his father.

42 His parents were killed by the Taliban when he was a
    teenager. He left his family in Afghanistan and arrived in
    Britain in January 2002 and was granted exceptional
    leave to stay. He was the only Afghan national to be killed
    in the bombings, and the last of the victims to be formally
    identified.

43 –

44 When he went on a three-month trip around Ghana,
    Senegal and Mali last year, he was satisfying a long-held
    ambition.

45 In 2003, she joined the specialist criminal law firm
    Reynolds Dawson as an assistant solicitor and worked as

a duty solicitor in court and police stations, specialising in fraud and extradition.

46   She came to London earlier this summer to get a taste of big city life.

47   She was full of high hopes when she gave her mother her usual goodbye kiss at Liverpool Street. Mother and daughter always caught the same train from Billericay and had developed the fond little ritual as they went their separate ways. Ms Taylor had just heard that her temporary contract as a finance officer at the Royal Society of Arts in the Strand had been made permanent.

48   She dedicated her life to helping children as a radiographer.

49   She was a personal assistant who lived with her partner in Islington, north London.

50   Coming to Britain from Ghana in the mid-1980s was almost an accident for her. The Lebanese bank manager she worked for in her home town was forced to move to London for his son's medical treatment and Mrs Wyndowa travelled with him to care for the family. When they returned to Lebanon, she remained in the UK, where she had made a new life.

51   He followed the same routine on the way to work every day for ten years. After leaving home shortly before 8 a.m., the IT specialist would take the tube to Liverpool Street, where he would join the early-morning regulars at Leonidas Belgian chocolate shop for a double espresso at 8.30 a.m. After half an hour quietly listening to others holding forth he would make the short walk to the offices of Equitas Holdings in St Mary Axe, where he worked.

52   Determined to improve his English, he headed for London shortly after gaining an IT engineering degree from the University Institute of Technology (IUT) in Saint-Martin-d'Hères, near Grenoble. He shared a flat in Kensal Green with three friends and worked in a pizza

takeaway. He sent any spare money home to his younger sister but managed to save enough from his modest wages to buy a computer.